Sex History Of France
and Its Erotic Literature

By
Henry L. Marchand

Fredonia Books
Amsterdam, The Netherlands

Sex History of France and Its Erotic Literature

by
Henry L. Marchand

ISBN: 1-4101-0529-6

Copyright © 2004 by Fredonia Books

Fredonia Books
Amsterdam, The Netherlands
http://www.fredoniabooks.com

All rights reserved, including the right to reproduce this book, or portions thereof, in any form.

In order to make original editions of historical works available to scholars at an economical price, this facsimile of the original edition is reproduced from the best available copy and has been digitally enhanced to improve legibility, but the text remains unaltered to retain historical authenticity.

CONTENTS

✤

INTRODUCTION   1

BOOK I MEDIEVAL AND RENAISSANCE

✤

CHAPTER   PAGE

I   13
SEXUALITY IN MEDIEVAL FRANCE
II   21
INDECENT FABLIAUX AND FARCES
III   31
TROUBADOURS AND COURTS OF LOVE

BOOK II THE SIXTEENTH AND SEVENTEENTH CENTURIES

✤

IV   45
THE SIXTEENTH CENTURY
V   61
THE SEVENTEENTH CENTURY

BOOK III THE EIGHTEENTH CENTURY

✤

VI   79
THE GOLDEN AGE OF LOVE
VII   100
ANTI-ROYAL AND ANTI-CHURCH LITERATURE

CONTENTS

CHAPTER		PAGE
VIII	*THE OBSCENITY OF THE THEATRES*	120
IX	*VENEREAL VERSES*	128
X	*SECRET CLUBS AND PERVERSIONS*	133
XI	*CELEBRATED PORNOLOGISTS*	140
XII	*OTHER CELEBRATED PORNOLOGISTS*	160
XIII	*PORNOGRAPHIA RAMPANT*	184

BOOK IV THE NINETEENTH CENTURY

XIV	*THE NAPOLEONIC REGIME*	199
XV	*BABYLON ON THE SEINE*	206
XVI	*THE HEYDAY OF OBSCENE ART*	224
XVII	*THE REIGN OF THE PROSTITUTE*	230
XVIII	*MASTERS OF EROTIC LITERATURE*	239
XIX	*PUBLISHERS OF EROTICA*	257
XX	*VENUS VICTORIOUS*	266

INTRODUCTION
THE EROTIC HISTORY OF FRANCE

THIS book sets itself the interesting and intriguing task of writing the erotic history of France and its erotic literature. Perhaps someone will inquire why we choose such a theme, and what profit is to be derived from a knowledge of the numerous piquant and gallant details that we shall meet on our quest. It is possible, too, that some reader will wonder about the latter part of the title: The History of French Erotic Literature. What is the justification for this phrase? Let us spend a few moments now in trying to understand why France should be chosen as the subject of an erotic history; why the history of the vast system of practices connected with the most unbridled and diverse expression of sex life in the land of the Gauls is of importance for us. Then we shall be in a position to realize the tremendous value of French erotic writings, which shall be our guides in our expedition through this land of love.

It is a nice question whether there is an essential and an all-pervasive difference between the different races of mankind. But whatever be the truth about this very moot question, it is an indisputable fact that France has for many centuries been renowned as the home *par excellence* of eroticism, and Frenchmen as the typical representatives of the erotic spirit and practitioners of the erotic art. This by no means implies that there is something inherent in the French which impels them to this type of activity. We are merely stating a fact which can be buttressed by numerous phenomena, historical and sociological. Many investigators have asserted the fundamental unity of all nations, and have even denied that there has been any development through the course of history, by which modern men, for instance, have come into the possession of new traits of character or elements of physical structure. The French critic—Remy de Gourmont—has gone so far as to develop a quasi-law of history which claims that in all ages and in all climes men are alike, and the same diversities which separated classes of men and individuals at a bygone age are still observable today, *mutatis mutandis*.

If this view is true, and we incline to believe that it is, then the sources for the development and importance of the erotic motif in French culture are to be led back not to certain structural peculiarities of the French people but to certain peculiarities in their history and sociological organization. Just at what date these traits first became manifest it is difficult to assert with precision. During the Renaissance period, when new blood began to run in the veins of the awakened and enlightened Europeans, and the first fruits of the new culture became documented in literature, we are already able to discern the strength of this motif. Of course at this time other nations of Europe, the Italians principally and also the Germans, were producing similar works. Indeed, the beginning of this literature as forsooth of the whole drive and potency of the Renaissance is to be seen in Italy; but at any rate this direction manifested in literature was the reflection of tendencies continued, developed, and augmented which at a later date made France the mundane residence of Venus in Europe.

There are so many items which testify to the importance of France in this connection that it is difficult—nay, impossible—to list them all. Only a few facts and illustrations will now be cited as witnesses to the truth of our contention. We appeal first to the testimony of language. The existence of certain words in a language prove that institutions represented by these words are found among the people speaking that language. If these words have been borrowed by other languages, it is clear that the institutions were borrowed from the people who first employed these words. Thus, many musical terms show their Italian origin; psychological terms their German origin; etc. Characteristically enough, the greatest number of erotic words spring from French.

Furthermore, France has long been recognized as the source of all types of art and literature connected with the erotic sphere. In modern times, France has been the producer of novels, tales and dramas dealing in divers ways and from exceedingly varied viewpoints with sexual love. France exported these products to every other nation of the world. Why is it, for instance, that when we think of the French influence we immediately conjure up certain notions about the naughtiness and venereal escapades of its characters? Why is it that the majority of erotic books are French? Why is it that naughty picture cards and various other indecent drawings have been marketed to the rest of the world from France? Do not these facts serve to bolster up the truth of our contention about the primacy of France in the erotic realm!

Finally, Paris has long been the center of modes in dress for the world, from which new modes are dictated and the chic of the world created. Any adult who has tried to understand the delirious and apparently chaotic alternation of modes and fashions and designs, especially in women's clothing, will conclude without any shadow of a doubt that the anthropologist is right. The latter contends that clothes were not invented because women were modest, but because they were immodest. That is, women did not cover their nakedness because they were disturbed at being seen in full view. Women concealed part of their anatomy in order to make themselves more seductive. In short, women concealed those portions of themselves which were not altogether esthetically satisfactory in order to increase their charm for men. Now when women reveal their nakedness today, or carefully selected and pampered portions of their nakedness, they are carrying out this motive attributed to them by the student of human evolution. Fashions change, apart from the sheerly economic motives of profit to designers and manufacturers of clothing, because it is necessary for new attractions to be revealed to unsuspecting man: a little more of the leg or a little less—a little more of the breast or a little less—a little different outline to the female form, more flesh or less—these are the dominant motivations for the unaccountable panorama of the mode. Is it, therefore, to be wondered at that Paris, which more than any other city in the world has cultivated the erotic, and has undergone a long and rigorous schooling in indulging every whim and every taste in the erotic, is also the arbiter of destiny in fashion?

These remarks on the importance of France as the center of erotic activity in the Occident during modern times will serve to justify the present project of writing an erotic history of France. We are now ready to take up the question about the sources of this history. To what materials or phenomena shall we turn for information about the successive stages of this development? There are many possible procedures.

One might go through the files of French legal archives and select all matters connected with the erotic realm. If we were to trace all laws, injunctions, prohibitions, litigations, etc. connected with this field, and then systematize and analyse them, we should certainly be on the way to tracing the history of these questions in France. Thus we might trace all the laws connected with the regimentation of brothels and prostitutes and thus arrive at the history of this question; or we might collect all references to incest, both prohibitions or records of cases, and thus develop the history of this aspect of erotic affairs, all the while proceeding on the very obvious assumption that whatever becomes recorded in the law is not an abstract invention or speculation but rather a record of actual existing conflicts in human affairs.

Closely allied to this procedure would be the analysis of the church's reaction to the domain of sex. If we were to collect the sermons, pamphlets, etc., composed on these themes, and if we were to collate the decisions of ecclesiastical bodies concerning the erotic, we should have an enormous mass of materials for tracing the history of this problem.

Another approach would be through the realm of medicine, medical history and vital statistics. Using this road we might for instance, examine all available records concerning the origin and spread of syphilis in France, and by tracing the distribution of this plague throughout France, and the references to it in various sources, we should be in a position to understand the significance of this malady and draw some conclusions about the conditions responsible for it. This would be a clear contribution to the erotic history of France and a compilation of such monographs would undoubtedly form a corpus of writings of great importance.

Another way would be to collect the low linguistic usages, the "bad words" of the French language, and by examining the data of speech, endeavor to determine where and whence certain words entered the language. By doing so and by studying the semantic changes in those words which have taken on a new and erotic coloring, we could write the erotic history of France from the philological point of view. This effort would be considerably supplemented by the cognate activity of collecting the folk songs and proverbs of the land, which would generally afford us fuller insights than single words.

Or we might make a collection of objects connected with the

domain of sex, all sorts of appliances for aiding and augmenting carnal pleasures, for abetting the normal and appeasing the perverse impulse. Such a collection properly labeled and understood, would be an invaluable museum for the illustration of actual practices to professional men and sociologists.

We come at last to a different method. If we were to examine all the paintings and sculptures that are concerned with love, nakedness, sex activity, etc., we should have an excellent method of seeing the impact of this problem upon successive ages. We are, therefore, now no longer dealing directly with the materials of sex life or their relation to legal, ecclesiastical, or medical history, but rather with their reflection in the mirror of art. The painter and sculptor hold the mirror up to nature, and the glimpses they capture and fix, remain forever. We can read to all eternity the message they wrote. The literary figure we have just employed brings us to another and perhaps the greatest art—the art of letters. There may be great and far reaching changes in literature as well as in the other arts. But after all, the meaning with which words are laden cannot be dispelled and forgotten. The word heard and spoken afar off, retains for us today, a goodly portion at least, of the efficacy and verity it possessed then. Hence, we shall choose to trace the erotic history of France as reflected chiefly in its literature, the most potent of the productions of men. We shall not altogether overlook the other methods we have enumerated, and whenever possible shall employ them, but primarily our concern is with what French writers, poets and prosaists, wrote; what they saw and immortalized in their words.

The Gallic spirit was well equipped to treat of these themes, indeed, in a fashion unexampled among other nations. What do we think of in the complex of vague notions that are comprised in *l'esprit gaulois*? A certain clarity and lucidity combined with a marvellous grace and finished levity. Freedom, wit, polish, are not these the inevitable characters of the French mind and language? Hence, in dealing with the enormous mass of materials connected with the most dominant impulse of living things after food-hunger, which among human beings may assume forms and consequences awful and unspeakably nasty; in addition to being responsible for exquisite joys, and happy, ordered lives, can we not see the importance of the French gifts of mind? It is their grace, and charm and wit that lightens serious issues; and their lucidity that clarifies them to us in proper perspective. The love of leisure of these people, their joy in the exercise of the body in all its senses, and of the mind in all its capacities—these qualities have made France one of the greatest and wisest nations in Christendom. And if we cannot condemn too severely their sexual unrestraint and perversities, let us remember that their high and ennobling virtues vastly outweigh their eroticism.

The merry French people love words and are happy in the exercise of the pen. They love their language as no other nation and for many centuries have so cultivated it until it has become the most flexible instrument in the hands of the trained writer. In France, one can say everything—and that which is said is tolerable even to the modest ear, because the magic of the language enables one to overlook the subject matter. On the whole, the opinion of Engel, expressed in his *Psychology of French Literature*, is quite true: that the preponderance of sexual matters in French literature is much less to be attributed to unrestrained lustfulness than to the love of laughter. The French are not so much sexually passionate as sexually witty. The jokes and amorous adventures of the middle ages known as fabliaux never show a trace of really glowing sensuality. They are smirking tales of doubtful content told and punctuated by the laughter of fauns. The everlasting butt of the humor in these tales is the deceived husband; and up to this day in the very latest *boulevard comedies* the husband bears the brunt of the laughter, even with a masculine audience. Moreover, Rabelais scarcely a page of whose work is free from sexual matters or suggestions, has treated the sexual relationship with rough rudeness but without any evil intent, without any secondary object, and merely as material for the satisfaction of his own love of laughter, and that of others. There is no question of earnestness, passion, or obscenity. The same is true of another old book, one of the worst of this sort: *The Hundred Merry Tales* of Antoine de la Sale in which we discover utter shamelessness, and reckless wit, but nothing that resembles real participation by the author in the sensual activities of the book.

Nevertheless, the conclusions of Engel apply to only one part of French erotic literature. One need merely mention the erotic writers of the eighteenth century: Sade, Bretonne, Dulaurens; and such nineteenth century authors as Maupassant, Zola, Flaubert, Gautier and Verlaine, to prove that all these poets and authors were very much in earnest about their eroticism. For them, it was not always the love of laughter, but vital interest in the material that directed their pens to their artistic tasks.

And now one word more concerning the plan of the book. The great age of uncontrolled love in France is the eighteenth century. More than during the Renaissance, and no less than the classic period of antiquity, sex ruled life at that time. Naturally, literature mirrored the reign of sex in countless productions which surpass any previous or subsequent period in the erotic history of France. This representation of the classical age of French love will be the climax of the book; the remainder will lead up to and away from it. The beginning will treat of the early period in France, the age of knighthood and chivalry, the rule of the church and the song of the troubadour. There will be passed in review the love court, worship of the Virgin, fabliaux, medieval farces and other sexual customs of that time. This will lead into the sixteenth and seventeenth centuries which foreshadow even greater vices and sextravagances.

Then the grand epoch of French love will be presented with its multitude of amazing personalities and startling incidents. This will be followed by an analysis of the nineteenth century, so near to us and still so responsible for so many elements of our life. The book will close with the last years of the nineteenth century—for most of the works produced by later writers are accessible to discerning readers. Perhaps at a later day it will be opportune to continue this history through the first decades of our own twentieth century.

All through this history there will be included significant surveys of the general sexual situation of the times. How free were conditions really? What of prostitution? And perversion? What were the most popular forms of esoteric amusement? All these and many other questions having been disposed of, we shall turn to an examination of the literature of the particular periods, first examining general trends and then describing the outstanding eroticists of successive ages. One very unusual feature of this history is the emphasis I have laid upon quotations from these erotic authors. Not merely are their most important works listed, but whenever possible I have given a synopsis of the plot, or quoted a typical extract. It is superfluous to indicate the value of this procedure. Many of these erotic classics are inaccessible and it is certainly necessary, in a serious history of this kind, to describe the contents of these works.

Finally, I must explain that the presentation which follows makes no pretence to completeness. Apart from the utter impossibility of writing a complete erotic history of France, such an attempt would necessitate the insertion of obscene details which it is neither my purpose nor pleasure to record. This volume has been written for serious adult students of history and I have deliberately excluded anything and everything which would appeal to pornographic-minded readers. For those who may be interested in more detailed information, the bibliographical works of Barbier, Brunet, Gay and Querard will prove invaluable.

BOOK I
MEDIEVAL AND RENAISSANCE

CHAPTER I
SEXUALITY IN MEDIEVAL FRANCE

IT IS important to recognize at the outset of our investigation into the erotic history of France that the instinctive endowment of men remains unaltered through all the ages and climes of the world. In our introduction we were concerned to establish the essential similitude of human beings in space—that is, to show that despite differences of nationality and race the fundamental and inexorable instincts are the same for every son and daughter of men. This fact must be remembered when we come to study the history of the manifestations of the dominant human impulse within the nation of France.

This sexual instinct, which its people share alike with the rest of the universe, has never throughout the ages suffered change or diminution. But in every period it has assumed different manifestations depending on the varied sociological conditions. Factors of politics and economics, of religion and philosophy, in short, real and ideal, served to build the channels for the flow of the stream—but the stream kept flowing unabated. Rich and poor, noble and serf, learned and ignorant, all were impelled by love and felt its sacred or, as the case may be, profane impulsion and acted out their instincts.

Now in the middle ages, what were the dominant forms of sexual activity? Or to put the question somewhat differently: how did the expression of the sexual instinct and the forms of sexual life differ from those current among us today? We all somehow have the feeling that in those dim, dark days of the medieval period all life was so much in the control of the church, that certainly the expression of the most heinous of all the instincts according to the church's doctrine must have been suppressed to the point of extinction. Before we can answer this question we must look at the structure of medieval society.

There were, as is well known, three strata in this social structure. At the top stood the king and his court of nobles, who owned vast tracts of land as feudal lords. These fortunate individuals were exempt from work; all the menial, necessary, productive work of the world was accomplished for them by their serfs, whom they owned bodily. All that they gave these slaves in return was protection, and in those lawless times this was not a small thing; there were continual wars between rival feudal barons and the life of the common man was of no importance. Between these two classes was the clergy, who ministered to both the upper and lower group alike, but was in inclination and position more nearly akin to the former.

Now to come back to the question of eroticism. Despite the lip service to poverty, chastity and obedience, despite the glorification of purity, the actualization of these ideals remained as impossible in the religious middle ages as at other times. Nature can only be conquered by obeying her, taught an ancient teacher; and the church was to prove for itself the essential verity of these truths. Each of the three classes, living on a different level of wealth, position, education and opportunity, gratified the sex instinct in its own way, but they had this in common: the public religiosity of the period which impressed the age, did not alter the course of their instincts. The church was very early to realize this and hence their institution of the confessional. What is the latter but a shrewd compromise with unalterable life? It must be admitted that men will

BOOK I: MEDIEVAL AND RENAISSANCE

sin. If the church is incapable of damming up the flow of passion, then let it at least retain some measure of control over its adherents by ascertaining where the flood has broken the dikes. Let them come and admit their sins. Let the church take cognisance of them and inflict some slight penalty for them. But this candid capitulation to sin and vice, this recognition of its inevitability, this assignation of slight penalties for it, are they not all admissions of defeat? Indeed are they not even greater incitements to wickedness? For if one can get off so lightly, why even make the attempt to live virtuously?

Let us begin with the lowest class—the serfs. Poor, miserable, utterly ignorant, worked to the bone, with their faces ground by poverty, the lives of this class were certainly nasty, brutish and short. It is no wonder then that there were frequent infractions of virtue among them. Here the church exercised its greatest effect but even here its success was slight. Chastity, continence, fidelity, were all too infrequent, and again and again we shall meet literary testimony to these evil conditions. Language was foul and coarse and there was a fierce delight in unmitigated ribaldry. Girls and boys lost their virginity very young—and hence they were married off as early as possible but not always in time, in spite of the hurry. The girls were continually at the mercy of the men of the upper classes, and pity the pretty or shapely one especially. Life was short and difficult—so sin was not infrequent, but the confessional made restitution. The poor had their own brothels, and divers other forms of amusement of a similar nature. Early they developed the coarse presentations which were combinations of miracle play and farce. The life of the poor was then what it has always been.

The general uncertainty of life, combined with the vast and fairly unchecked power of the king, and to a lesser degree of his nobles, set the pace for their life. It is no wonder that they led licentious lives which occasionally assumed titanic proportions. We shall read later of the sumptuous gatherings of high born ladies and men where the foulest talk circulated; and of the almost unbelievable richness and pomp of some of their orgies in which were enacted in the flesh, by living actors, the most intimate and passionate scenes. Again, one motive for the Italian invasion of Charles VIII was his desire for Italian women, and as we shall see later, he has left us vivid records of his incredible exploits with the winsome daughters of Latium. But, we are inclined to ask, what of knighthood? Surely there was a portion of medieval society which was different, was resplendent in its purity and high ideality. Unfortunately we discover to our great disillusionment that this institution was ridden by numerous foul and vicious elements; that very early whatever nobility there may have been in knighthood disappeared, and the service of woman became pretty confined to one area or function of the woman. If the knight did battle for the lady and went to extravagant lengths in his ostentatious fidelity to her, like wearing a lock of her hair, it was for a purpose. This lock of hair was not infrequently plucked from his lady's *mons veneris* as we shall see later. This institution ultimately gave rise to such ugly and pervasive abuses that it had to perish.

In connection with knighthood and the service of women a word should be said about the medieval cult of love which found its expression in the Minnesingers. These songs composed by troubadours and less frequently by knights, are part of the witness to the importance of woman and the strength of love even in the middle ages. As we shall learn the tone of these songs is none too exalted and the most passionate praises are sung to the physical beauties of the beloved, and particularly to her sexual attractions. A most interesting and unusual feature of the middle ages were the so-called courts of love. Here tournaments of words are supposed to have taken place in connection with questions of love. Or to vary the

BOOK I: MEDIEVAL AND RENAISSANCE

image, and to bring out the full meaning of the title, certain questions of the love life, occasionally ideal, but more generally very obscene, were argued as though before a court; and at the close of the "litigation", a verdict was rendered. These decisions were frequently later embodied in the actual life of the given groups among whom the "court" had been held.

But if knighthood was not all a flower, the church was not all a cloud of sacred incense. Indeed, it would appear as though the most consistent and violent transgressions in the sphere of sex were committed by those appointed to preach sanctity and exemplify it. The idleness, power, and ignorance of the priests combined with their unexampled hold upon their flock due to their status, gave them an unlimited field for the exercise of their lusts. Outside of the church and within it, the minds and bodies of many of the church's servitors served not the Christ but Priapus. Priests were known as vigorous lovers and were sought after because of their prowess and discretion. Indeed all doors were opened to them. Their churches were occasionally even decorated with indecent pictures; and the monasteries and nunneries were the homes of the most indiscriminate perversions. Many cloisters were virtually brothels. The suppression upon the sexual instinct of its clergy that the church had sought to enforce in its injunction of celibacy proved a boomerang. Not only was the body not conquered but the soul was frequently lost.

Hence it is no wonder that the priest became the target of the most vitriolic criticism and condemnation. His immoral life was an outrage to any moral sensibility and when there was so much to lash, we must not be surprised at the quantity of anti-clerical literature or its intensity. This was one of the dominant motifs of medieval erotic literature and has lasted into modern times. Another and related theme was anti-royalism. The life of king and court was also soaked in pornographic lubricity and its putridity stank to the distant clouds. The incessant and multiple erotic diligence and application, the insatiability, cruelty, and folly of king and noble was at the base of the mass of anti-royalist writing. Another motif, and indeed one that was prior to the ones just mentioned, was that connected with the Virgin Mary. This innocent Mariolatry was, as we shall presently discover, strangely intertwined with erotical elements of all sorts, some of them rather shocking. Indeed, from being the symbol of immaculateness and pure unsullied mother love she occasionally became the patron saint of unchastity. This transformation is interesting in correlation with the decay in the service of women noted in connection with knighthood. What is most striking in many medieval writings is the utter disrespect for women, the unspeakably low estimate of the whole female sex, who are representative of all that is base and wicked in human nature. This notion, partly derived from experience, partly also from the low status of woman, was however to a great measure influenced by the circulation, at this time, of a whole cycle of Buddhist stories. In these of course, the poor female of the species is nothing but a sinner and a snare for the entire race of men.

Let us say a word now about the literary forms of medieval France in which these records of her erotic life are preserved. A good number of these were distinctive of that period and have not survived it, while others have been transmitted but have assumed different forms. We will content ourselves with a mere mention of them here, and leave their explanation and illustration for the next two chapters. There are the fabliau (the tale), the farce, the tensor (the report of the court of love) the dramatized farce, the chanson (lyric) and brothel poetry, and the chronique scandaleuse.

One final remark about the progress of medieval French erotic literature. As we first find it we see something primitive, coarse, un-

BOOK I: MEDIEVAL AND RENAISSANCE

differentiated. In the early periods there are few genres, and in the very earliest but one, the fabliaux, aside from the panurgic anecdote which circulates among the people. These are rough, rude, and have no adumbration of artistic skill. As time goes on and culture becomes somewhat more differentiated, more genres develop and every type in turn becomes refined and hence amenable to artistic treatment. During the twelfth, thirteenth, and fourteenth centuries, under the influence of the troubadours and knightly gallantry, much is achieved. Poetry is developed to a high degree and even becomes precious and affected. The lyric poetry of the fifteenth century shows sophistication and already gives finished expression to satire. It is useful to remember, although it is not entirely relevant in this connection, that in this century syphilis began to ravage Europe, fixing men's minds to the realm of sex as never before, and giving literature many new themes both in tragedy and in satirical comedy.

By the end of this century all the genres of the medieval period have been invented and are in active currency. Thus the fifteenth century can also show an admirably simple and genuinely homely lyricism in Villon for example. The gradual growth of cities and the rise of the middle class created a need for a new type of writing more suited to the activities of this group. The highfalutin, pampered, precious gallantry of knightly writing was no longer to the taste of these groups, for it corresponded to nothing in their life. In the sixteenth century we see by the side of the romance of gallantry like *Amadis* with its false sentimentality, erotic productions that are lyric, naturalistic, coarse and finished—in short, eroticism that covers the whole range of the field. The foulest brothel poetry was to be found, but also the most delicate and tender emotional depictions; earnest reflectiveness and lewd buffoonery both were to be met in the extensive erotic literature of the century.

THE EROTIC HISTORY OF FRANCE

And this plethora of works with all the anti-clerical and anti-royalist broadsides and bawdy outlines of sex continued into the seventeenth century. The growth and development of all these types was of course only a reflection in letters of the intensity and development of the actual erotic life in France. We now turn to the history of this life as reflected in these literary forms.

CHAPTER II
INDECENT FABLIAUX AND FARCES

The literature of the middle ages is undoubtedly much beholden to the formation and propagation of the legends clustering around the Virgin. The immaculate conception, in particular, occupied the medieval poets considerably. One gets this impression not merely from the frequency with which this matter is referred to, but also from the intensity of the efforts many of the poets display in espousing and establishing their belief. To what extremes this adoration of the Virgin could go, may be surmised from the fact that the monks of the Order of Mary drank up dish water and licked the afflicted parts of lepers in order to show their reverence for their saint.

Mary first appears in the old French fabliaux and jokes as the guardian of virginity; but she frequently also comes to the aid of those who have gotten into difficulties of their own making. Thus, one of the fabliaux tells of a woman who is surprised by her husband as she sports with a cleric. The latter dashes out of bed and hides. When the husband lies down beside his wife she jumps out of bed and simulates insanity, all the while invoking the virgin; while the deceived husband seeks to calm the apparently hysterical wife, the cleric departs.

Although Mary is everywhere represented as the guardian of virginity, there is one story of an abbess famed for her piety, chastity and service to Mary, who has become pregnant. The night before delivery she fervently implores the help of the Virgin to save her from the impending shame; whereupon the former accompanied by two angels comes and delivers the abbess, keeping her body intact, and then leaves the child with a hermit. There are other stories in which the Virgin aids in illegitimate enterprises, notably the one of Cæser of Heisterbach in which she substitutes herself for the lady superior who is leading a whore's life outside the cloister.

The aid of the Virgin is invoked in many other needs and distresses: The young priest who has fallen in love with a young girl calls upon Mary to help him in his suit; and the lover abandoned by his love, prays for a change of heart in the beloved, or offers his love to Mary who is faithful and never deceives a lover. In this feeling there are many sensual elements as numerous fabliaux will attest (collected in the book of Coincy). Thus Mary reproaches a young priest who has been unfaithful to her and reminds him that for love of him she can open the heavens and admit him to her private chambers where a rich bed holds great pleasures of love in store for them. Or when a pious sacristan desires to kiss her feet she presents her face instead. Or when a young priest slips a ring on the finger of a statue of Mary but becomes unfaithful to her, she soon permits herself to be won back for ever, despite her jealousy. In these instances the mother of God is entirely divested of her divinity and is regarded merely as the loving, yielding woman.

This conception is rooted in the amalgamation of earthly and heavenly love, whose essential characteristics are its duality, and the exclusion of any other loves. Man cannot love earthly and heavenly beings at the same time; if he chooses the latter, then there is an end to loving the daughters of men. Mary takes complete possession of the lover's emotions and for that reason she concentrates upon herself not merely the heavenly, but also the earthly love.

BOOK I: MEDIEVAL AND RENAISSANCE

Comparatively early, however, certain frivolous elements appeared by the side of this reverence for Mary. Faithless women invoked her as witness to their "innocence", and the formulas were more than coarse. *'Por le cul Sainte Marie'*, *'por le cul dieu'*, *'par les boiaus sainte Marie'* are very frequent; as are also *'par le cortez'*, *'par les mamelles'*, *'par les denz'*, *'par la gorge'*, *'par la teste'*, *'par la cuer Sainte Marie'*. Among the common people such thoughtless and frequently vulgar invocation of the Virgin was customary. In the church poems of Jesuit Jacob Pontanus, the poet can think of nothing more beautiful in Mary than her breasts, nothing sweeter than her milk, nothing more excellent than her belly.

It is easy to understand the great reverence in which she was held when one realizes her utter readiness to help even in the most difficult situations—a fact continually taught by the priests. Indeed when only a simple prayer was necessary to avoid unpleasant consequences and to snap one's fingers at righteousness, every man and woman really received a charter of license.

It is well known that the later comic poets, especially those of Italy and Germany, owe much to the French fabliaux, which exercised great influence and inspired a very large number of derivative works. What is a fabliau? Pilz defines it as the poetic representation of an adventure that takes place within bounds of normal life. It belongs to the class of epic, or epic-didactic poetry, and its chief aim is to amuse and to arouse laughter. It is this general character which is indicated by the designations employed by poets to characterize their works, viz: *une trufe, une bourde, une risée, un gab*. Later on a moral was gradually added. With few exceptions they are composed in octosyllabic rhymed couplets. They are the poetry of the rising citizenry as opposed to the ideals of the courtly-sentimental poetry. Three elements have participated in their formation: the stream of Oriental stories with their Buddhistic ideal of the contempt of women, the low status of the minstrels, and the moral decadence of the clergy.

The Buddhistic conception denied woman every right and personal dignity, regarding her as the inescapable burden of man. She it is who keeps him in the bondage of sensuality and thus prevents him from achieving the true life. Its pronounced ascetic character inclines to emphasize the virtues of celibacy. These notions reappear in the fabliaux verses in their low valuation of marriage and in their tendency to attribute every fiasco and error of the man to the woman.

The motives that actuated the low-born minstrels, to whose satiric streak many a fabliau owes its existence, can scarcely be called noble. Ostentation, combined with the poverty of the singers and the hope for jingling rewards if they would flatter the opinions of their audiences, supplied ample material for laughter. This resulted in a conscious effort to pander to the demands of their public which demanded amusement and which was beginning to feel a definite antipathy to the knightly ideal of reverence for women. Furthermore, the disrespect of women is also to be attributed to the disastrous influence of the clergy from whose pens so many fabliaux flowed; celibacy, too, and its consequences were subject matter for satire.

A rude peasantry as yet untouched by refined culture tends to seek amusement in relating the occurrences of everyday life, since they still lack what seem to us to be higher interests. These tales treat of the most natural things, and they always excite the laughter of the ignorant peasant whose greatest joy is to play a joke or tell about it later. This hearty and even pleasant tone so common in German jokes despite their coarseness is alien to the Frenchman who toys with everything, titters over everything, is always on the lookout for the humorous and pursues it relentlessly with a measure of pride in his own superiority. Yet he is not malicious; he is merely light and frivolous. Thus he laughs at the stupid husband who has had horns conferred upon him; for has he not done the very same many times? He laughs at the prostitute cheated of her hire, and at lovers. He laughs at stories of priests which may or may not end happily, because their conduct in erotic matters is so rarely in accordance with their cowls and calling. Above all, his laughter is aroused by the cunning of women, their sensuality, their fickleness, falsehood, wantonness and gluttony. In most of the fabliaux the whole story turns on an erotic situation and the erotic joke is rarely lacking. The greatest joy is derived from those obscene stories where woman is drawn in the blackest colors possible. This leads us to the conclusion that these stories must usually have been recited in the absence of those censured.

Many of these tales excel in obscenity—and a few of the important ones will now be mentioned. *Le sot Chevalier* treats of a stupid knight who is instructed by his mother-in-law in his marital duties. In *La demoiselle qui ne povoit oir parler de foutre*, a young man learns of the daughter of a certain knight who can't hear the word *foutre* spoken without falling into a faint. He decides to try his luck with her and offers his services to that knight. He is very well received for the reason that he too becomes unconscious whenever he hears lewd words. The girl falls in love with him and they become a happy pair. *De la demoiselle qui neot parler de fotre qui n'aust mal au cuer* treats of a similar situation. For his *Bijoux indiscrets*, Diderot borrowed from the work of Garin: *Le chevalier qui faisoit parler les cous et les culs*. This ability was conferred upon a certain noble knight by two fairies in reward for his conduct. The third fairy promises that he will be well received everywhere. The prophesy is fulfilled and he becomes a wealthy man. In *De l'Escui-*

ruel, young Robin uses the inexperience of a girl in order to win his love.

The wanton life of women is what makes most of the fabliaux so obscene. These women enjoy foul words and coarse jokes, and delight in cynical *doubles entrendre* and filthy oaths. It is apparent from many references in the poets Preine and Bedier that women were present at the narration of such obscene tales and farces; and Jean de Conde does not hesitate to put into the mouth of a noble girl obscene words and sentiments which are never uttered today.

For these reasons women can very easily be won, and the most threadbare grounds will suffice, if the poets' words are to be believed. Thus, a priest gets into the bed of a virgin who struggles against his attack and seeks to call for help. He asks her to remain quiet for no one will now believe in her innocence; she is persuaded and capitulates. And why not? Girls have the greatest enjoyment in sensual pleasures; and no matter how inexperienced they are, as soon as the first bite is taken of the apple, they are greedy to devour the rest. A girl will wish to be married only to a young, strong man. Should her wish not be gratified and should her parents compel her to be married to an old man, she will bewail her years. The young woman will then experience as much discomfort in her enforced continence as will one whose husband, whether owing to stupidity or inexperience, does not fulfill his connubial obligations. In these cases of course the lover must suffer. When a shield-bearer laments the fact that he has slain his love by the intensity of his embraces, another one entreats him for the same death; but this does not happen. And no wonder, for according to the poets one woman can suck the marrow out of the bones of a hundred men before she will be satisfied, and to prove this point they resort to a remarkable exegesis of two verses in the Bible (Prov. 30, 15-16). Even the nunneries, which should

BOOK I: MEDIEVAL AND RENAISSANCE

be the seats of pious discipline, are the scenes of the most lascivious lusts. From the newest novice to the abbess, all feel the prick of the flesh. Three nuns have found an obscene picture, according to another version *un vit grossier et plenier*, and bring it to the abbess to assign it to one of them. The latter settles the dispute by declaring it to be a miniature from her psalter and keeps it for herself.

The standing figures in the fabliaux and farces are the priest, husband, wife, maid, procuress, knight, student and serf.

The priest is represented as a seducer much more frequently in the fabliaux than in the middle high German tales. He was very much sought after as a lover and there were good grounds for this, as a daughter once explained to her mother. "The knight and the slave will spread abroad their exploits with me; but when I have lain with the priest he must shut his mouth and keep still." It was to his advantage as well as the girl's, to keep the matter secret. As a result of his inactive and voluptuous life, he became a *bon ouvrier en lit*. His wiles to achieve his aims are numerous; but once apprehended in a love scene he is revealed as a ludicrous, tremulous coward.

The stories about husbands generally do not deal with the wise, superior husband who sees through the intrigues of his wife and understands how to revenge himself upon the seducer, or how to enjoy some escapades of his own; but rather with the common figure of the cuckolded and henpecked husband. Generally the husband is old, ugly, stupid, naïve or anxious—all of them justification for his wife's extra-marital pleasures.

Woman is seldom absent in these tales. Generally her beauty is drawn in all conceivable colors. The breast especially appears to be an important fact of feminine pulchritude: it must be round and full, but not too big. For the designation of more private parts rude words are used. The more beautiful a woman the more she wishes to shine; and it's a short way from her vanity to her fall. Consequently the unfaithful wife is the usual type in the fabliaux, false, daring, unhesitating, mendacious, always ready for love and always with enough presence of mind to avoid being caught in her escapades.

The virgin is usually naïve. She knows nothing of love but is quite willing to be taught. This playing with naïveté and erotic innocence so attractive to the German and Russian writers, is also employed by the French, but in a much coarser way.

What was the reason for the pessimistic evaluation of women? It certainly was not dictated exclusively by the ascetic notions of the middle ages about the inferiority of women and marriage. At the end of the middle ages such harking back to the Bible or church fathers was rare. What gives these satires their force is their tone of personal experience. Thorough knowledge of the female is at the base of these poets' warnings against marriage—for girls are much different after marriage than they were before. A favorable judgment about women would be very difficult if we had to depend only upon the meagre words of praise in these tales. Nevertheless, behind this entire catalogue of female vices there slumbers the conviction that the female mind is superior. The constantly reoccurring circumstance that the woman emerges as victorious, after having taken advantage of the unworthy characteristics of the man—his credulity, fear, clumsiness, inertia and jealousy—is an indirect recognition of her power, which one must have a knowledge of, if one is to escape it.

The subject matter of these tales and farces has frequently been traced. Le Grand D'Aussy and Barbazan-Meon have followed, in their editions of the old French fabliaux and contes, the treatment of this subject matter throughout many centuries and in many

BOOK I: MEDIEVAL AND RENAISSANCE

Romance languages. Bedier has investigated their sources in his *Les fabliaux*; and his general conclusion is that the raw material does spring from the Orient, but that the French poet has so developed these themes as to make his stories a pure product of the *esprit gaulois*.

After the lapse of time, these dramatized farces were acted out. They generally consisted of one hundred to three hundred verses. Few of them were ever written down and still fewer printed. All that have come down to us, about 150 pieces, date from the period 1440-1450. After 1450 there appeared the *soties*, closely related to these farces but having real fools or clowns in the chief rôle. The Guild of lawyers, the Basoches, was most instrumental in developing the farces. Miraulmont, their historian, tells us that at set times during the year they would present pieces in which they would ridicule their own individual members and in editions *secrettes galantes des maisons particulières*. On Shrove Tuesday they would hold a session and satirize the law just as the choir boys did to the church service at Christmas time. They would deal with an imaginary legal process usually of a very coarse nature. We don't know much about the repertoire of these societies but here are some examples dealing with litigation: Whether a baby born six months after the wedding can be considered legitimate; a defloration case; the *farce du pect* (*pet*) where man and wife accuse each other of breaking wind in formal legal manner; or *Les femmes qui demandent les arresages* in which the woman brings suit for non-fulfillment of marital duties but later becomes reconciled to her husband. Again there is no lack of farces dealing with unfaithful wives. Thus we find the story of a one-eyed man whose wife covers that one eye while her lover escapes; and then that of the fool whose wife is confined much too early. The cunning tricks of amorous women play a great rôle in these farces, and there is no dearth of obscenity, but on the whole there is more of the latter and less of wit in the Germanic productions of that time than in these French farces or in the Italian *beffe* or *burle* tales. The gallantries of the clerics were also dramatized. In general it may be said that only a small fraction of the farces can be regarded as dramatized fabliaux which were but little used. However, the primitive joy in piquant and panurgic situations is not to be mistaken in them.

CHAPTER III
TROUBADOURS AND COURTS OF LOVE

ONE must not judge too harshly the licentiousness of the people, for joy in erotic matters has been found among the high and the low in the gray mists of antiquity as well as in the present. The higher classes of that time were no exception. The plays which were publicly produced in France during the reign of Henry IX were exceedingly offensive. Thus, *The funny tale of the physician who cures all diseases and makes the nose of the child of a pregnant woman;* or the boisterous and merry tale which describes the dispute over a girl between a young monk and an old gendarme, held before the God Cupid. At the time of Louis XI and Charles the Bold there were representations comparable to those of antiquity—with absolutely naked girls participating in scenes like the Judgment of Paris, the History of Noah, etc. Schnaase reports some of the doings at a party that Philip the Good gave at Lille in 1454 on the occasion of a summons to a crusade issued by Pope Pius II, with all the accompanying revelry and license. At one end of the board was a naked girl covered only by her long hair and a thin veil, whose breasts poured forth Hypocras a favorite drink; and on the table there was a naked boy who scattered rose water in an even more naïve fashion.

The paintings and the tapestries of the rich showed the same scenes. William Pepin, a preacher of the fifteenth century has this to say: "The paintings and tapestries frequently display such disgustingly lewd matters that passions are aroused in even the most tranquil dispositions. These are usually found in the castles of the nobility. Would to Heaven that none were even seen in the residences of prelates and the clergy. But I cannot deny that I have even seen certain lewd paintings in the interior of a famous church which was decked out this way in honor of Easter. I had them removed and carried them elsewhere." The palace at Fontainbleau, which Italian artists built and decorated for Francis I, had a mass of lewd paintings according to the fashion of that time. Sauval says that one could see represented in them gods and goddesses, as well as men and women indulging in unnatural and horrible excesses. In 1643 the regent queen caused many of these paintings to be destroyed; and the loss amounted to more than half a million francs. The handwritten prayer books were decorated with miniatures; and collectors saved those which portrayed offensive matters.

Brantome's writings constitute an inexhaustible source for evaluating the moral conditions of the higher society of that time. He writes: "The gallery of Count du Chateau-Vilain, known as Seigneur Adjacet, was visited by a horde of women in the company of their admirers. Their eyes were entranced by the splendid and rare paintings that hung in this gallery. They saw a very pretty painting which portrayed beautiful women at the bath embracing one another and doing one another various other kinds of love service; upon observing which, even the coldest nun or hermitess could become ardent. One of the women whom I knew suddenly turned to her lover and kissed him excitedly, intoxicated with the amorous madness depicted on the wall: 'I can't stand it any longer. Quick, into the carriage and home. I am burning! Come on! We will extinguish the fire.'" How widespread this love for exciting pictures was, can be gathered from a sarcastic remark made by the Marquis d'Argens apropos of Mary Medici's destruction of a number of these paintings: "She had better set all of Fontainbleau aflame if she wishes to have some measure of success in her enterprise."

Brantome also relates the following: "I knew a prince who purchased from a goldsmith a beaker of gilded silver which was a masterpiece. All around, and even inside, it had delicate but clear representations of some figures of Aretino and many scenes of cohabiting animals. During the feasts that this prince gave, the beaker would be passed around to the women who had to drink from it and who found great amusement in it." And again: "At the time of Henry III a nobleman of my acquaintance presented his love with a picture book, representing 32 ladies of the court disporting themselves in venery with their admirers. Among them were certain ladies who had two or three or more lovers each, and these 32 exemplified 27 postures of Aretino. The pictures were perfect likenesses—some fully naked, some in the same clothes and coiffure that they always wore; and the same was true of the men represented. In short this book was splendidly made. It cost about nine hundred thalens, and the drawings were colored." Brantome further relates that when one of the court ladies thus represented saw these pictures of herself she didn't feel at all insulted, but rather experienced a high degree of excitement. Obscene amusements were the order of the day with the gallant ladies of the court, as contemporary writings demonstrate.

Something more should be said concerning knighthood. This institution possessed indubitable merits but it also was disfigured by many defects which are not at all in accordance with the notions commonly held about it. For generally it is supposed that knighthood and the Minnesingers were based on, and culminated in, the highest degree of reverence for women. Yet it was anything but that. To be sure, the poet-lover of a given lady regarded himself as a vassal of his love, and assumed the obligations of this vassaldom—and its privileges. The lady love was the feudal lord and he served her in the expectation that his services would finally be recompensed with the desired, ultimate boon. In this concept of mutuality there lay a deeply immoral moment which was soon to become the point of attack for the annihilating criticism of knighthood. Since this mutuality was nearly always carried into the realm of the sexual, the homage to woman soon was lost. Why? Because there had to result a gradual demolition of all marital relationships, and a revaluation of all moral conceptions concerning marital fidelity and purity of family life.

This strong emphasis on sexual matters was aided by the thorough occupation with love in all its phases which characterizes the didactic poetry of that time. In the Minnesongs for example the preponderant theme is the corporeal attraction of the lady who is being solicited, and the joys of physical love. No attention is paid to the spiritual qualities of the woman, who indeed has value only as an object for serving man's insatiable passions. Consequently, pleasure in woman is confined to the externals; if she possesses physical merits these are glorified by her knight in songs of appropriate praise. But what if these corporeal attractions decay? Then they become disesteemed, as are from the start all those women who have not been dowered with beauty, and are cast upon the junk heap. The Minnesongs can be pronounced to be immoral in the wide usage of the term, if only for the reason that it is always a married woman who is the mistress of the poet's heart. And since there was no lack of jealous husbands at this time, the singing troubadour was frequently compelled to use fictitious names and allegorical signs in order to conceal the identity of his lady. It is this circumstance that to a considerable degree spoils the naturalness and truth of the experiences in these poems. But

BOOK I: MEDIEVAL AND RENAISSANCE

this reserve does not extend to the physical charms of the beloved which were always placed in the foreground and celebrated with utter candor. Her most intimate beauties and private favors were poetized and revealed to an interested world, and what woman could remain deaf to music so flattering to her ear! The forms which the Minnesingers assumed were frequently very grotesque. The knights wore the shirt of their beloved, saved their hair, often their pubic hair, and were present to lend a helping hand when their lady-loves disrobed and retired. Ulrich von Lichtenstein (1276) drank with great relish the water of his beloved's bath, had his lip operated for her sake, etc. Once the lady's favor was won, the happy lover did not have to wait very long for the satisfaction of his impatient desire. These relationships took place without delay and quite openly, and were sanctioned, indeed demanded, by society. To such a pass did matters reach, that the husband was often compelled to be content with a secondary, inferior position in his wife's favor. Certainly one cannot become very enthusiastic about the moral conditions of that time.

It is not extraordinary, therefore, when the poet inflamed by the charms of his beloved and reveling in the memories of sweet hours of intimacy, gave such free rein to his fancy that his words were somewhat too outspoken for seminary girls. It is even pardonable, for these songs are the expression of a genuinely experienced emotion. Not quite the same justification exists for the composition of erotic verses which are calculated to dazzle or to amuse by their brilliance, since in this case there is no inner feeling struggling for expression that might, however slightly, excuse the license of speech.

The low moral standard of the Minne-poetry is also attributable to the fact that it was not always knights who were the composers of these songs, since a certain measure of talent is necessary for their composition, which cannot be learnt. For the most part, itinerant singers, troubadours dependent on the kindness of the knight, were the creators of this poetry. Troubadours (from *trouver*) denotes discoverer, poet. They flourished in the period between the middle of the twelfth and fourteenth century. Their productions include violent satires against the clergy, didactic poems, but above all, love songs and abstruse speculations anent the nature of love. They sought to establish their fame in the *Tensons*, in which questions posed at various courts of love were treated in pedantic fashion. These tensons consisted of dialogues in alternating couplets in which these various speculative opinions were expressed. In their own land the troubadours led an idle and uncertain life but they found a cordial welcome at the palaces of the nobles where they consorted with low villains. This afforded them a fine opportunity to gather the anecdotes and the *chronique scandaleuse* of the day which they afterwards utilized for the benefit of their hearers, with due corrections. The unquestionable beauty of many of their songs is nevertheless disfigured by numerous failings. Thus the tales are sometimes extravagant and more often offensive, not merely in expression but also in content. Many obscene matters are even put into the mouths of women.

Love is represented as an art by this poetry, and reduced to rules. Hence the expression, *Saber d'amor*: to be wise in matters of love. It is very likely that manuals were composed for this art, for which Ovid served as preceptor.

It has already been mentioned that there existed a great predilection for investigating the nature and essence of love; and this brings us to the courts of love with their questions of the Minnesingers, frequently very free ones, too! *The Roman de la Rose* is an excellent example of this pedantic inclination to a scholastic consideration of love. Even the privileges and obligations of the lovers

BOOK I: MEDIEVAL AND RENAISSANCE

were codified—in such works as the *Love Court* of Raymond Vidal; and the *Liber de Arte honeste amandi et de Reprobatione inhonesti Amoris* of Andreas Capellanus. There were debates on such questions as these: Which lover shows more affection—he who is so jealous as to be disturbed on the slightest provocation, or he who is so prepossessed in favor of his love as not to be jealous even when substantial proofs are at hand? Which lover owes more to his love—he who has won her heart after a long siege or he who has not to solicit so long? Which lover demonstrates his love more—he who at the behest of his love absents himself from a tournament that he desires to witness, or he who, again at the request of his love, accompanies her to a tournament he would rather have missed.

The existence of these courts of love is certified by numerous poems of the troubadours. What we are not certain however is whether they were regarded as pastimes, or whether the decisions of these courts really had any effect upon the courtly society. The first of these suppositions seems the more likely. Probably these questions about love were brought up at social gatherings for the delectation of the guests. Aretino would also seem to be of this mind. Schultz is doubtless right when he says: "It is highly probable that both ladies and gallants who had been following the suit of a certain young man with interest, would discuss the matter to determine whether the lover had already attained the final favor or whether he was to suffer much longer." But this sort of amusement and the court of love which gives decisions according to the writings of Andreas are quite different things.

The distortions of the knightly service of women, and the moral excesses of the time afforded ample material for didactic poetry and satire. There were those preachers who babbled about the good old times and who wished to lead their misguided and neglected contemporaries back to morality and honor. These attempts were made in a very formal manner by Maitre Ermenen, for instance, who composed *Breviari d'Amor* (1288), a handbook of love which treats of its subject with all the available knowledge of that time, starting from divine love and ending in earthly love. Raymond Vidal composed a volume in which he imparted wise doctrines to lovers. Peire Giullem composed a novel in which love, and her attendants, grace, shame, and frivolity, appeared as allegorical characters.

All these attempts and numerous others pale by comparison with the *Roman de la Rose* of Guillaume of Louis (ca. 1260) which Jehan de Meung completed about 1300. In certain respects he stands on the threshold between two periods. The earlier knightly gallantry to women had been succeeded by a satirical and superior sort, and the art of love was taught out of the treasure trove of rich experience. The pruriency and voluptuousness of the representations were in accordance with the taste of the time. The satirical treatment of the errors of society, combined with an amazing erudition, lent a prestige to this work which it maintained throughout the fourteenth and fifteenth centuries, even though there rose up among the attacked many who defended the old order.

Lyric poetry of the troubadours had but a shadowy existence in the fifteenth century. Its rare and precious forms, its affectation, its concealed allusions did not appeal to the new taste, which sought genuine, homely lyricism. Among those who satisfied the new demands were Froissart, Besselin and especially Villon, who was born near Paris, in 1431. He came to Paris to attend the university but the loose student life attracted him much more than did science, and he was drawn deeper and deeper into the whirlpool of pleasure. His chief occupation was *aimer*. When one of his sweethearts dismissed him he revenged himself by composing a satirical poem, for which he was publicly flogged. Thereupon he left Paris but not before he had composed (in 1456) his will—the *Small Testament*.

BOOK I: MEDIEVAL AND RENAISSANCE

His miserable circumstances compelled him to perpetrate two felonies for which he was twice sentenced to the gallows and twice pardoned. The date of his death is unknown but it falls between 1480 and 1490. His chief work is the *Grand Testament* which he composed in the shadow of imminent death by hanging. It was a collection of ballads and poems in which he bequeathed to his relatives and cronies that which did not belong to him and which the heirs would have to steal to make their own. To his enemies he bequeathed a jest or a term of abuse. His roguish songs were collected by a friend under the title *Repues franches*. All his works make a peculiar impression upon us with their rapid alternation of the coarsely erotic, and the noblest and purest of sentiment. With great candor he reveals to us his evil characteristics, and even his crimes. All his works are characterized by melancholy, humor, and a naïve devotion to his impressions of reality; all his works breathe a deep truthfulness. His expression is frequently foul and obscene, and the wordplays which he skillfully scatters throughout his verses have nearly always an obscene allusion. Despite all his shortcomings, Villon remains the best folk poet before Marot, and stands in conscious opposition to the lascivious, sentimental, idyllic poetry which was the accepted thing in France since the *Roman de la Rose*.

In the realm of the humorous story the two outstanding productions are the *Mensa Philosophica* and the *Cent Novelles Nouvelles*. The first was printed in 1475 and is attributed to Michael Scot. The author's purpose is, in his own words, to teach his readers what and how to speak at the table. The fourth part contains a collection of "honorable, merry" stories that are adapted for table amusement, and include a great number of indecent stories. Bebel has borrowed a number of his *Facetiæ* from it, Boccaccio's *Decameron* (VII, 5 and IX, 2) is beholden to it, and Gargantua's table amusement looks back to it as prototype. Michael Scot, who died in 1291, can unhesitatingly be regarded as the author of the first three treatises. The fourth treatise, however, which includes the erotical tales is very likely the production of a Dominican monk. The *Mensa* served as model for the later narrators of humorous tales.

The *Cent Novelles Nouvelles*, so called to distinguish them from the *Cent Nouvelles antiche*, were produced about 1460 but did not get into print before 1486; they may be regarded as the first French book of tales which was consciously produced for this purpose. Neither the first printing of Verard nor any of the subsequent ones give the name of the author; all sorts of guesses have been made, even the name of Louis XI having been suggested. At any rate it was assumed as certain that they sprang from the King's table. The Marquis d'Argens mentions that the favorite table talk in that monarch's refectory consisted of obscene love adventures, and these stories doubtless gave the impetus to this book. It remained for Wright in his edition of the work (1858) and the Grisebach, to establish that Anthoine de la Sale was the author. The latter was born at Provence in 1388, journeyed through Italy, Brabant and Flanders and in 1415 took part in a military expedition to Portugal. After his return he became a judge in Arles, and tutor to the Dauphin and to the sons of Count Saint-Pol. Little is known of his last years, except that he was past seventy when he died.

The form of the stories resembles Boccaccio's. A group of young noblemen, just returned from the hunt are gathered round the fireplace, and as they feast they regale each other with coarse, humorous stories. The stories are told broadly, are rooted in a rude, rough eroticism, and are scarcely fit for female ears. Fifteen of them are borrowed from Poggio, and Boccaccio too contributes some material; furthermore, the author took much from the fabliaux of the twelfth and thirteenth centuries. But La Sale has revised all

BOOK I: MEDIEVAL AND RENAISSANCE

his sources so that his work can really serve as an accurate mirror of the morals of his days. Lusty cavaliers, faithless and frivolous wives, jealous husbands, cunning monks and lascivious nuns pass before our eyes in colorful alternation. All their thoughts are concerned with the satisfaction of sexual desire. Yet even the most delicate matters are represented with smooth grace, which seems to be instinctive in the French people.

La Sale is also the author of another very well known work which appeared anonymously, *Les quinze joyes de mariage*. The edition of this work issued with many lacunæ, by Jehan Treperel in Paris between 1495 and 1502, contains a foreword which gives the name of the author in a charade. This riddle was not deciphered until 1830 when Dr. Andre Pother, municipal librarian of Rouen, wrote the solution to a certain bookseller Techener. This work is not merely a collection of obscenities but a striking and mordant satire on marriage, and though done in an admirable style, is quite pessimistic and misogynous.

BOOK II
THE SIXTEENTH AND SEVENTEENTH CENTURIES

CHAPTER IV
THE SIXTEENTH CENTURY

SENTIMENTAL love reached its peak in the flood of *Amadis* stories. During his imprisonment in Madrid (1525) Francis I had read some of the Spanish *Amadis* stories by Garcia Ordonez de Montalvo. These stories of adventures and love appealed to him so much that he requisitioned d'Herberay des Essarts to translate them into French. The task was completed in 1540 and despite its long winded title aroused the intensest interest and gave rise to numerous imitations which were failures. In all of them the erotic element was dominant.

It is in the heroic romances of gallantry, in fictions like Amadis and in the pastorals, that songs of praise are sung to sexual love, which constituted the chief desideratum of life. It is almost a tradition that all heroes of the Amadis romances must have been the fruit of premarital unions; and the knights who extol the notions of free sexual relations always find ladies of like mind. In the heroic romances of gallantry there is not quite such a degree of freedom; indeed it was the part of courtly perfection to apply a curb to erotic passion and to paraphrase matters almost sanctimoniously instead of employing the blunt word. But this does not imply that a nobler conception of love had come to be entertained. From contemporary descriptions of the moral life of the period, we know that at the court of Louis XIV chastity was by no means regarded as an ideal worth striving for, and that sexual pleasures were more highly valued than anything else; only, it was held that to display one's erotic desires to the whole world was not compatible with the dignity and honor required of a courtier. Madame Scudery is a prototype of the poets who composed these romances. Although she lost much of her popularity after Boileau's biting satire, the public continued to favor these romances; and in Germany they were even more popular than in France.

However, this fare of false sentimentality which our modern appetites can no longer enjoy, did not hold the sole place in the esteem of that period. Other genres, more substantial, were also favored; and the grotesque, the piquant, the ribald found as many lovers as the Amadis romances, or even more. The chief representatives of each variety will now be mentioned.

The first place is without a doubt occupied by Master François Rabelais (1483-1553) with his Gargantua and Pantagruel, which is more than a grotesque-humorous fiction. There is unrolled before our eyes a satirical picture of the times, which has never found its equal. There is no need for us to give a more detailed analysis of the work since this will be found in any history of literature. This world famous satire owes its origin to the suggestion of his publishers, who requested Rabelais to write a popular work to indemnify them for the poor sale of that author's medical works. So Rabelais composed his *Pantagruel roy des Dipsodes, restitué a son naturel avec ses faicetz et ses promesses esponentables; composez par feu M. Alcofribas abstracteur de quintessence* to which he soon added the revised satire *La vie tres horrifique de Gargantua, pere Pantagruel j'adis composée par M. Alcofribas, abstracteur de quintessence.* In the first book Rabelais lets the giant Pantagruel journey through all provinces of folly. Everywhere he punishes fools and protects the righteous. His companion is the infinitely amusing Panurge, who addresses him in all possible languages following the evil custom of the scholars of his time; and they exchange experiences. Rabelais lashes the crimes of the church and the monks and their lascivious life with unsurpassed, vigorous humor. In line with the comic content, the narrative is adorned with speeches and words in foreign languages, and with linguistic frills of all sorts which despite their nonsense, give a most just characterization of the persons represented.

Naturally this book was a thorn in the side of those whom it attacked, and it would have fared ill with the author had not the royal hand protected him. Francis I in particular took great delight in the unrestrained merriment of the delightful work. However, Rabelais never aimed at lewdness in these books. Even as prudish a historian of literature as E. Engel admits that while certain chapters in Gargantua are so immeasurably indecent that it is impossible to give even a list of its headings, it must nevertheless be admitted that Rabelais is never lewd, no matter how far he strays beyond the bounds of what is permissible to the writer or artist, or how much he indulges in offensive and monstrous nastiness. He never aims to excite the reader sensually, though he always and quite without scruple, uses the shocking word to designate the shocking deed. In other words, although he revels in the vocabulary of coarseness so that many chapters are complete lexica of pornography, which have no equal even in the wide realms of French literature, he never smirks, and only uses such words to portray faithfully coarse men and raw situations.

In the rhymed foreword to Gargantua, Rabelais expresses himself unequivocally about the purpose of his work:

Mieulx est de ris que de larmes escrire
pource que rire est le propre de l'homme.

The hostility of the theologues is quite understandable for even Protestant literature cannot show more witty and malicious mockery than Rabelais offers in the chapters 49 to 54 of the third book, and chapters 3 to 8 of the fourth book of Pantagruel. His work is a splendid antidote to the literature of libidinousness and pruriency—like a mudbath. His piercing scorn is also directed against the female sex, particularly against the immorality of his feminine contemporaries. What a grotesque impression is created by his account of the unusual condition of the *laborator naturæ* (clitoris) which in some women is so long, large, thick, fat and vigorous, that they can twine it around their bodies five or six times as a girdle, or actually use it as a lance in certain circumstances!

How insatiable the women of his time were may be gathered from the following anecdote from Rabelais: One fine morning Panurge met a fellow who was carrying two baby girls of about two or three years of age in a double knapsack, slung across his shoulders—one in front and the other on his back. Panurge who had but little respect for the female species asked the man immediately whether the children were virgins. To which the man replied that he had been carrying them about for two years; that the one in front whom he carried on his chest—he supposed that she was still a virgin; but as for the one whom he carried on his back, he could not undertake to speak with certainty.

Quite in the spirit of Rabelais, but not at all a part of literature, are the *Erreurs popolaires et propos vulgaires touchant la médicine et la régime* of Laurent Joubert (1578). The very headings betray the roguish wantonness of the author: why one should not meet women before going to bed; the abuse of women who bathe in order to become gravid; how it is possible that a woman should bear nine children at once; whether it is good for a woman to sit on a hot kettle or place the night cap of her husband on her belly to assure an easy parturition; are there sure signs of a girl's virginity; etc.

BOOK II: THE SIXTEENTH CENTURY

Obviously the roguish author of this coarse humor has caught the breath of Rabelais' spirit.

Guillaume Bouchet, who lived between 1513 and 1593 and was a bookseller at Poitiers, has also long been famed as an imitator of Rabelais. He wrote the *Series*, fifty gallant "jokes" which have the effect of well-told anecdotes in their pregnant setting. One reads here of the lady who has to sit on the *pot de chambre* and gets pinched in her private parts by a crayfish; of the dreamer who dreams of gold but who receives turds; of the cuckolded husband who must get into the privy at once but who cannot open the door because his wife and her lover are having a very important conference there. Whereas the stories of the *Heptameron* and the *Nouvelles Récréations* still contain much that is superfluous, the tendency toward the pure form of the anecdote appears ever more clearly in the last decades of the 16th century, to assume final form in the work of Bouchet and Beroalde de Verville. In these anecdotes of the *Series*, and of the *Moyen de parvenir* soon to be discussed, with their condensation and pointedness, the material of the old French fabliaux assumed the form of the modern French *conte*. A few illustrations will prove this.

¶ A pregnant woman feels that her hour is due. The midwife supports her and desires to put her upon the bed. Whereupon she cries: "No, not on the bed; that's where I met my misfortune."

¶ A group was conversing about the slightness of hand found among gypsies, and one man related how they took a stone, enclosed it in their fist in the sight of all, and were so skilled in making it disappear that no one could tell whether it was still there or not. His wife who had not been listening very attentively remarked, quite naïvely: "Tush, that can't be so difficult. I always know whether it is inside or not."

¶ A newly married couple had just gone to bed and the husband was praising his wife for her chastity during their betrothal—that is, for not having granted him that which he had been so fervently desiring. Thereupon she said to him, "Yes, dear, I took great care not to let myself go in spite of the fact that I desired you, because I had already been deceived too many times in such matters."

Des Periers the valet, secretary and page of Margaret of Valois, also wrote witty anecdotes. Gay gives a full report about his life and works. Bonaventure des Periers was at once philosopher and author. He was born at the end of the fifteenth century and stood in relationship to Clement Marot and Rabelais. By Catholics he was suspected of Protestantism, and by the latter of licentiousness. In 1537 he published *Cymbalum mundi*, a collection of philosophical dialogues. Immediately, the whole edition, with the exception of two copies, was placed under embargo and destroyed. Of these two, one is in the Bibliotheque Nationale, the other in the municipal library of Versailles. The protection of Margaret of Valois saved him from persecution and the following year another edition was issued by a different publisher, Bonn of Lyons. For a short while he belonged to the intimate circle gathered around Margaret which was devoted to the cultivation of *bel-esprit*. In 1543 he committed suicide in a fit of insanity. After his death his works were issued by his friends, and among them were *Les Nouvelles*. The following are some of the erotic stories of des Periers that may be considered characteristic of his time:

¶ Concerning the three unmarried sisters who give witty answers to their husbands on the night of their marriages.

¶ Concerning the procurator who has a girl from the country come to minister to his needs, and his secretary who enjoyed her too.

BOOK II: THE SIXTEENTH CENTURY

¶ Concerning the Scotchman and his wife who displayed quite an unaccountable skill during the first skirmish.

¶ Concerning the poor bumpkin who found his lost ass thanks to an enema that his physician had given him.

¶ Concerning a superstitious physician who would play with his wife only when it rained; and of the great good fortune that befell her upon his death.

¶ Concerning a priest who let himself be castrated at the instigation of his housekeeper.

¶ Concerning the trick that a young woman of Orleans employed in order to ensnare a young student to whom she had taken a fancy.

¶ Concerning the lawsuit that a mother-in-law brought against her son-in-law because he had not deflowered her daughter on the first night.

¶ Concerning two youths of Sienna who were in love with two Spanish women, of whom one in order to help the other attain the pleasures of love, went through great dangers, which subsequently brought him much joy and satisfaction.

In much the same way Nicolas of Troyes, the saddle master, wrote down the humorous stories that came to his ears. He lived about 1530 at the time of Francis I and composed his stories just before the Heptameron. His stories depend on Boccaccio, La Sale, *Cent nouvelles nouvelles*, Gesta Romanorum, old sermons and books of legends, the dialogues of the holy Gregory, Jacob de Vitry and others. In order to characterize the stories a bit, we will summarize the contents of some of them:

¶ A young woman engaged to be married has her duties knocked into her by the barn thresher in order that she may be a ready worker by the time she is married.

THE EROTIC HISTORY OF FRANCE

¶ A merchant purchases from a priest the sacrifice of all the women whom the latter has had. But the man's own wife who has been one of the company, subsequently deceives him again.

¶ A priest is enamoured of a woman painter and what happens to him after he represents, entirely naked, the crucified one upon a cross.

¶ A youthful couple were married. Once the husband leaves for a short trip to Paris and when he returns his wife asks what he has done with the little ploughman that he used to have before.

¶ A certain baker is in love with a maid and embraces her whenever he comes for the dough. Her mistress lies in wait for him one day, gives him his dough and gets in return what was coming to the maid.

¶ A young wife is persuaded that she has caused her husband to be pregnant. Whereupon his wife consents to have him transfer his pregnancy to the maid whom he promptly impregnates.

¶ A certain girl is unwilling to marry any man who has the generative organs of the male.

¶ A youth bound for Lyons lies with an abbess while en route. A hermit presents him with a ring that adds half a foot to the stature of his member. A certain bishop finds the said ring and encounters many strange adventures.

These tales are valuable to us for the historical materials they contain. Aside from this, however, the circumstantial narratives of the upright artisan are neither of literary nor cultural value.

Infinitely more alive is the master of the droll tale, François Beroalde de Verville (1558-1612), whom we now consider. He was born and raised as a Protestant but after his father's death he went over to the Catholic church, and at thirty-five became canon

BOOK II: THE SIXTEENTH CENTURY

of Saint-Gatien de Tours, in recognition of his extraordinary erudition and superb gifts. He was the author of a series of novels including *La Pucelle d'Orleans* but none of these would have rescued his name from oblivion had he not hit upon the happy notion of collecting piquant anecdotes. The volume titled *Moyen de Parvenir* appeared about 1610 with no author's or publisher's name and no place of publication. Subsequent editions bore other quaint titles, as *Le Coupçu de la Mélancholie* and *Vénus en belle humeur*, etc.

We have here a collection of extremely free tales related round the festive board. The modern reader needs much patience to read Beroalde who makes many demands upon that particular virtue because he is very prolix and repetitious. The boon companions spin their yarns to great lengths indeed. Most of the anecdotes have to do with the genital and anal regions; and it would appear as though this strong, and not at all prudish nation, took particular joy in swimming in cesspools. Beroalde finds special pleasure in putting the juiciest jests and anecdotes into the mouths of famous writers like Sappho, Rabelais, Calvin and many other scholars whom he vulgarizes before us. His influence was very considerable and for a long time his work was attributed to Rabelais. Even today we find some of his witty tales included in contemporary works.

A few examples will illustrate how coarse these anecdotes are. Several characters are conversing:

¶ THE OTHER: I will tell you all about it. Gaffer Genebrard had married a young, pretty, and dainty wife, and in due course they went to bed. He kissed her and fondled her to his heart's content (he was soon content) and then tapped her gently, saying: "Roach, sweetheart, roach." Next Friday the maid was charged to go to the fishmarket, and asked her mistress what she should buy. "Whatever you please," said the lady. "Shall I bring some roach?" (The name of a common fish.) "The devil take you! I never hear anything but roach in this house!"

¶ GAUPIL: *Roach* is a good name, considering the care that nature hath to ward off *encroachments*, otherwise women would be perpetually hoarse. But it is a wondrous thing how this mystery of nature can come together again after it has been parted.

¶ SAPPHO: It came about when Jupiter severed the androgyne. He bade Mercury sew up the bellies of the two halves; and thus the belly is tender to the touch to this day. The lace he used to sew up the man was too long, so the end hung down in front; and when he came to the woman he took too short a lace, and there was not enough to finish her; hence for want of a stitch a gash remained open. Do you understand that? Then lay it up in the cedar chest by the hearth. Know you, learned sirs, what are the seven wonders of the world? You say not a word. It is evident that I can teach you some rare doctrines, so make ready to listen. Don't you know that though the hen and the cow live in the same field neither eats buttered eggs! I will tell you greater secrets which contain the marrow of all the sciences. The seven miracles are as follows: 1. A black hen, which lays a white egg. 2. Claret, which goes in red and comes out white. 3. The spigot that has no ears, and yet hears well enough when there is talk of grappling. 4. The vessel which has its mouth at the bottom, and yet lets nothing out. 5. The bow which bends of itself without a winch. 6. The rose which sucks the marrow of men's bones, and yet does not break them. 7. The anus which opens and shuts like a purse, without any strings. Ah, ha! What do you say to that?

Here is another example from Beroalde, as witty and as coarse as the preceding excerpt and no less characteristic of the age:

¶ It fell out once on a time that as Brother Laillee was journeying to Angers, he spent a night in the house of a good woman who had long known him; if I am not mistaken she was called La Coibaude. When he was in bed they put a chamber-pot on the stool beside him, and on the same stool was a round and hollow rat-trap; not one of the traps with a door, but with a spring that gripped the rat by the middle of the body. This trap was at least half a foot in diameter, it was ready set, and the spring was stiff and strong. In the night Brother Jean woke up to micturate, and took hold of the trap by the rim, thinking it had been the pot. He then presented John Chouart to the instrument, and as it stretched down as far as the catch, the spring went off, and grabbed hold of the Greyfriar. He bawled out loudly enough to awake the Seven Sleepers, and they brought a candle, and set him free.

¶ The maid laughed at him with all her heart, for she was now avenged of an ill turn he had done her when he was sleeping there before. It was in summertime, and the house being full, he who was a familiar friend slept in the lower room, where the good wife and her maid lay in another bed. The rascal got up to take the air, and the night being dark, he called out to the maid: "Marchioness, I have lost my way; prithee, come and set me right." The poor wench got up and went to him, and in the meantime the friar had tucked up his shirt and was holding his arms high above his head. "Prithee, take me by the hand," said he. "Alack!" quoth she, "your fingers are mighty thick; no, it's your arm. Why, what's this? Go away, I will have nothing to do with you." With that she gave him a push and left him in the dark.

In marked contrast to Beroalde's naturalness and primitiveness is the courtliness that emanates from every line of the *Heptameron*, despite its attention to sexual matters. Marguerite de Valois, born on April 11, 1492 and dying on 21st of December 1549, stood at the center of the literary circle gathered at the court of her brother, Francis I. Rabelais thought a great deal of her and dedicated the third book of his Pantagruel to her. Clement Marot who poetized about her was regarded as her lover. The fruit of this social intercourse was the *Heptameron des nouvelles* which was written in conscious debt to Boccaccio. The seventy-two stories are spread over eight days, and the introduction as well as the general scheme of the book reminds one of the great Italian masterpiece. A company of ladies and gentlemen who are journeying to the Pyrenees to take the baths, take refuge in a monastery in order to escape a storm and flood. To beguile the tedium of the enforced delay, everyone of the group tells a love story. Besides certain very tolerant opinions springing from the spirit of a sophisticated humanitarianism, there are some extremely forceful attacks on the evils of the time, especially on the abuses of the church, and the immorality, pride and superstition of the monks. French literature owes its first fluent and merry book of entertainment, free from excessive erudition and bombastic euphuism, to Marguerite.

In her introduction the authoress relates how the Dauphin, and Madame Marguerite (that is, herself) had resolved jointly and with the further assistance of other ladies, to write a collection of stories like Boccaccio's, whose work but recently translated by a secretary of the king, had met with great success. Lotheisen believes that the stories were not meant for publication but were intended only for a small circle of friends. In 1550 the first edition was issued by Pierre Boaistuau under the title: *Histoire des amans fortunes* but it did not bear Marguerite's name. However, since he had mutilated the text Marguerite's daughter, Johanna of Navarre, caused to be issued in 1559 a more conscientious but castrated text, under the title by which it has come to be known: *The Heptameron*. Later editions contain the unmutilated text.

The authoress set as her task the narration of real occurrences and historical incidents, in the form of the very short stories that her age loved. Generally they are of a prurient nature but told with a seemingly naïve candor. However erotic they may be, they are told quite undisguisedly but they do not aim to excite the reader through lascivious descriptions. Marguerite's pen was moved by joy in writing these venereal anecdotes which are well able to arouse even the modern reader's laughter. Marguerite was thoroughly aware of the daring nature of her material but it was part of the age and she was certainly no prude among her contemporaries. And sometimes, when an extremely erotic tale is told, Marguerite was shrewd enough, aping the hypocrisy of her time, to make it yield a pious moral.

Beroalde de Verville, des Periers and Margaret of Valois are then a few of the most significant representatives of French writers of funny tales. Their work is by no means diminished in importance because they borrowed most of their material from popular sources. Karl Amrain (Anthropophytheia x, 248) gives a very illuminating explanation of the wandering of such stories. He holds that the female domestics who are notorious for their love of tattle put into circulation all the intimate details, love talk, panurgics, obscenity, and chit-chat of their sensual and loose mistresses, the high born ladies whom they prepared for love. The tales then ran the gamut of the lower classes and the best were embellished and magnified. Finally the poets and collectors of facetiæ gave them piquant form and thus they reached the upper classes. This explains the frequent recurrence of similar stories in collections far removed in space and time. There is no question of plagiarism at all. Even today there are extant among people jokes and anecdotes which first appeared hundreds of years ago.

When we discussed the *Heptameron* we mentioned the name of Clement Marot. Born in 1495, he early became a page at the court of Marguerite where his charm and wit brought him much success with women. As valet to the king, he stood in close relationship to Diana of Poitiers. He accompanied Francis 1 on the latter's expedition into Italy, was wounded near Pavia and captured, but was soon released, and in 1525 was back in France. All sorts of gallant adventures together with the suspicion that he inclined to Calvinism brought him to jail, but he was released at the command of the king. He then went to Geneva where he became a member of the reformed church, but owing to his amorous exploits was banished from the city. He went back to Italy where he returned to Catholicism, dying at Turin in September 1544 in comparative poverty.

Of his many writings only the *Epigrams* are readable today. No matter how brilliant his other poems are they are vitiated by the defects of the style of the time, the obsolete emotion and ponderous pomp. For erotica however Marot found the clear classic form of the epigram whose master he was. He was able to enclose a whole Italian story in eight lines of verse; and so great was his skill that this morsel contained all the spice of the original. The age he lived in with its intense joy in love gave him the material for his maddest inspirations and he created pictures which recall the strength of a Goya. Marot's epigrams entertained and corrupted the dazzling court of Francis, and they still sparkle, like little mirrors, with all the license and insouciance of that time.

The driving force of Marot's period, the force that colored and ruled over its thought and emotion was the erotic. It has been suggested that Charles VIII of Burgundy, to whom all Europe is responsible for the spreading of *lues* (according to Bloch) undertook his Italian expedition merely because he yearned for Italian women. He and his men were received with great enthusiasm. For over one hundred and twenty days and nights, the king and his soldiery revelled in a limitlessly giddy life, until the defeat at the river Tarro on July 6, 1495. He was just barely able to force his march with a part of his baggage. The Veronese physician Alexander Benedictus who was an eye witness related that among the booty there was found the illustrated diary of the king in which were inscribed the names of all the beauties whose lover he had been, and each one

BOOK II: THE SIXTEENTH CENTURY

was pictured therein with all her charms. In this way did the royal libertine hope to perpetuate the memory of the pleasures of his insane sensuality in various Italian cities. But this catalogue has been lost. The loveliest and noblest of the creatures arranged a grandiose spectacle at Chieri on September 6, 1494. They wanted to wish the monarch luck upon his arrival and proclaim him the protector of the fair sex. Among other scenes which they portrayed for his royal delectation was an actual confinement.

There is one authentic eye witness who has depicted the unbridled life of pleasure characteristic of his time with clarity and fidelity, namely Pierre de Bourdeille, Seigneur de Brantome (1539-1614). His childhood was spent at the court of the queen of Navarre. Henry II bestowed upon him the abbey of Brantome, by which name he has come to be remembered. After journeys through Italy, Spain, England and Scotland he participated in the campaigns of his time and finally in a sudden fall of his horse sustained grave injuries which kept him in bed for four whole years. During this period he devoted himself to study and to the writing of his works. On July 5, 1614 he retired to his castle which he had built at Richmont, a mile and a half away from the abbey. His most famous work, *Gallant Ladies*, is entirely subjective throughout. We see and hear the courtiers who have been born and reared in fastidiousness, and how they trifle away their days. Everything amuses them, for everything has a ridiculous side. Brantome is a brilliant chatterer, nonchalant and amusing, who blurts out the secrets of discreet alcoves with cunning little eyes and corked ears. We moderns are attracted by the impartiality of his presentation, and with the unconcerned manner in which he treats the most intimate things. But the charge of frivolity cannot be maintained against him. There are many contributions to sexual pathology in his work. And not alone for this reason is it of definite value to the physician as well as to the historian.

His chronicle of scandals contains seven treatises on the following themes—1: Concerning women who cultivate love and make their husbands cuckolds. 2: What has the most charm in love—the emotion, the face, or speech. 3: Concerning pretty legs and their charms. 4: Concerning older ladies who are as eager for love as their younger sisters. 5: How fair and honorable ladies love valiant men, and the latter, courageous women. 6: Why one should never speak ill of women, and of the consequences that follow therefrom. 7: Concerning married women, widows and maids, and which of these are the best to love.

These seven headings by no means exhaust the contents of the work. Brantome no sooner begins his theme than every name and expression calls up an anecdote which he promptly sets down. This in turn provides material for interesting parallels, and so he laboriously returns to the starting point—but he doesn't stay there very long. For very soon another *bon mot* or piquant story ensnares him which he cannot for all the world pass over. He gives homage to the beautiful and "honorable" women who grant their love despite marital shackles, whenever and to whomsoever they please, and his sympathy is entirely on the side of the fair sex. A tremendous amount of interesting material is revealed to us in this work which is of great value in the history of culture and manners, because it reveals to us a clearer and more consistent picture of that period than could be derived from a thousand sermons.

CHAPTER V
THE SEVENTEENTH CENTURY

"THE good old times" to which harmless old souls always refer, never really existed. They are merely a utopia, a beautiful and pious wish, but alas! no more. Every century has its merits and its weaknesses. No age is really better or worse; it is merely different. The personal viewpoint of the historian is responsible for his drawing one age in gray and another in rosy colors.

In sixteenth century France we already find all genres of literature and erotic writers, from the most delicate emotional depictions to the foulest brothel-poetry, from the serious learned writer to the coarsest and most unintelligent buffoon. And in the France of the seventeenth century, there is no lack of erotic light literature, nor of anti-royalist and anti-clerical pamphlets, nor of free chansons, nor of lascivious popularizations and outlines of sex.

Thus for instance we might mention the pamphlet which Adrien de Montluc directed against the government, entitled *Infortune des filles de joie suivie de la Maigre* (1648). In this brochure the author espouses most energetically the interests of the *filles de joies* whom there was talk of compelling to settle outside the walls of Paris. *Lupanie, histoire amoureuse de ce temps* (1668), attributed to Blessebois, is generally regarded as a satire directed against the Montespan, but erroneously, since this short erotic story portrays a middle class milieu. This same Pierre de Blessebois was also the author of another work: *Le Rut*, which contains an indiscreet and candid account of his relations with a Mlle. Scay. In addition, there are extant a number of scandalous stories about Alençon which the author terms a modern Sodom.

Every one of the crowned heads served as a target for obscene jest and satire, despite the extremely strict censorship. For example there is the *Description de l'isle des Hermaphrodites* directed against the bisexual Henry III, and the *Histoire secrete des Amours d'Henri IV* by Caucont de la Force, which exposes the love-life of Henri IV.

The immoral life of the clergy and the inmates of the convents are criticised in *Le libertinage secret de cloitre*, (1683) and *Le moine au parloir* (1682). The latter work is a collection of more than bold tales and anecdotes, in prose and verse, whose chief headings will give one a notion of the contents: *les tétons naissants, la réligieuse en chemise, l'accouchement, le chat, le ventre libre, le bon office*, etc.

Collections of chansons are very numerous. I will merely mention the *Le nouveau cabinet des Muses gaillardes* (1660), reprinted frequently in the eighteenth, nineteenth and twentieth centuries.

Among the most important works in the popularizations of sex, should be mentioned *Tableau de l'amour conjugal* (1685), by Nicolas Venette, often reprinted, and *Le nouveau jardin de l'amour* (1671).

In other words, in this erotic history of France no lengthy proof is needed that lascivious literature existed there in the seventeenth century. Indeed, contemporary writers confirm the inclination of their contemporaries to excesses, and to a naturalistic conception of the sexual. Nevertheless, their testimony must be accepted with great reservation, for the greatest failing of most historians is the tendency to generalize from but a few if true particulars. It would be absurd to brand an age as evil and barbarous because immorality

BOOK II: THE SEVENTEENTH CENTURY

and brutality were immoderately widespread. There is no doubt that erotic manners occupied a predominating place in seventeenth-century France; but it is equally certain that there were to be found unprejudiced and incorruptible men who did not permit themselves to be swept away by the whirlpool of sensuality but kept their heads cool in order to judge the weaknesses of their time. A few such will now be mentioned.

Chief among these writers is Gideon Tallement des Réaux (1619-1692) whose *Histoiriettes* is of the first importance for a knowledge of the manners and morals of the time. What Brantome was to the age of Francis I, Tallement is for that of Henry IV and Louis XIII. While Brantome is lengthy and detailed, the later writer is brief, succinct, and hence pleasant to read. For a long time the manuscript remained unprinted. In 1803 when the library of the Castle of Montigny was sold, the Marquis de Chateaugiron purchased it for twenty francs, had the 798 folio pages copied. Later, when the society of French Bibliophiles was organized, he turned it over to them for publication. Since 1833-36 when the first edition appeared there have been numerous other editions.

Another writer of significance is Bussy-Rabutin, the notorious author of the *Histoire amoureuse des Gaules*. He sprang from a very distinguished family, entered the military service very early and earned great distinction. During the war of the Fronde he first served Prince Conde but then took the side of the King. Until 1659 he was lucky, but afterwards a series of misfortunes descended upon him. The most improbable rumors were circulated about him. Thus he was reputed, in the company of three cronies, to have celebrated the black mass during passion week; and again, to have exhumed a corpse with which his drunken fellows danced crazy dances. The penalty for these rumored extravaganzas was a year of exile. What made his transgressions worse in the eyes of the king, was the growing distribution of the *Histoire amoureuse des Gaules*. Bussy had hit upon the idea of writing down the gallant adventures of great ladies, partly for his own pastime and partly for the delectation of his mistress, Madame de Monglas. Only four or five persons were permitted to read the manuscript but one of these few was a traitor. Madame La Baume divulged the contents, and what was much worse for the author several courtiers were able to persuade Louis XIV that his mistress had not fared so well in this work. The embittered king didn't hesitate to sentence the foolhardy pamphleteer, who had had the additional audacity to send him the manuscript, to thirteen months in the Bastille. After his release, Bussy had to retire to his estate, and it was not until 1682 that he regained permission to reappear at court. In 1693 he died at the age of seventy-five. There is no doubt that Bussy owed his incarceration entirely to the king's personal displeasure for there was nothing novel in the *Histoire* to justify his punishment. At the same time various other works and collections of courtly gossip had appeared and their authors were not molested: *Histoire d'amours d'Henri IV avec diverses lettres escrites a ses maitresses, et autres pieces curieuses* (1664); and *Les Amours du Palais Royal* (1665). All of them sought to show that under Henry IV and Louis XIII marital infidelity was a pastime, under Louis XIV a rule, and later an obligation. The cuckolded husband was regarded not as a tragic person but always a comical creature at whose expense one had lots of fun; indeed, not even crowned heads were immune from the fate of wearing horns. The various editions of the *Histoire* were naturally secretly printed and distributed.

Bussy-Rabutin can also be regarded as the author of an extremely obscene comedy *La Comtesse d'Olonne* which was circulated in many editions. The play is enacted in the bedroom of the Comtesse of Olonne. Argenie, who represents the countess suddenly awakes

BOOK II: THE SEVENTEENTH CENTURY

in her bed, in a fright induced by a nightmare. In her dream she sees her former lover and husband, the duke of Candole. As she berates him for his neglect of marital duties he breaks out into imprecations, and prophesies the impotence of Argenie's next lover. The account of the dream is interrupted by the visit of a friend, the Countess Fiesko. Argenie, who has a violent passion for Count Guiches, sounds her friend about the latter, and is informed that he is a zealous skirt chaser. This news doesn't discourage the countess at all and the next scene finds her in a love episode with the object of her desires who at first labors under the curse foretold in the dream. It is only after many repeated exertions that the Count triumphs and then both lovers compliment each other upon their venereal prowess.

An important contribution to the history of morals was made by Count Anthony Hamilton (1646-1721) in his *Mémoires du Comte de Grammont* (1713), in which he describes the loves of his brother-in-law, Count Philibert of Grammont, at the court of Charles II of England. The *Mémoires* of Duke Saint-Simon also contain much important material.

When we turn to *belles lettres* we find that light literature in general which has no artistic aims but is created for no higher purpose than entertainment, does not evince a particularly high moral conception. Stories were proliferated in whole series as well as in single works, and no country, historical epoch or personality was safe from exploitation as a possible theme. There was nothing that could daunt the insatiable commercial ambitions of the writers of this fustian. If one series failed, it was refurbished with a new title and was once again sent into the world. The curiosity and libidinousness of readers was aroused by such titles as *Les amours de* ——, *Histoire amoureuse*, etc. By the end of the seventeenth century this genre which had been losing in artistic value every year was only fit for supplementary readings by the unlettered.

In all these tales the word "love" occurs constantly, and accompanies man from cradle to the grave. Children live in expectation of future love, and the aged revel in memories of past loves. But withal this "love" is no emotional content. It is merely a means of pleasure without any depth, nothing more than gallantry. This was perhaps induced by excessive prudishness for in the attempt to appear "decent" these scribblers fell into affectation. The effort to remove all sensual elements from the sphere of love led to the same folly as the converse effort to banish all ethical elements.

Despite the reign of the precious, mannered style there were none the less dissenting voices. Moliere in his *Les Precieuses* led the battle against the current folly and lesser figures helped to prove that original wit still could be found. In his humorous novel *Francion* (1622) Sorel de Souvigny poked fun at the idyllic and precious tales of his period and included a number of dirty stories for the sake of the moral effect.

Gradually the sexual note became more audible in the higher type of novel and play. For the first time a courtesan was displayed, without any camouflaging, in the *Gustav Vasa* of Madame de la Force. Soon the password of the time was *Volupté*, the sentimental ecstasy which exercised complete control over the senses and the souls of men. The olfactory organ of upright and unprejudiced apprentices accustomed to the strong smell of the stable could find but little joy in the close odor of the perfumed salon. By the side of the ethereal poesy of the precious, the century can show a number of strong erotics which have not yet lost their original attractiveness, especially the *Aloisia Sigea* and *L'école des filles*.

Undoubtedly the most famous erotic work in world literature after Aretino's *Raggionamenti* is the *Aloisia* or *Luisa Sigea*, as it is

BOOK II: THE SEVENTEENTH CENTURY

titled in English. These dialogues of love appeared in 1660. The supposedly Spanish authoress who was as a matter of fact a descendant of French stock and later became court lady to Donna Maria of Portugal, was born about 1500 and died in 1560. Her chastity and virtuous deportment brought her many admirers throughout the Spanish realm. But this did not hinder the real author from bringing her name into connection with erotic obscenity *par excellence*. It was perfectly clear to the thinking people of that time that no such book could have been composed by a woman, least of all by one who led such an exemplary life. Nor has the supposititious translator, the famous professor of the University of Leyden any relation with the dialogue; for the real author, the lawyer Nicolas Chorier of Grenoble, composed it in the Latin language. The latter lived between 1622 and 1692, became a doctor of laws at the age of seventeen, *procureur du roi* in 1666, and later was raised to the nobility. He enjoyed a pretty unsavory reputation and was, for example, accused of having stolen three capitularies from the archives of the Archbishop of Grenoble which he later shamelessly sold back to the cleric at considerable prices. At the expense of a M. de May, the attorney-general of the Parlement, Chorier's dialogues were published by a Grenoble bookseller, one Nicolas. The latter had to shut down his business and flee to escape worse punishment, which was only stayed at the intervention of very powerful friends. Search was instituted for the author but Chorier was passed by since Aloisia contained two Latin verses composed by him and published in 1680 among a volume containing his own Latin poems. He maintained that these verses had been stolen and inserted into the Aloisia to mislead the public.

In the introduction the author, anonymously of course, employs a trick dear to contemporary authors of erotica. He describes himself as having miraculously come into possession of the lost manuscript of Meursius: "It were a pity to withhold these dialogues from our generation. Who could be so dull and insensible as not to grieve over the deprivation of such piquant, such pleasant, nay, such instructive percepts of a merry life?" Chorier had living models for the characters of this Sotadicum but we have no key to identify them by. Alcide Bonneau claims that there was one copy of this work in which a contemporary had indicated the key in notes scrawled across the margins of his private copy. According to this, the heroine of the tale narrated by Octavia in the Fascennine dialogue was a certain Anastasie Serment whose beauty, wit and free life in Paris were celebrated by Corneille and Quinault. Perhaps too Chorier composed preliminary studies for the dialogues since he speaks in his memoirs of a book, designated as Anecdota, neither published nor shown to his friends, in which he had described ninety-five intimate and scandalous portraits of men and women known to him. If these anecdotes are not identical with *Luisa Sigea*, as Bonneau hints, we must lament the loss of a valuable work.

Despite the fact that Chorier's authorship was so successfully concealed as to prevent agreement even by recent authorities, the fiction of the translation from the Spanish seems transparent enough. Had the manuscript been translated from that tongue and were the authoress a Spanish lady, it would appear remarkable that practically all the action takes place in Italy, and that all the characters are Italians. If examples are chosen from other lands it is France and Germany but never Spain that is called upon. Chorier probably saw the force of this point himself as time went on, for in the Geneva edition of 1678 he added a seventh dialogue which is enacted in its entirety upon Spanish soil and by Spanish characters; but there is no word in explanation of the addition.

BOOK II: THE SEVENTEENTH CENTURY

It is perhaps possible that Chorier entertained hopes of revising the whole work to make good the omission, but the plan was never carried out. It is much more likely that he left many gaps in his work which would at once give verisimilitude to his work and thus lend it greater plausibility as well as diverting suspicion of its authorship from himself. In the latter ambition he was entirely successful and he remained unmolested, for no proofs could be obtained against him. He was careful not to give any sign that the work was his own except for a few small hints in other works. Thus in his memoirs, no longer accessible today, he mentions two youthful works one of which was of a sotadic nature, which may refer to the dialogues. Then too, the edition of 1678 contains a short poem which had appeared in the edition of his Latin poems published in 1670. Now this poem contains practically the same denunciations of one Tubero, who was probably a personal enemy of the author, so that we must assume a common authorship. Furthermore, in 1660 he caused the work to be printed in the same format with his other works. Finally, the style is the same, and the same figurative use of words leaves no doubt of Chorier's authorship.

The six original dialogues are entitled: The Skirmish, Tribadicon, Fabric, the Duel, Pleasures, Frolics and Sports. In choice, flowery language, with copious erudition derived from Latin writers, Ovid particularly, Chorier describes with his unexampled frankness, brilliant wit, humor, and masterful gifts of observation, the shameless and lewd conduct of the higher classes of his time. He employs the same fidelity as Aretino in the latter's depiction of the mad economy of the Roman procuresses and their world. Indeed, Aretino's influence is undeniable—not only in the author's high praise of this "divine genius" but also in his assigning of the action to the same period as the *Raggionamenti* (about 1530), and in the use of the names of Aretino's friends for his chief characters.

THE EROTIC HISTORY OF FRANCE

The other famous work of this class bears the title of *L'école des filles*, etc. This original edition (1665) is lost today, but in the municipal library of Breslau there is to be found a reprint dated 1667. The author is concerned to instruct in matters of love those young girls who still live with their mothers, in order that they may afford genuine joy in the sport of Venus to their future husbands or lovers. Hence the whole art of love is covered in two dialogues.

Robinet, a young Parisian merchant of the time of Louis XIII, loves Fanchon who is too naïve to know what's expected of her. In order to get what he wants, he asks Susanna, a girl of experience, to light the flame in Fanchon. The incendiary does her task so well that Robinet soon finds a willing ear and perfect delight in Fanchon. In the second dialogue Susanna again visits the other girl who describes the events of the devirgination. Both compare experiences and what one lacks, the other supplies. Poems of praise are sung to the genitals of both sexes, and there is a discussion of those vicarious devices of love which may fill a woman's solitary hours. In brief, we have here a whole compendium of the art of love. The author Helot, Milot, Millitot or Milliot, as designated in the preface, got into very hot water because of the publication of this book. He had to flee, his book was burnt under the gallows and his effigy hung upon them.

They were not very forbearing during that period in their treatment of authors of such pornographic works. As early as Louis XIII it was felt that the art of printing might become a disturber of the public peace and a corruption of its morals. Hence from 1660 until 1756 some 869 authors, publishers and printers were sentenced to the Bastille for works inimical to religion, the state, or morals. For a libel against Mme. de Maintenon, two printers were hung in 1694, and the other participants severely punished.

BOOK II: THE SEVENTEENTH CENTURY

But a generation earlier such a hard fate was already the lot of one Theophile de Viau whose life reminds one strongly of Villon's except that the latter remains much more sympathetic. A collection of very bawdy verse appeared which found but little recognition at first, but in 1622 a reprint was issued, augmented by numerous piquant pieces which were attributed to Colletet (1598-1659) and Viau (1590-1626) under the title *Le Parnasse des poètes satyriques*.

The earlier work bore Viau's name upon the title page. Viau denied authorship but his denial did not help him for very long. A year later, the hostile Jesuits accused him of irreligion and immorality. A bench of judges selected to convict him found the charges true and sentenced our poet, after he had fled to Chantilly, to death by fire. Bertholet was sentenced to the gallows, and Colletet to nine years of exile. On the very day the verdict was rendered, Viau's effigy was burnt under the gallows. Shortly afterwards, he was arrested and languished in jail for two years awaiting his fate. At the expiration of that time Parliament quashed the original sentence but banished him from France.

Today we regard Viau's punishment as harsh for there were other collections of erotic verse which were tolerated freely. One example is *Les Muses gaillardes* (1609). No fuss was ever made about it though there is very little difference between it and the *Parnasse*. From this and other cases, we must conclude that the reason for Theophile Viau's persecution was not his immorality but his irreligiosity.

A far greater popularity was enjoyed by a subsequent collection: *Le cabinet satyrique* (1632). This collection is one of the cleverest products in the field of panurgic poetry. It is one of the few works whose originality cannot be denied, nor should its literary value be underestimated. An impartial reader cannot refrain from admiring the graceful treatment of single thoughts, and the pointed expressions. One must go back to Martial for a similar treatment of equally clever thoughts. Anyone of experience knows how monotonous the erotic theme can become unless wit and humor can discover new angles for treating the novel suggestions. Hence we can give the full meed of praise to the genius of this much maligned poet. The *Cabinet* is not a whit more decent than the *Parnasse* but remained unmolested by the persecutions which beset the latter, because the author was careful enough not to attack religion and the church.

Perhaps a few examples of these witty epigrams will help to show the nature of the work. The author would agree perfectly with Coleridge that all thoughts, all passions, desires, whatever stirs this mortal frame, all are but instruments of love and minister to his sacred flame. He would even go further and insist that the sexual embrace is the paramount, propulsive, central goal of all human activity. But this embrace is entirely dependent on the whim of the Master Iste.

Hence an impotent man cannot be counted in the council of men who can calculate their happiness in accordance with their priapic perimeters. Thus a youth who craves the highest favor of his lady but who has been but poorly provided is answered by her: "Remove it! I'm afraid it's a caterpillar."——If a maiden loves to play the flute, the poet knows another instrument for her artistic efforts.——Or, "Madame, I bring you a beautiful bird."—"But this is no bird." "Well, I admit there is a slight difference. Whereas other birds hate to get into cages, this one yearns for it so much that it weeps with joy."

The more or less skillful pretenses of girls who give themselves if the man is only daring enough, are jeered at ironically. "I told her that I wanted it. She was angry when she heard it. But when I did it a little while later I noticed that she thoroughly enjoyed it, although

BOOK II: THE SEVENTEENTH CENTURY

she hadn't with her ears shortly before."——A young man tells his sweetheart: "I am so full of love I can't sleep nights. You don't believe me? Very well. Just let me sleep with you and you'll see." ——The newly wedded wife asks her husband on the wedding night: "Am I not sweet?"——"Yes," answers the newly wedded husband, "but the devil take the man who taught you it."——A cuckold returns home in a dark night and uses his marital privileges. But when he begins to speak, the loving wife sighs disappointedly and murmurs sleepily: "O, it's only you."——When Lisa's song is praised "you mustn't say she sings like an angel but that she sings as though she were being loved up."

It is questionable who is more versed in the art—men or women. A lady promised a large sum of money to a poet if he would lead her into Eden's lovely paradise ten times in one night. "Very well," he replies "count out the money and get ready." Occasionally the debt to Martial is very obvious, giving the impression of a translation. Thus in the case of Lisa who once received a fortune for her favors but has since sunk so low that no one wants her even gratis. Or when a man sends one of his friends Aretino's postures but advises him to have a girl around lest he become a husband without a wife.

Aside from these verses on special incidents there are many of a more general nature: the defense of breasts worn exposed, blasts against courtesans, jeremiads inspired by gallant disease, comparison of the instruments of love with all possible things, comparison of the two genital apparatuses, pæans to the male organ, and lyrics on the female parts. These few comments will afford some notion of the highly interesting contents of this compilation.

The lion's share of this compilation was borne by Mathurin Regnier (1573-1613), a priest who led a fairly loose life in which, to be sure, he differed but little from many of his colleagues. But intellectually, he stood head and shoulders above them and became the founder of the so called classic satire in France. Possessed of a thoroughly sensuous nature, he exercised no inhibitions on the choice of his expressions. His presentation is naturalistic, but not earnest; factual, but merry. His purpose was to make those whom he attacked ridiculous, and every means, including obscenity, was valid for this purpose.

Nevertheless, despite their undoubted importance the mass of such writings and writers are known only to students of the erotic history of French literature and to a number of book collectors of erotics. But there is one man of this century who still lives, Jean La Fontaine (1621-1695). He is proof of the contention that to achieve immortality it is not necessary to have contributed epoch-making discoveries or profound investigations in some realm of human research. La Fontaine did none of these things. All he did was to write light verse about common themes filled with the charm of his own personality. With the same openness and grace that characterized his fables he later versified the themes of the old French fabliaux, of Boccaccio, Ariosto, the Hundred Merry Tales, and Rabelais.

In 1655 the first volume of his *Contes* appeared which owed its composition to Marie Ann Mancini, duchess of Bouillon and niece of Mazarin, the French cardinal and prime minister under Louis XIV. The second volume appeared in 1666 and aroused the king's displeasure. At a time when the precious bluestockings set the tone and when d'Urfée's *D'Astrée* was the popular book of high society, the open eroticism of La Fontaine could not elicit undivided applause. The publication of the third book took place in 1675, at the instigation of the clergy. Yet on the same day on which M. de la Reinie had officially prohibited the distribution of the *Contes*, as a sapient man, he privately invited the author to lunch.

BOOK II: THE SEVENTEENTH CENTURY

When the prohibition seemed to have been forgotten, the fourth book was issued (1685). The poet never suspected that his elegant and amusing verses could give offense. When he lay on his deathbed the shameful character of the book was mentioned to him. Whereupon he asked in all naïve wonder: "Are they then really so bad?" He enjoined his friends to atone for his sins in this manner. One hundred copies of his tales should be sold and the proceeds given to the poor. In the tale, *The Geese*, he explains with considerable persuasiveness that his efforts couldn't possibly do harm; that all the furore aroused by his merry jokes was so much ado about nothing and that hence it were best to let his work go unmolested.

La Fontaine's tales are better than their reputation, which doesn't say much because they enjoy a vicious reputation. Why? They are no better and no worse than the other gallant tales of Piron, Grecourt, Gresset which that century and the following one were very fond of. If La Fontaine was the first to achieve excellence in this craft, it certainly is not to be taken as a proof of his immorality, but rather of the playful dallying taste of his age and the mood of the people whose child he was. These tales are immoral if we accept the moral code of prudes. It is platitudinous that every age has its own moral code. La Fontaine is an admirable chatter-box, giving the impression that he is having a pleasant chat with the reader. Moreover, often he deliberately digresses to present some good-humored moral reflections, which justify him to the reader all the more. None of his countrymen ever again achieved such a graceful tone, such a flexible form as La Fontaine's, who was the crowning glory of the erotic literature of seventeenth-century France, and the most truthful historian of the morals of that period.

BOOK III
THE EIGHTEENTH CENTURY

CHAPTER VI
THE GOLDEN AGE OF LOVE

IN THE cultural history of the Occident there have been two great periods of erotic literature—the period of imperial Rome and the rococo. To be sure, Greece and the Renaissance contributed considerably, but there is little extant of the former and the achievements of the latter are far surpassed in magnitude and quality by the two first mentioned. But the first two are themselves very different. Rome may be considered cynical, raw, crude, coarse, extremely frivolous. Yet it cannot be accused of producing witless things or aiming merely to arouse sensuality, although there were a number of such works according to some of the writers preserved to us.

Utterly different was France of the last half of the seventeenth century. Louis XIV with his basic tenet of *L'état c'est moi*, and his court set the tone. There was now no room for free participation in politics, for independent activity in public life. Everything was decreed from above, so interest in politics declined. The personal element pressed to the front. One lived for sensation only and gave in to every excess provided it promised some pleasure. One lived for pleasure, took unlimited joy in the commonest of pleasures, that is, the sexual; and one ordered one's whole life to achieve a maximum of it. Later, while the ageing king was under the spell of the pious Mme. de Maintenon all this joy had to be taken in secret. Etiquette was the supreme law and style engendered the changed mood. Coat tails were made stiff with wire sieves in order to make them respectable and quite unapproachable; collars, cravats, and gloves were strengthened; the mighty and uncomfortable Allongé wig forced one to keep a gravitational posture.

When the Regent came to power all was changed at once. Grace supplanted honor and everything was cut out for ease. Grandeur in clothes and in externals had already played their rôles; the perukes wandered into the old lumber room; now the hair was worn powdered and loosely dressed in order not to hinder fast movement. Dwellings became less formal and more seductive. No more high cold rooms of state, no more grand ostentatious chambers opened only on grand occasions. Daily life was now enacted in pretty discreet boudoirs, in small salons warmly cozy and dimly lit with a soft perfumed light seeping through shades of colored silk. Voluptuous paintings beckoned from the walls where blue and white predominated; and gold-framed, crystal mirrors reflected pictures of ardent pleasures; to these the swelling sofa with easily displaceable cushions and the soft yielding fauteuil with its soft pillows clamorously invited. Orgiastic perfumes which sweetened every healthy and natural odor hung in the rooms and were good panders for amorous pleasures, served with multitudinous refinements. This joy was more pleasurable since virtue, marriage and fidelity were but poorly marketable wares.

Virtue was regarded as an empty nought. The virtue of most creatures seemed only the creation of masculine virtue, and it was difficult to guard a treasure to which all men had the key. Marriage was regarded as a free hunting ground in which anyone could poach to his utmost satisfaction. Mutual love and fidelity—how ridiculously was it considered, how insipid, how commonplace! The man found all possible joys of marriage with the lovely girls of the ballet and the opera; and the woman could have the familiar

BOOK III: THE EIGHTEENTH CENTURY

family friend. Marriage was the charter for erotic needs, and in this connection Mirabeau's confirmation is interesting. In his letters to Sophie he speaks of his relations to the daughter of Mme. Vence who one day thus addressed him. "Milord, after she is married you may do it as you both please, but pray, permit her to become married first."

It need not even be sensual lust that spurs one to infidelity, it may be just curiosity. Certainly curiosity played an important rôle in predisposing women to infidelity but the desire for change was also a motive for inconstancy. The following judgment of a contemporary writer does not by any means correspond with the facts. "The times are not become better, they can't be any different, but some change may be discerned even if it springs out of tedium and disgust with shamelessness. There will be a return to virtue to a certain degree because it affords pleasure. At present nothing is as much decried as marital fidelity but the prejudice is too strong and cannot last forever." There was no need of curbing one's desires, or one's lewdness, for the Regent set the example for all of France. After his accession to the throne he continued the same dissolute life he had lived before. Towards evening he would lock himself in the Temple, the former dwelling of the lords of the Temple and now the residence of the Princes Vendome, with his mistresses, his singers and dancers, and together with ten or twelve associates would hold wild orgies, heavily punctuated with obscenity and blasphemy.

The corrupting life of the court became worse than ever when the king of all rakes, Louis XV came to the throne. The rule by mistresses had already become the subject of satires and literary criticism during the reign of Louis XIV but the "solar" king didn't exactly appreciate the humor of these sallies. Thus, he banished one day the Italian comedy-players who had been at the court since 1661. Saint-Simon makes the following remark anent this affair. "So long as these players did no more than discharge their filth and their irreligious blasphemies they were greeted with laughter. But one day they got the idea of producing a piece by the name of *La fausse prude* which was unmistakably aimed at Mme. de Maintenon. Everyone flocked to see it, but after three or four performances the theatre had to close and within a month the actors had to leave the kingdom.

Louis xv, on the other hand, left all shame behind. The large number of his avowed mistresses did not suffice to quench his tremendous lust, whereupon at the urging of the Pompadour and the Abbé d'Aigre he caused a private brothel to be established for his own usufruct in the notorious *Parc an cerf*. At the head of this stood the Pompadour who would have to supply fresh goods continually, if she intended to keep her place at the rudder.

When the ex-brothel-inmate Dubarry was advanced to Pompadour's place as royal court strumpet, many vitriolic pamphlets were directed against her because she carried over her brothel manners to her new post, and remained open to every flattering courtier however inferior—provided he was potent in love's lists.

But these active, private orgies didn't satisfy the glowing senses of the royal scapegrace. So he had to feed his lust anew. Thus, he chose to pander to his libido by becoming a sort of vicarious *voyeur* in the following fashion. He now insisted that the Paris police inform him at regular intervals and in all piquant detail all obscene occurrences, and all scandals and sex crimes. Of these, there were plenty.

At this time Rousseau's influence began to make itself felt. If nature is good, then pleasure that does not offend her, is both permitted and justified. The feelings of shame and religious sensibility are merely the result of societal influence. Better give men unlimited

BOOK III: THE EIGHTEENTH CENTURY

sex freedom. But this cannot be accomplished by one alone; it requires a complement in others. Away then with modest yearnings, with coy wooing for a favor which if granted, one must conceal as something prohibited. Ridiculous sham! If love is something natural, one should give oneself naturally!

But the physical receives a value only when the desired pleasure bathed in beauty hightens the pleasure. Because the sexual domain has always been ruled by women, so women give the tone to love when fashion makes sexual pleasure the crowning joy. Never before or since has woman had such a dominant place as in the rococo period. Despite the fact that she lacked all legal rights, she occupied this exalted position due to a coincidence of the factors mentioned: a strict but moribund despotism, an educated but disintegrated society, sharp class differences and rising democratic levelling, political weakness conjoined with mental alertness. It was the period of tense lull before the tornado; those with weak nerves had to play at all costs in order to forget. Now in matters of pleasure woman knows no middle way. Once she has put away shame, she far surpasses man in shamelessness. Whatever she desires, she grasps firmly; even if the interest isn't deep, it holds her spellbound. Because her whole thinking and doing is concerned with the erotic, she will reveal herself without any concealment whenever man's influence is but slight. This influence man had shuffled off. Man was nothing more than a lap dog to play with, to heighten joy and arouse ecstatic feelings. In this loosening of morals man bore the greatest responsibility by permitting himself to be harnessed to the triumphal chariot of the loved one. Inactivity led to effeminacy.

This shallowness and effeminacy was stamped on science too, and especially on philosophy. The crass materialism of a Holbach, Helvetius, La Mettrie and others, led directly to the hunt for pleasure. If life is only a short span between birth and death, if there is nothing to hope for or fear after death, then all feeling, thought and action are to be concentrated on this life. Ideals which one could grasp at for support no longer existed for this sceptical group. It was folly to suppress one's impulses, since one could not hope for any reward and could find no satisfaction in such a struggle and victory. What remained therefore, except to exploit life and enjoy it as pleasantly as possible? Duty and self mastery were forgotten words; whatever was not tangible or pleasurable was hurled out. Morals erect walls and forge chains; therefore, the walls must fall and the chains be broken. It followed that soon all ethical norms were denied not out of any deep conviction but because they were felt to be uncomfortable. One further step, and marital infidelity is regarded merely as the activity of enlightened spirits and the natural satisfaction of corporeal hungers.

However, as artists of pleasure it will not do to forget that the bare material delight without intensification of joy, without the ecstatic embroideries of the spirit will finally bring ennui instead of perfect satisfaction. It was just this to-do, the costly preparations, the measuring of powers, that conferred a value upon the desired goal. For men and women alike the joy in the smart play of "wit" was paramount. Care was taken not to give one's self completely at once for the acme of refined pleasure required an alert, if brief, contest between the sexes. What was desired was to bind the other, couple him (or her), to strip the character of the other completely, all the while remaining oneself aloof. Coolness of heart is the indispensable element in these curious tournaments of sentiments. Every pleasure is the result of a fine education, resting on the mobility of the spirit which acquired its routine and perfection in the salon. All life had the character of the demi-mondaine, why not amusement?

It is so easy and pleasant to become accustomed to the shocks of a gallant conversation. See the laughter on their lips as the company

BOOK III: THE EIGHTEENTH CENTURY

listens to the naughty stories, the erotic jokes, the intimate details of the *chronique scandaleuse*. The most scabrous details won't elicit the start of dismay or the blush of surprise; but the downright and forthright recital of known and countenanced facts will bring the displeasure of the company down on the head of the uncouth narrator. Occasionally in a small company one would remove all restraint and completely indulge the desire for obscene words; and in this pastime women were in no wise outdone by the roués. Thus, it is narrated of the gorgeous lady de Sainte-Julien that when she was at table with gallant Abbés, she just loved to say the dirtiest words; and so astonishing would the words sound coming from her beautiful mouth that she turned the heads of all the men by this unrestraint of speech.

In the salon of Fanney de Beauharnais the receptions lasted from eight in the evening to six the following morning. Her chief admirers were three realistic poets: Dorat, Mercier and Cubieres, who heaped abuse at the classics and earned the title of the *truimvirat du mauvais goût*. In her salon Cazotte and Restif read their audacious works. When the actress Quinault retired from the theatre in 1742, she instituted a weekly meeting at her home of choice spirits such as Duclos, Abbé Voisenon, Count Gaylos, Crébillon, Marivaux, Voltaire and Piron. In this *Société du Bont-du-banc*, as it was known, things were very lively. Tribute was freely paid to the Muses and every free joke was applauded, every piquant anecdote laughed at if only it was clever.

If the women as rulers of the salon lowered the level and sanctioned complete revelation how much more would this undressing process take place in the realm of letters. Everybody wrote gladly, wrote well, jested wittily and gossiped blithely; there was no trace of faultfinding anywhere and one was greedy for success only in the art of pleasing. At the early age of fifteen or sixteen the young lady would leave the cloister, the general educational institution for the highborn, and inaugurate her literary career in the following fashion: Mama would present daughter with a darling little secretary, and a perfectly cunning little key. Every night when dear mama would shut her eyes in slumber, daughter whose eyes had already been opened, would slink to her little secretary and pour out her little soul in languishing letters which dallied with eroticism or celebrated joys already tasted. But alas! one grows older. The mirror shows it every day; and what was formerly genuine emotion is now pushed into the background, and weighed down under a mass of reflections, genuine or more probably factitious. The once genuine feeling has become literary and the epistolatrix is concerned only with her reflections and the reception of her efforts. The whole task is undertaken because it is pleasurable in the doing, and because it confers pleasure later when one sees one's influence upon others. Thus one escapes ennui.

It could not be otherwise than that women should set the pace here too. At the age of eighteen, Mme. de Stæl, then Miss Necker, wrote highly erotic epistles. Other ladies of the court described their first loves, extra-marital loves, etc. in obscene letters. Nor must it be supposed that gentlemen did any violence to their feelings and suppressed all traces of them when they approached letter writing. Everyone knows the erotic letters of Mirabeau to his two sweethearts. Because of their obscenity the letters of Montesquieu were kept under lock. Saint-Simon tells of a love relationship between a very high cleric, Dom Gervaise, and a nun, and the resulting correspondence. "The whole letter was a mass of vulgar expressions mixed with the filthiest words of tenderness and jests of a shockingly dissolute monk; her delights, sorrows, and sexual yearnings are all depicted with utter frankness and license."

That this mode of panurgic correspondence was not confined to

BOOK III: THE EIGHTEENTH CENTURY

great writers of sentiment or significant personalities but was a very widespread practise, the collections of Beardsley, Paul Dublin and Grand Carteret will attest. Some of these letters are very attractively set up indeed. Naked cupids, hearts and arrows serve as letter heads; letter papers are used which open and close like shutters. When the pretty one opened the shutter she would see the cupids drawing a classic phallus out of a drum, or two grenadiers presenting arms.

Along with such letters stood the *Mémoires* which were nothing more than clever gossip and scandal. Since they were responsible for many uncomfortable revelations their appearance was not greeted with unmixed pleasure and they were criticized rather unfavorably. On this point the remarks of Count Tilly, one of Marie Antoinette's circle, are interesting: "What is most to be censured in these people is not so much the indecency of their representations (I do not speak of the intentionally coarse depictions of the orgasm) as their foolish intention or desire to delude and persuade that the private vice of the great world is the public morality of that whole world. That indecent conversation conducted in the boudoir is also conducted in the business office; that young ladies of the world are puppies and snot-noses who employ the most bizarre and improper jargon for their language; that finally the school of the refined court etiquette in France is a sort of quackstall where one hears nothing but candied foulness, broad jokes and elegant nonsense. These are the figures drawn by those gentry when they desire to depict the morals of the great world. Such depictions, in which the most barbarous absence of taste is shown, deserve much more censure than isolated sketches of single immoralities which are no longer novel or rare in a century accustomed to hear such things without shame or blush."

In order properly to evaluate the worth of the literary productions of that period, we must keep in mind how the society then was organized. The king was first and last!—the sun to which the planets owed their light. His opinion was decisive for society, at least for the nobility grouped around his throne. At that time Paris was much smaller than it is today. Trains, autos, and other means of locomotion were not yet in existence, and people were condemned to greater fixity and immobility. Encounters were not for a little while only. Only at Paris and Versailles did the royal sun shine. Indeed, both the monarch and the powerful lords profited from the royal graciousness, for Louis found no joy in solitary rule. He needed praise, admiration, incense—all of which he could obtain from a group whose gratitude he won through his great generosities. His own person had very little that was lovable. On the other hand, the pleasure-hungry nobility and clergy could not do without the king's open hand. For after one had grown accustomed to the charms of Paris and Versailles it was impossible to think of living without them. The income of the neglected estate at home was scarcely sufficient for this extravagant life within the confines of the royal residence. Therefore the king who desired to assemble a rich and luxurious court about himself and to raise the nobility and the clergy above the wealthy bourgeois class, assumed the responsibility of supporting an aristocratic class in accordance with its rank. For this pomp and splendor tremendous funds were necessary. Since there were not enough positions in the royal establishment to fill with the horde of noble parasites, and since the illusion had to be maintained that the sinecures and pensions were granted for some real service, new posts were created upon paper with impossible names and functions. Those interested in this aspect of the subject would do well to read Taine's *La France contemporaine*.

Two vicious results from this profitable dependence upon the

BOOK III: THE EIGHTEENTH CENTURY

king were: (1) extravagance, with all its evil consequences and (2) the delight in gossip, which derived from the joy of scandal and nourished it. The élite, following the example of their ruler, were a weak group not made for serious work. But the dreadful idleness would have to be filled with something, and in this they were wondrously expert. Funds were never lacking, so no wish need go unfulfilled; and the more easily they were gratified, the more they were magnified. There was no longer any regard for the natural, so one sought the unnatural, the vicious; and great perfections were achieved in this search. Whoever did not lend himself willingly to abuse and did not permit himself to be drawn into the whirlpool of unlimited pleasure, was impelled to sacrifice his strongest principles by the sound and shimmer of gold.

What was not purchasable? Love of parents, children and mate—all fell under the sway of the glittering metal. Since virtue was listed so low on the exchange, the favor of the fair one could be won by him who had the most wealth, and who was, consequently, able to drive his rival from the contest. Expenditures and needs should be balanced, but alas! human demands are often in excess; hence there results a mad rush for gold, a wild pursuit of the favor of the king from whose open hand all gifts come. It is, after all, the king who will decide whether this or that noble parasite's desire shall be gratified.

The less favored one must think of other means to reach his ends. Accordingly, he launches hidden attacks, sometimes more efficacious than those of the rich and powerful. The most popular weapon is the libel, gossip, or the pamphlet. Always the gossip must be brought into connection with the person of the king if the latter, the dispenser of gifts, good and evil alike, is to be enlisted against the libeled one. That is why this sort of gossip is common, raw, cunning, poisonous, and untrue; for usually no basis exists for the accusation. But what of it? The goal has been reached. The libeled one has lost, the grace of the king has been gained, and the scandalmonger has ingratiated himself into royal favor. Even when there is no question of displacing a rival, one still scores a point with his royal majesty, who swallowed the Parisian police reports with such lusty avidity and who knew well how to price such gossip especially if it were filthy enough.

This was the public, less attractive side of gossip. The other which profaned private secrets was less reprehensible. One had so much time—and these petty fellows had very little business to attend to. One had enough means to gratify all one's desires and enough time to gossip about one's neighbor's affairs. Each knew the affairs of the other, and since life was regarded from the joyous side, judgment was not very strict. Why pretend to a morality which has no validity? One merely sought pleasant amusement and as such, gossip is invaluable. It was whispered that Count X found his wife in the arms of the singer Y, that the bosom of that renowned beauty was not quite so youthful and fresh as a score of years ago; that the pretty Clarice never goes to bed at night without having made at least three lovers happy. Today the Marquis dealt a pair of horns to the duke, tomorrow the revenge has been given, and the other head wears the horny emblem. Or a few days ago a certain ladies' man got a venereal disease, and some weeks later it is whispered that the intimate friend of the household bears the same cross. This ominous coincidence arouses laughter but no shudder; at the most there is a word of sympathy for the hard luck. For it was no more than that in the eyes of this frivolous company, since tomorrow some indiscriminate sexual union may bring us to the same pass; so let's forestall the evil interpretation now.

Not only cavaliers enjoyed the favor of women, powerful servants or stable attendants were also welcome at all times. Nerciat

BOOK III: THE EIGHTEENTH CENTURY

tells us the reason: "Since the gentlemen cavaliers and officers, in short all who once boasted polite behavior, gallant conduct and honesty, have lost their civility and set no more store by elegant deportment which has much of charm for us, the servant who is generally well built, well dressed and proud of the attention we bestow upon him, is much more serviceable for our pleasures. Moreover, he is more trustworthy, and less likely to be hazardous to his lady both before and after the relationship."

In these memoirs the most intimate female charms are described with a lack of ceremony that is amazing. Madame Tallien depicts for us her bosom and her thighs with the same fullness of detail as she expends upon her face. In the diary of a contemporary belle, Mme. Celie-Epomine Dupont occurs the following note: "Which of my gorgeous dresses shall I wear? It's no matter, for they're equally transparent. Recently at a *souper* a friend made a wager that my whole garb including rings, anklets and shoes weighed more than two silver pieces. I forthwith disrobed and won the bet."

The number of these secret memoirs is legion, so only a few characteristic ones will be mentioned. The life of that time is most faithfully mirrored in the memoirs of the prince of all adventurers, the likeable Giacomo Casanova, Chevalier de Seingalt, born at Venice, 1725, died in Bohemia, 1798. Casanova is another proof of the contention that the personality living in perpetual war with the laws of the normal citizen has much more of interest than the lives of other men, who abide by the conventionalities of social life. Today we incline to call him a rascally swindler, but the terminology of his time recognized no such designation. Crowned heads sought his presence. Frederic the Great sought to attract him to his court but the arch-restless one could not long remain in one spot and the strictly regulated life of the average bourgeois was an abomination to him. His restlessness is responsible for the uncertainty, the ups and downs of his life. Today journeying through the land in a chariot accompanied by two servants, his pockets stuffed with gold; tomorrow once again deprived of the most elementary needs, driven to sell his watch for a bit of bread. In order to obtain the means for his luxurious life he did not hesitate to deceive the credulous. When he played at cards or other games of chance he did not hesitate to cheat quite shamelessly; to him it was merely to *corriger la fortune* and he passionately praised his tactics. He was frequently brought into contact with the stolid guardians of the law who were naturally unable to appreciate his extraordinary ability; he was also compelled to make the acquaintance of the leaden prison of Venice but here too his audacity and astounding nerve saved him.

However, when we think of Casanova today, we do not remember the extraordinary wealth of his adventures. He is for us the type of all erotomaniacs. Indeed, his name would be known to merely a few scholars had he not possessed so inflammable a heart. For him love is the sum of life; thus, when, after the inexorable flight of time he lost his power over women, he became bitter and resigned and withdrew from the world. He never had one definite ideal of beauty; it was woman whom he desired. In his round of love, red, blonde and brunette sisters lend each other a hand. Young or middle-aged, slim or plump, virgin or whore—all alike tempt him. He bestows his ardent embraces upon dazzling beauty no less than upon repulsive ugliness. With imperious candor he reports his orgies with two and three, without applying any moral criterion to the situation. Undismayed, he follows his natural inclinations and never avoids the pleasure they hold in store for him. And despite the breathtaking frankness of his narration we do not lose our sympathy, for Casanova avoids all perversity, merely regarding woman as an object of natural pleasure to be discarded

BOOK III: THE EIGHTEENTH CENTURY

as soon as hunger is appeased. He does not love with his senses alone, he gives all of himself and his personality, desiring to be loved for himself. He remains true to each one so long as his restless heart has not been caught in new bonds. In every temporary sweetheart he sees a person of like rights with himself and extends the same consideration to her desire for pleasure as his own. Hence the joy he is preparing for is greater than the experience. His love wishes to encompass the object of his interest completely, body and soul.

Witty chatter is an indispensible concomitant of physical surrender; hence his great love for bed-talk. Sometimes his desire is doomed to disappointment, and frequently enough the object is merely a vessel of impure lust; then he is compelled to appeal from Venus to Mercury. But the gods have endowed their favorite with healthy blood and soon he has expelled the poisons from his body. Such little wounds sustained on the battlefield of love are not sufficient to turn him into a hater of women. No, indeed not. He sings the Canticles of Woman who alone makes life worth living. Women know how to appreciate and reward his utter surrender. When the delicate hands of one inclination loosen, and the restless one is driven to a new garden, to dust the petal of a new flower, there are occasionally tears which embitter the farewell; but no hatred ever pursues the fickle one. Sometimes, when his love has died, a long friendship blooms in its place. The actual process of all his loves, the conquest and the liberation from fetters found galling, Casanova relates in unadorned truth and pleasurable pride. Yet his vanity doesn't lead him to leave everything in a rosy glow. He reports his misfortunes in love, the blanks he has chosen in the lottery, with the same candor and admits that in his case too, Master Iste has had his whims, and on occasion has brought him into the most fatal situations. This love of truth at the cost of his reputation, is quite a sacrifice to his *amour propre*. It constitutes the best guarantee of the documentary value of these writings dealing with the social life of his time. It is this quality which has raised Casanova's document far above the great number of contemporary memoirs.

There is another work which reflects the erotic morals of France during the eighteenth century quite as faithfully, although it is not composed on so wide a background. This is the compilation of the *Mémoires secrets* by the Royal Censor, Matthieu François Pidausat de Mairobert. He was born in 1707 and committed suicide in his bath in 1779, when it became known that certain pamphlets directed against France which had appeared in the English press, had been composed by him. In his compilation of anecdotes not every bit of gossip is garnered up without criticism. All the little scandals that had been aired with gusto in the salon of Madame Doublet de Person by the daily visitors like Madame de Tencin, Du Deffand, Geoffrin, Lespinasse, Voisenon, or Piron underwent a very strict criticism as to their truthfulness; only after truth had been conscientiously sifted from fiction were they written down by Bachaumont and his successors. It would be more correct to say that Bachaumont wrote only the first form and half of the fifth volume between 1767 and 1771; and Pidausat de Mairobert took charge from 1771 and continued until his death in 1779. Then the author of the *Private Life of Louis XV* assumed control and together with a few others accumulated material until the year 1789.

These articles and memoirs contain more than mere gallant anecdotes. Politics and religion likewise play important parts therein but the gallantries occupy chief place. Particularly interesting are the notices concerning erotic writings and pamphlets. Naturally these memoirs are not to be regarded as trustworthy historical sources, for many of them are obviously a result of prejudice, and there is certainly no denying the delight in piquant indecencies.

BOOK III: THE EIGHTEENTH CENTURY

By and large however they constitute an unsurpassable reflection of contemporary social life.

The second work of this class is *L'Observateur Anglais* (1777-78), reworked in *L'espion Anglais* (1779). This too is probably the product of Pidausat's pen although there is no certainty on this point. At least this much is certain, that many remarks and verbatim quotations from this work were found scattered among his other writings. The work contains a collection of satirical and free pieces and is a most important source document for the study of prostitution in eighteenth-century France. The infamous Mde. Justine and equally notorious Mde. Gourdan maintained the most lavish brothels in France. They were figures of national importance and exercised great influence on the moral conditions of their time.

There were many supplements to the memoirs of Bachaumont and Pidausat. The Marquis d'Argens, for example, served up some very saucy details concerning the amorous relationships of the French kings combined with anecdotes and satirical verses in his *Mémoires historiques et secrets* (1739). And there were many other scandalous chronicles. The most infamous penny-dreadful journalist of this time was undoubtedly Thevenot de Morande (1748-1803) who proliferated a great deal of smut and obscenity. He led a rather active life. At the wish of his own family he was held in the Bastille for a while, and upon his release journeyed to England. Here he published the *Le philosophe cynique* and the *Mélanges Confus* (1771), both of which caused considerable scandal and brought the author a considerable profit. Since his business was flourishing, he devoted himself to the accumulation of further scandals and anecdotes of a similar type.

He made a sally against Du Barry with a satiric blast: *Vie d'une courtesane du dix-huitième siecle* (1776), and at her instigation he was pursued by the London police. As early as 1774 she had sent the police inspector Receveur to London to bring the pamphletist back to France, but in vain. Persons of high and low degree feared his sharp tongue and pointed pen. Hence it was not considered at all queer to enter into negotiations with this dangerous pamphletist. For a second pamphlet which had already been printed, Du Barry paid the author 32,000 lires and assigned him an annual pension of 4800 lires, whereupon the edition was destroyed. It was only later in 1784 that the Marquis de Pellepart dared to lash Morande's shameless career in his *Diable dans un bénitier*, but he himself brought out many scandalous stories about Dubarry, Gourdan, and others.

Thevenot de Morande wrote another amusing work which was not quite in the vein of his other satirical blasts. It is called *La Portefeuille de Madame Gourdan* (1783). A strongly augmented edition appeared the following year but still the work found far from sufficient recognition. The author states that he had come into possession of the letters which comprise the volume through a visit to Mde. Gourdan and was now giving them to the public. This lady was called by the pet name of *La Comtesse* and was, as we have mentioned above, one of the most notorious brothel-keepers of her time. She practised her extremely lucrative profession together with the equally notorious Justine Paris from 1759 till her death, probably from poisoning, in 1783. This work presents a paragraph in the erotic history of France far better than many thick folios of that time. Here are a few specimen letters to be found in Morande's work.

From Mademoiselle Savigni,
Paris, July 15, 1779.

Dear Mama,
              The officer who supported me has had to return to his regiment because his furlough is over. I don't know what to do and am turning to you for help. You know that I'm a good

BOOK III: THE EIGHTEENTH CENTURY

girl, afraid of nothing, and that everything's all right with me provided I am well paid for it. I am not of the class that demands that everything be done according to rules of decency. That's nonsense. What do men expect to find? A regular whore is everywhere at her post and has every privilege. I hope that you will praise my principles and not forget your loving child.

From Mademoiselle Rancourt, July, 8, 1781.

Madame:
At the Italian theatre yesterday I saw in your company a young pretty person. If you can get her for me for one night I shall pay you six louis d'or. Entirely yours, R.

From Mademoiselle Sophie,
Paris, February 25, 1783.

Dear Mama,
I've gotten into a hell of a hole with your damn Carmelite. He has gotten me into a terrible condition. Never in my life have I been so sick. My physician, for whom I have sent this morning, informs me that I shall be sick for at least two months. I hope that you will help me and not leave me in this condition. After all, I got this wound while under your standards. Please send me by this messenger, two louis. You will greatly oblige. Yours gratefully, S.

From Madame Berbier, Paris, April 9, 1783.

Madame:
My daughter is not able to comply with your wish at this time. Immediately after the ballet she had a miscarriage. As soon as she will be well again, however, she will present herself at Madame's, and will be ready for service.
I have the honor to be your very devoted servant.
Mrs. Berbier.

THE EROTIC HISTORY OF FRANCE

From Mademoiselle François,
Arpajon, May 27, 1783.

Madame:

I'm only a simple country girl but that I am pretty, no one can deny. I am an orphan, and not yet eighteen years old. I've heard the servants at the castle say that I have a maidenhead which would be bought dearly at Paris and that for you Madame, I would be worth much gold. Hence, I have obtained your address from them, who laughed at my request but gave it to me none the less. If you want me, you have merely to summon me and I shall come with my maidenhead. I don't know yet what it is, but they say that you will take care of everything. I remain very respectfuly,

Your devoted servant.

From M. T., Paris, 23rd June 1775.

Madame:

My daughter is turning fourteen. If you wish we can talk about first fruits. It will not be at all difficult to win the youngster. With a few bonbons and a little courtesy one can do with her what one wills. One only needs certain preparations. It will be necessary that you take her to you as chambermaid. Please specify the time and I will come with my daughter and we shall settle everything. I have the honor to remain in all respect, your very devoted.

F.

From Monsieur de B., May 1, 1776.

Madame:

I possess a collection of the positions of Aretino in forty pictures. Since I am going to Rome I should like to dispose of them. It seems to me that as a room decoration nothing would be more suitable for you. They cost five thousand francs. Only a year ago I was unwilling to part with them to (Duke de ——) for a hundred louis. If you wish to inspect them I shall remain at home all day tomorrow.

BOOK III: THE EIGHTEENTH CENTURY

From Mr. D. (Book Agent), June 22, 1780.

Madame:
　　　　I have just received from Holland editions de luxe of the *Virgin, Portier des Chartreux, Margo, Positions of Aretino, Ode to Priapus, Futromeni, Discourse of Two Nuns,* for the instruction of young dames who want to enter into society. If any of these appeal to you, madame, please inform me at what time to bring them.

This sheaf of letters from the portfolios of the notorious and powerful panderess gives us some insight into the nefarious life which she and countless others of her ilk led, and the infinite mischief and corruption they engendered.

CHAPTER VII
ANTI-ROYAL AND ANTI-CHURCH LITERATURE

ANYBODY might become the target of the storm of satire which has been just mentioned, but it is obvious that those in high places would be most exposed to it, and could find least refuge from the downpour. Perverse dissoluteness has always found a fierce pleasure in tearing the veil from the most intimate matters of one's self or the other fellow's. It is a debauched delight to display the nakedness of another to a band of spectators, and it is accounted an even more voluptuous delight to display one's own. Hence there can be nothing more piquant than the publication of these detailed enumerations. Is there any wonder, therefore, at the colossal proportions this shamelessness assumed in eighteenth-century France when the highest classes engaged in the composition of such scandalous works?

The Duke of Richelieu, one of the greatest heartbreakers of all time, set down the reminiscences of his youth at the court of the Regent. He mentions in his memoirs that a book had been composed by Madame de Tencin, describing the most obscene practises of all the rakes before the eighteenth century, which was destined for the personal use of the Regent. These regal voluptuaries sowed wind and reaped the whirlwind. Louis XV, one of the greatest of libertines, with his corps of mistresses certainly gave ample provocation to the most vitriolic satire. One of these satires, with its witty allusion to the frigidity of the Pompadour, cost the royal minister, Maurepas, his post. During his banishment he assembled all possible erotic works and bound them in red morocco adorned with his coat-of-arms.

The King and his mistresses were the targets of the most obscene pamphlets. Pompadour was not so sensitive to these malicious squibs. In her letters she speaks of a pamphleteer who had composed some vulgar verses at her expense but had been compelled to flee to London in order to escape her wrath. "He can always return," she continues. "Though I am a woman I can forgive insult, and what's more I can reward my friends and compel them, if not to love me, at least to have a measure of respect for me". These letters are most probably forged. Dubarry was not able to exercise such magnanimity and we have seen above that she took very stern measures against Thevenot de Morande. Her published letters too must be regarded as historical sources, but are nevertheless of some interest for the contemporary moral situation.

With the ascent of Louis XVI the ball of satire had gained such momentum that there was no stopping the stream of anti-royalist literature which was directed not so much against him, as against Marie Antoinette. As a foreigner she proved an excellent object for national hatred, and in addition she provoked public opinion in many ways. Her ostentatious aversion to "crapule"; her secret nocturnal outings to disreputable inns where firmly believing that she was unsuspected, she carried on her undisguised affair with the King's brother, the Count d'Artois, a notorious wastrel; and the visits to her private theatre where frequently the performances were indecent. These and similar matters were not calculated to arouse the sympathy of the people.

In his memoirs, Count Tilly seeks to defend her. "Her appearance on the terraces at Versailles where the beautiful evenings and enchanting music called forth the groups of strollers, was a new pretext for libel and malice.... In these nocturnal strolls were sought and found the weapons which finally dealt her a fatal wound. The mask-balls at the opera and the theatre, the intimacy between her and the Princess of Lamballe, her long friendly connection with the Duchess of Polignac, offered enough material for accusation. Her aversion to court coercion and to the precise obedience of the etiquette proper to her class, were regarded as neglect and disrespect of royal duties. And though no one knew better than she how to act the rôle of queen with dignity and grace when she so desired, still they interpreted her unforced freedom as immorality, and her aversion to some people as irascibility." But Tilly is too partial, as he needs must be, to a queen who was very generous to him. And it should be recalled that he was not a regular member of the inner circle, so that he was not altogether enlightened. Nevertheless, despite his partiality for the queen, he admits that she had two love affairs—with the Duke de Coincy and Count de Fersen.

One of the most successful of the anti-court anti-Marie pamphlets was an obscene satire describing her amour with the Count d'Artois—later King Charles x; the supposed impotence of the King is mocked and the Queen is represented as a model of licentiousness. At the behest of the court, the whole edition was bought from the booksellers at the price of 17,000 francs, and burnt in the Bastille. Naturally, a few copies escaped this destruction, and later this piece was reprinted by Mercier de Compiegne in his *Momus redivivus*. The notorious story of the necklace was the occasion of the pamphlet *Le bordel royal*, which describes a secret conference of the Queen with Cardinal Rohan. Of equal obscenity is the *Bordel patriotique*. The Queen and Madame Theroigne decorate the statue of Priapus with flowers, and use their hands upon the statue in a very obscene fashion. This Theroigne woman instituted a patriotic brothel, and in the freest of language makes known the prerequisites and conditions of the brothel business. Of a similar nature is the *Messaline Française*, in which the author doesn't hesitate to slander the Queen for having had intercourse with him. Of like scope is the book *L'Autrichiene en goguette*, attributed to Mayeur de Saint-Paul. The interest here centers, as in dozens of others, in a lesbian scene between Marie Antoinette, the Duchess of Polignac and Count d'Artois. It is especially amusing since all the erotic events take place behind the back of the sleeping King.

A pamphlet directed against the whole courtly society is the rare and remarkable *Bibliothèque de la cour* (1781). The peculiar thing about it is that every person is characterized by the possession of an eroticon which is somehow suited to his character or life. Thus, Cardinal Rohan has the *Liaison dangereuses*; Chevalier d'Eon whose sex will always remain a mystery, has *Description de L'Ile des Hermaphrodites*; Talleyrand, the Archbishop of Lyons, has the *Traité sur l'apostasie*; the Archbishop of Paris has the *L'Art de péter*; the Abbess de Polignac, *Traité sur les accouchements*, and so on almost indefinitely.

Most of these writings were distributed from England or Holland since France possessed in the Bastille, an excellent means of silencing these malicious tongues. For England and other lands, there was another remedy. Out of fear of these poisonous pamphlets one entered into negotiations with the authors, through intermediaries, and sought to buy their silence. This practice, begun during the reign of Louis XIV, roused the greed of the malefactors. It became a good business, this mulcting the great and near-great. It became a regular trick for these wallowers in mud to warn the Chief of Police at Paris concerning the impending publication of a libel, and then to negotiate for the very profitable sale of the manuscript. The breadgiver of these unsavory folk was one Brossière, a former lackey who had barely escaped the gallows.

If in a land as absolutistic as France, the throne could not escape these attacks, it certainly is no wonder that the clergy was ferociously set upon. The immoral life of many priests, who could not be represented as other than "loving", provided enough material for fierce satire. The anthologies too, received enough cynical verses which censured these clerics in rounds of profanity. It was not unnatural that religion itself should finally be blamed for the continuous misdeeds and abominations of its professionals. Cause was mistaken for effect and the devil exorcised by Beelzebub. Thus Evariste Parny wrote *Les Galanteries de la Bible*, in which he attempted to make the Bible ridiculous by retelling its love episodes in a frivolous manner.

The first place among anti-clerical pamphleteers was occupied by the Parisian lawyer, Charles Gervais de Latouche (1718-1782), with his classic *Portier des chartreux* which appeared under the title of *Histoire de Dom Bougre*. *Bougre* derives from Bulgaria, from which land pederasty is supposed to have spread. The book first appeared about 1745, though the exact date is uncertain, and may be regarded as the naughtiest and maddest mockery of clericaldom, especially monkery. No other book of its kind aroused such a furore and was so frequently reprinted; no other represented the monks in their degradation with so much wit and savage satire. At the same time, it was a breviary of the art of love perfectly suited to the erotic taste of France during the eighteenth century. Naturally the offended priests moved heaven and earth to have the book destroyed, but in vain; for despite all persecutions the reprints were as numerous as mushrooms after rain. Everyone with any education read it. Lichtenberg mentions in his Aphorisms and in

BOOK III: THE EIGHTEENTH CENTURY

a letter to Dietrich that he has read it, and remarks that it is a very witty if a very dirty book.

Its history too is interesting. It is first mentioned by the Marquis de Paulmy in the manuscript of his catalogue. This edition was provided with twenty-three engravings by Catylas, well cut but poorly drawn. Today there is but one copy owned by the noted English collector Hankey. The Marquise de Pompadour had a very handsome edition, richly bound and decorated with twenty-eight miniatures drawn on parchment. She was very fond of this book with its daring philosophy, genial composition, magnificent style, and not least, its obscenity. In a letter to Vicomte d'Herbigny she speaks of it in terms of the highest admiration and urges him to get a copy at once as it afforded her so many hours of pleasant excitation. Pompadour's copy later came to the collection of Berard and was doubtless destroyed with other books of the Arsenal library. Of the third edition printed at Versailles there is again but one extant copy in the Bibliothèque Mozarine, with a dedication to Marie Antoinette. A most valuable and attractive edition of these *Mémoires* is the one published by the Cazin press in 1787, distinguished for the absolute accuracy of its text and decorated with twenty-four lovely engravings by Borel and Elluin. This edition, of which one copy is found in the library of the Palais des Arts, is also very rare.

Because of its great importance in the history of French erotic literature the contents of the story will be briefly summarized. The author looks back upon his stirring life and sees the array of all his conquests and achievements. He is presumably the son of a peasant couple but in his paternity all the brothers of a cloister were participants. It is quite by accident that Saturnin is inducted into the mysteries of Venus. One afternoon he is aroused from his siesta by the sound of sighs and groans. Through a hole in the wall he sees his supposed mother in the most intimate posture with the family confessor. Thoroughly aroused by the sight, he sings the song of Hymen with his own hand. As a result of this experience many things become clear which have hitherto been obscure, and all his wishes are hereafter directed to doing that which the Pater had done with his mother. His sister Susanna appears to him to be a likely object for the satisfaction of his lust. He finds her picking flowers one day and after some hesitation decides to take her by force. But she defends herself pluckily, so he desists, especially as he sees their mother approaching. Next day they both visit the religious preceptress of Susanna who is suspiciously tender to both but particularly to Saturnin, who is daring enough to venture some amorous contacts. The untimely arrival of the administrator prevents him from using his advantages, but he is invited to come another day. On the way home he again seeks to make Susanna comply with his wishes and to his great surprise learns from her statements that she knows much more about such matters than he does. After some struggle she informs him how she came by this knowledge.

One night while she was asleep at the cloister where she was being educated, Sister Monika had slipped into her bed and initiated her into tribady. In the ensuing conversation Monika sings a pæan to the male organ and is astounded to discover that Susanna doesn't know the names for the genital parts. Monika confesses that while very young she had felt intense sex desires and had made various efforts to cool her heat. Since the manipulations of manustupration no longer satisfy her, she casts her eyes upon the brother of one of her schoolmates. She offers no resistance to his approaches but they are discovered while still in the preliminary stages. A strict investigation ensues and Monika is sentenced to chastisement but she defends herself so wildly that six nuns are no match for her. In the

BOOK III: THE EIGHTEENTH CENTURY

scuffle there drops from the pocket of one of them a godemiché which Monika attempts to use as soon as she is alone. When she finds no success in this she desists in great disappointment but decides to revenge herself for the treatment she has received, and then to disappear. The Mother Superior reproaches her severely for her conduct of the previous day, but becomes all kindness when Monika shows her the instrument, as an example of the sort of thing that goes on in the cloister. At once it becomes obvious from her embarrassment that the Mother Superior is the owner of the article. When Monika's mother arrives in answer to a summons, she is informed by the Superior that her daughter is perfectly innocent and that the summons had been a misunderstanding.

During the night Monika has an erotic dream and realizes when she awakes that it has been no dream but reality, for she finds herself in the arms of the valet to the nunnery chaplain, and had thus painlessly lost her maidenhood. One night of love succeeds another and soon Monika notices that she is pregnant. Tearfully she informs Martin, her valet-lover, who comforts her with the assurance that his master has a medicine which can remove the disagreeable consequences. This medicine has been used successfully by Angelica, one of the six nuns who had sought to punish Monika. This he knew from Angelica's letters to his master. Thereupon, Monika decides to have her revenge and orders Martin to bring her the letters—and the medicine. She succeeds in getting the letters to the Mother Superior, and the latter, jealous of the favors of the chaplain to another, incarcerates Angelica. The chaplain suspects Martin of having purloined the letters and dismisses him. The end of the narrative brings another love scene between Monika and Susanna.

This lengthy recital has excited both Saturnin and Susanna considerably, and the former, tense with passion, is now convinced that he will meet with no opposition if he is but able to assure

Susanna that there will be no evil consequences. Just then he gets an idea. He takes the girl up to his room and lets her be the eye witness of the sex play between Pater Ambrosius and Toinette. Susanna is so overwrought that she makes no resistance whatever. Attracted by the noise, the Pater and Toinette become aware of the others' game. The latter is at first speechless, then takes Saturnin into her room to instruct him in the mysteries of Venus. The Pater who had remained with Susanna was not quite so fortunate. Since the boy is in the way of the Pater and his love, he is sent away to the *pension* of the local priest. From here he visits Susanna's nun who gives him happiness. On one of the following nights he seeks to gain his end with the priest's niece but misses her door and enters the room of the old governess instead. The next day he enters the cloister, and with this the first part is concluded.

The second portion deals with the experiences of Saturnin in the monastery in which he finds himself very uncomfortable at first. With no women present, he once again falls into the sin of self-abuse. A fellow inmate once comes upon him as he is engaged in this pastime and invites him to become acquainted with the excesses of the brothers in the church. The novice participates in these orgies, and at one of them makes the acquaintance of his real mother who requests him to cohabit with her; a vestige of shame restrains him, for which the monks praise him. After an excursus concerning the delights of venery and cloister life, Saturnin tells of his impotence induced by excessive indulgence. An old Pater, in whom he confides, advises him to become father confessor—for the piquant confessions of the lovely confessors are not to be despised as aphrodisiacs.

Saturnin follows this advice and soon feels himself in possession of his virile powers. In his new potency he rapes a pretty confessor, who turns out to be Monika, Susanna's bosom friend and mentor.

BOOK III: THE EIGHTEENTH CENTURY

She reports that she had carried on a simultaneous relationship with Verland and the valet Martin, who had come to blows when they discovered their partnership. Hence she had fled to Saturnin, and wished to remain with him. He decides to have her participate in the orgies of the cloister but his plan meets with failure. In his absence they find Monika, and to escape punishment by his order, he flees to Paris where he meets Susanna in a brothel. Despite her struggle and her warning that she is sick, Saturnin cohabits with her. During their sleep there is a raid and in the confusion they are separated. He finally gets to the hospital in a grave venereal condition, the outcome of which is that he is eunuchized. Susanna dies of her sorrows, and with these tragic events the book closes. Thus are the ways of sin rewarded.

This book which may justly be regarded as the standard work of erotic anti-clerical literature had an enormous vogue. Frederick the Great found it in the equipment of French officers. It was therefore natural that in a time which was almost delirious about sex, it should call forth a host of imitations. The chief of the followers of Gervaise who sought to justify their debaucheries by attacking the church, is indubitably the Abbé Henri Jos. de Dulaurens (1719-1797). All his life he harbored a berserker rage against the Jesuits. He was finally rendered invulnerable; the last twenty years of his life he was confined in a mental hospital. He it was who said that he knew God only from heresay. His most famous works *L'Arretin Moderne* and *Le Compére Mathieu* are cynical in the extreme.

The first book is preceded by the almost prophetic phrase: *Parve, nec invideo, sine me, liber ibis ignem.* This work contains an obscene criticism of the Bible and religious observances in twenty-five stories. In keeping with the ideas of the time, the book is an apologia for vice. It is an endeavor to remodel ethical values and to defend the lax morals of the author. The wish to appear original is transparent but the proof of the positions assumed are mere sophistry, and the inner mendacity and emptiness of the author leers at us all the time. This whole offensive against the clergy lacks wit and the book has been worsened considerably by the frivolities that weigh it down. What for example does Dulaurens hope to accomplish by the silly tale of the godemiché? A Father Superior has impregnated a nun and enlists the aid of an old witch who advises him to feed the unfortunate one mandragora roots and other ingredients to the accompaniment of magic incantations. He follows this advice and the nun gives birth to no human creature, but to a godemiché. This comforts a number of nuns and he finally breathes his last while in the arms of the decrepit sorceress. This tale does not stand alone in its absurdity.

The fifteenth story is the most cynical and paradoxical—it deals with the theme of *L'Utilité des vices*. Dulaurens takes the position that vices are more useful to society than virtues. The latter are sterile, uniform, monotonous—in short, chimeras to keep men in darkness. Vanity and egotism are necessary if the world is to go on. Crimes are many and diverse and nature itself develops the seeds of our vices. Love is the indispensable sin for society. Passion is the favorite child of nature. A passionate girl affords more joy than a virtuous one, and it is lust alone which makes us love women. It takes a man who embraces a virtuous girl a long time to experience the joys he can find among the girls of Montigny. Man cannot be satisfied with one woman. How many days are there when his wife is inaccessible to him owing to menstruation, pregnancy and childbirth! Hence, he must wander to other pastures; and while society is condemning him to continence, by opposing it he has made many additions to the population. Passion performs a public service for it prevents hoarding and keeps money flowing into industry.

BOOK III: THE EIGHTEENTH CENTURY

Of similar scope is the second work, *Le Compére Mathieu*. In his customary blending of frivolity and blasphemy, Dulaurens represents religion as something unnatural, and he establishes the relativity of good and evil; wherefore, all is permitted and punishment doomed to pass away. This is the true evil and the source of it all is the state which is also fated to disappear. A third work by the same author, *La Chandelle*, is an obscene mock heroic poem concerning the fortunes of a strumpet healed of her illness through the intervention of the Virgin Mary. It depicts with great clarity the female practices in the nunneries. In this same fashion, writers like Evariste Parny, Voltaire, Voisenon and Mirabeau wrote. Parny's work on the war of the gods and the gallantries of the Bible, *La Christainide*, was strenuously suppressed by Napoleon and during the Restoration it was finally bought up by the government and confiscated. These anti-clerical attacks fell in with the taste of the time whose influence few could escape.

A most important work, perfectly typical of erotic eighteenth-century France, for it contains more fact than fiction, is the work *Thérèse philosophe*. Although the authorship is doubtful it may with strong probability be attributed to the Marquis d'Argens who was the author of other erotica. There are many grounds for this attribution, and that it was suspected a long time ago may be seen from the following interesting anecdote. Frederick the Great had painted the most important scenes of this work and ordered that chief figures be painted to resemble Marquis d'Argens and Madame Cochois. Once the Marquis' room was secretly decorated with these pictures which "greatly astonished milord but pleased him little". In reality, however, this fuss about authorship is vain for we are not dealing here with creations of fancy. The contents of the book are based on actual incidents which had taken place some time before. Catharina Cariere (Eradice), the pious and beautiful daughter of a rich merchant, had entered the native confessional institution for women established by the Jesuit Girard Dirrag. The lubricity of the monk immediately directed itself toward this shy young creature. By using her dreams and visions for his shocking purposes and invoking an attenuated sex mysticism, he finally succeeded in making the girl accessible to his erotic desires. The uninterrupted orgiastic erethism and the excessive spiritual raptures induced a grave hysteria in Catharina; and when she became pregnant the Jesuit knew how to employ an efficacious abortive. The matter finally got to the courts and despite general disappointment, the court freed the man and, what is worse, sentenced the unfortunate girl to pay costs for libel.

It was this true material which the author employed in a devastating satire against the clergy and religion. A supposed eye-witness, the philosophical Thérése describes the proceedings, informs us of her own reactions to them, and throughout her views concerning the rational satisfaction of human love needs. Although there are obscene incidents aplenty, these are overlooked, due to the paramount importance of the book as a source document of social and erotic history; for this reason it has defied all attempts at suppression.

In order to characterize the style and thought content of the work two excerpts from different portions are appended. It is obvious that the doctrines are by no means harmless, and are calculated to induce considerable confusion in the minds of readers who lack judgment.

The first aims to disprove freedom of the will. We are compelled to act by various factors not in our control. The kind of organs, the distribution of nerves in our body, a certain type of movement, the absence of particular juices, all these variables control our passions, whose strength determines our will in the most

BOOK III: THE EIGHTEENTH CENTURY

important relationships of our life. Accordingly there are passionate people, wise people and crazy people. The last mentioned are no more or less free than both other types for they also act in accordance with the same fundamental laws. If we are to assume that man is free and follows his own will, we set him on a plane with God. Foolish people to believe that you have the power to suppress the passions implanted by nature! Shall human creatures, the handiwork of God, suppress their passions or destroy them and thus attempt to appear mightier than God? Let things be as the old creator has made them, for all is good and must be as it is.

We can see at once that if the freedom of the will is denied, and passion is not to be opposed because it has been placed in us by God, every man is free to give himself over to debauchery according to the measure of his power. Indeed he *must* do so, for "God wills it".

The second quotation is an abridgement of the seduction scene, expurgated to omit all the obscenities of detail and description. The Pater enters the confessional room and asks his pupil: "Is the stigma that you have on your breast still in the same spot? Let me see it?" Eradice immediately uncovers her left breast beneath which the stigma is located.

"Ah, it is still there, rosy and red. Saint Francis still loves you. And I have once again brought with me a piece of his rope which we shall use at our exercise later. We shall have great reward, dear daughter, if you fulfill your obligations. This holy exercise will shower you with ineffable bliss, thanks to the rope of the sacred Francis and your own pious contemplation. On your knees, my child. Expose that part of your flesh which arouses God's wrath! The pain you feel will bring your spirit into connection with God. I repeat: forget yourself and let everything happen to you."

Eradice obeyed at once in silence. Holding a book before her, she kneeled and lifted her skirts and undershirt until her girdle, discovering snow-white and perfectly formed buttocks carried by two splendid thighs.

"Raise your skirt higher," he ordered. "Now that's better. Now fold your hands and lift your soul to God. Fill your spirit with the thought of the eternal bliss destined for you." He kneeled down, raised his cowl high, tied it with his girdle, and brought forth a thick bunch of long rods which he gave the girl to kiss. She obeyed silently. The Pater feasted his eyes hungrily on her thighs and whispered to himself: "What a beautiful bosom. What charming breasts." Presently he arose and murmured a Biblical phrase. Nothing escaped his lascivious curiosity. Finally, he asked the beautiful penitent whether her soul was in devotion.

"Yes, worthy father. I feel that my soul is becoming separated from my body, and I beg you to begin the holy work."

"That suffices. Your spirit will be satisfied." He said a few prayers and then administered three light blows upon her hind quarters, followed by another verse. Finally, the holy rope got into action. One can readily understand what sort of rope it was.

Of course every one at all acquainted with the history of French culture realizes that the case of Pater Gerard does not stand alone, and that intimate relations between confessor and penitent were not infrequent in those days. Today such a contretemps would not raise so much dust though every year a number of such are reported in the newspapers. One may compare the similar case of the Abbé Reginald Outhier who however defended himself very skillfully in his *Dissertation theologique sur le péche du confesseur avec sa pénitente*.

In 1760 there appeared *Les Delices du Cloitre* and *Les Lauriers ecclésiastiques*, the work of Jacques-Rochete de la Morlière, the famous author of Angela. This La Morlière (1719-1785) was a bad

BOOK III: THE EIGHTEENTH CENTURY

sort. Originally destined for the law he was disqualified, entered the army and had to flee because of a scandal. Having been disowned by his family, he turned to writing romances in the style of Crébillon the younger. Difficulties with the police resulted in his flight. Upon returning he took to the drama but was hissed off the stage. In desperation he became a cliqueur and gradually sank deeper into misery. The first of the above mentioned writings scores those parents who still believe in the purity of cloister life and immure their inexperienced girls without consideration for their love desires. He believes that there is no better way of lashing the wicked life of the cloister than a frank exposure of the vices that teem in those institutions. His exposé is never obscene, though perhaps too informative. His moral lessons are obvious and persuasive. Two nuns, Julia and Dorothea are conversing. The first reports that the cloister physician is preparing for an amorous affair with her and describes his palpations and her shyness. Dorothea enjoins her not to permit her lover to languish in vain. Julia takes her advice and the next scene discovers her surrender.

The other story, based largely upon facts, departs somewhat from the scenes of clerical life and journeys merrily into high society. The Abbé Terray, a contemporary of La Morlière, visits his uncle and becomes acquainted with the latter's *soul-friend* who after some hesitation grants his love-request. Their pleasure is heightened because they take their joys on the same bed on which the cuckold reposes and in his immediate proximity. But the happiness of the lovers doesn't last long. A young serving maid has fallen so violently in love with the abbé that she finally goes to his room and declares her love. The happy man must now share his love with two women. The Marquise promptly discovers this through her spies. Her jealousy is aroused to such a pitch that she has the young abbé transferred to a distant abbey and the little chamber pussy cat married to a bourgeois.

The exiled one takes his luck with him, however. On the way he meets a charming lady whose coach has broken down. He offers her the use of his own vehicle, becomes useful in other ways and on the morrow receives the *summum bonum*. But he soon realizes that he is sharing his beloved with a brawny Franciscan. He and two cronies administer a solid drubbing to the latter when they find him *in delicto flagrante* with the charming lady. In the meantime, the father of the young abbé has died and the latter must return home. He has a slight dispute over some boundaries with a neighboring duke which he settles in favor of the latter. The duke is so overjoyed at this eventuality that he presents the abbé to the duchess, while the lady is still in bed, and leaves the two alone. He assists at her *levee* and, though disturbed by an untimely visitor, proceeds to the onslaught successfully.

But for the nth time, he finds that there are other men in the world, for he surprises his Dulcinea in the arms of her servant. He foreswears the unfaithful one, and returns to his uncle where he is present at the investiture of a most beautiful nun, whose parents are compelling her to assume the veil. He falls in love with her and all obstacles are overcome. At the death of the girl's parents, both renounce the clerical life and the abbé leads the nun home with him.

In another important book of a similar nature, *Venus dans le cloître*, which appeared at the close of the seventeenth century but was many times reprinted in the eighteenth, two nuns, Angelica and Agnes, chat about the amorous regimen current in the cloister. Free indulgence is defended with philosophic clichés, and counselled as a way of life. This book also shows that erotic literature was well known to the ladies of the cloister. *Luisa Sigea* comes in for a special meed of praise, and in one place a catalogue is given of a series of porneia, all lost today, but whose titles amply testify to their strong anti-clerical tendency.

If these works were occasionally written for a purpose, they nevertheless in their totality constitute a true picture of the immoral deportment of the church and many of its servants. Indeed, we possess enough historical witnesses to confirm the truth of these pamphlets, for instance: *La Chastété du clergé dévoilée ou Procès-Verbaux des séances du clergé chez les filles du Paris. Trouves à la Bastille* (1790). This is *authentic* material. Here we find the exact names, status, and residence of those clerics who were caught with prostitutes before the Revolution. The list is long though only a small proportion of these debaucheries became public since most of them were naturally carried on secretly.

There are two more far-reaching works which have to be considered, since their revolting cynicism opens invaluable perspectives upon French society of that time. The first is a book of six songs, each of which contains three hundred verses. The title is *La Foutromanie*, and the author Senac de Meilhan. Gods and man alike have joy in foutromanie, the former to dispel their ennui, the latter for their very happiness. Mlle. Dubois, actress, of the Comédie française, cannot be without it. Mesdames Arnould and Clairon with their parner Count Valbelle are passionately devoted to it; and Mme. Allard has probed the utmost refinements of it with Duke de Mazarin. At the conclusion of the first song the duchesses and court ladies march in and have dalliance with their lackeys. The second song is opened with a description of the corporeal delights of a virgin who has fallen into the clutches of a roué. After the interpolation of Chrysostom against sexual debaucheries in the cloister, there is broadly related how one afflicted with satyriasis enters a monastery and how he ministers to his blazing desires. This affords the author the best opportunity to attack the vices of tribady and pederasty. Towards the close, de Meilhan mentions syphilis which forms the transition to the third song, almost entirely dedicated to this disease. The author cannot sufficiently praise the now perfected means of curing the malady. Many luetic lovers are adduced and the luetic prelates come in for special mention. The song ends with a praise of Aretino, the discoverer of the plastic positions. The fourth song emphasizes the great advantages of the bordello. A hymn of praise is sung to the great procuresses: Paris, Gourdan, Montigny, d'Hericourt Carlier, etc., and then we are permitted to witness passionate orgies in these dives. The song is concluded with a praise of German women and a curse upon Italy where the author had lost health and money. The fifth chanson seeks to allay the fears of syphiliphobes. Not all women contain this abominable ailment. Montesquieu, Rousseau, Marmontel dared and came out unscathed. Finally the timorous are encouraged by pointing to the example of Maria-Theresa, Catherine II, the King of Poland and the deceased Queen of Denmark. The last song is a pæan to Dr. Agyroni who has cured the author of his disease. After a display of his medical knowledge on the subject the song culminates in a repeated eulogy of Foutromanie as the pillar of the world.

This book served as a model for *La Masturbomanie*, in the foreword to which the author states that he sings the incomparable joy of Onan, the independent self-created pleasure of man, and one most worthy of a philosopher.

The other far-reaching work that serves as a companion piece to *Foutromanie* is *Parapilla*, a book of five songs written by Charles Bordes. It tells the story of a wonderful instrument which is the joy of all ladies. Rodric receives it direct from heaven; from him it gets to Donna Capponi, to a nunnery and finally to the hands of Lucrezia Borgia. This affords the writer an excellent opportunity

BOOK III: THE EIGHTEENTH CENTURY

to describe the wild life under Alexander VI. Although this work was not published until 1775 it was known earlier; in 1773 Voltaire in a letter to Bordes had termed it one of the "best books of this genre that we possess". In his memoirs, Bachaumont makes some perspicacious remarks concerning this book. He points out that despite the obscene subject matter there is not an obscene word to be found in it; in keeping with his theme the fabulist had drawn very free pictures but always veiled and with the most decorous means. He asserts that there never was a merrier or lighter volume than this short epic of folly and choice taste.

The readers for whom the above mentioned works were intended did not, naturally, belong to the circle of those normal, naïve people who find pleasure in bathing nymphs and enraptured shepherds. For the readers of this erotic literature of the eighteenth century, strong stuff was needed, cynical and unnatural, for their jaded senses would not react to ordinary or high literature.

CHAPTER VIII
THE OBSCENITY OF THE THEATRES

The theatre has always been the best mirror of morality in any age. When life became more than free, the boards swarmed with frivolity and obscenity of every kind. In twenty-three theatres the muse wore her skirt as high up as possible and pornographic clubs multiplied and came out of their concealment. Pamphlets, comedies, vaudevilles, even parodies upon operas and musical pieces had to include the erotic touch. One contemporary avers that the works of Crébillon junior were moral by comparison with these small pieces which laughed hilariously at all virtue. But no matter how far some had gone, there were still many poets and mimes who refused to say obscene things. However, in a small intimate circle there is no need for any inhibition, not even of the most extreme perversity. Hence private theatres were established in which no bounds were set to any word or deed. Behind the grated lodges of these small secret theatres, the noble ladies of finest society might witness the erotic plays which showed priapism and philosophy in strange mixture. The famous dancer Guimard had such a theatre in her country home at Panin for which Collé supplied the shows. We must not make the mistake of concluding that these secret theatres were the original creation of the rococo period. They are as old as the theatre itself and as justified to a certain type of human being as when the *odi profanum vulgus* was first uttered. The wealthy lover of the theatre provided for himself a stage on

BOOK III: THE EIGHTEENTH CENTURY

which those plays that would gratify his own taste would be produced. This is no more unnatural than the corresponding fact that poets will always be found who will drive their Pegasus to a watering place of excrement for the sake of money. The old French writers of farces may here be remembered; and that Bussy-Rabutin's *Comtesse d'Olonne* is as characteristic of its century as the *Theatre de la rue de la Santé* is of the nineteenth century. But it does remain true that the rococo period has the doubtful distinction of being richest in these erotic theatres.

The indiscreet deeds at nunneries form the subject of derision in various pieces. Collé composed a skit about four bishops called *Accidents*, which by his own testimony was so obscene that he dared not print it. Very numerous were the revolutionary comedies directed against church, state and monarchy. In 1791 there was a public theatre at the Palais Royal where a so-called savage and a woman performed coitus before a crowd of people of both sexes. Finally both actors were summoned before the justice of the peace and it turned out that the *savage* was some rascal from the suburb of St. Anthoine, and the woman a common whore who had earned considerable sums by such pandering to the pruriency of the public. If the latter could not be actors in these spectacles at least they could be spectators; and La Mettrie remarks in his *L'Art de Jouir*: The sight of others' pleasure is our own.

To obtain some insight into these orgies of the better society one should read *Confessions generales des Princes du sang*, otherwise one will never understand the lewd royalistic tragedies which existed at the time. Or failing this, one should thumb *La France foutue*. These are the indispensable documents for the history of erotic elements in political caricature. On the title-page one sees Louis XVI sitting on the penitent's seat in line with other penitents. On one side kneels a high courtier and on the other a princely

THE EROTIC HISTORY OF FRANCE

strumpet. A brief resumé of the plot is now appended. The char acters are:

LA FRANCE
ENGLAND—*brothel mistress who owns a brothel at the Duke of Orleans' castle.*
MLLE. VENDEE—*a lady of honor and intime of France*
DUKE OF ORLEANS—*brothel monger*
COUNT DE PUISSAYE—*king of rogues*
FREDERICK WILLIAM III
FRANCIS II OF GERMANY
CHARLES IV OF SPAIN
Three knights, five English women, five pages of the Duke of Orleans, troops and citizens.

The action takes place in the private chambers of the Duke of Orleans at the Palais Royal. The theatre represents a luxurious boudoir equipped with many sofas.

ACT I

Frederick William III, Francis II, Charles IV and the Duke of Orleans are engaged with an equal number of Englishwomen, each one on a sofa. One bares the bosom of his woman and kisses the breasts, another fondles the dorsal hemispheres, after he has hiked her skirts up to her girdle, a third uncovers his wench aft and explores the decks there. The women are standing or sitting on the knees of their men, depending on the position of the latter. England lies on a couch in the center in a very indecent position.

ACT II

In the instant in which the three kings carry Madame France to the couch, the five Englishwomen enter, each carrying a different object: a bidet, a pot of water, a sponge, perfume bottle, and finally underwear. Puissaye makes an obscene gesture to the Vendee woman and draws her to a sofa alongside them. Duke of Orleans hies him to the opposite sofa with England and exer-

BOOK III: THE EIGHTEENTH CENTURY

cet actum de retro. *Francis and Charles stand behind the couch as expectant observers and* manustupratione se delectant, *while Frederick rapes France.*

Act III
In this scene Orleans, Puissaye, followed by the Englishwomen, enter the stage from the rear. Armed citizens also enter the rear and the sides. After them, grooms enter on the right and pages on the left. The citizenry in battle formation take their place in the rear, the pages fall on the women. At the command of the Duke of Orleans to his satellites a stall slave comes forward, two others approach from another side and all assume obscene positions. In the background the Englishwomen are seen with their pages; presently the armed ones push the pages aside and demonstrate the vice of sodomy. In the foreground, Puissaye sits on his sofa and attempts to rape Vendee but she struggles viciously. Suddenly the duke cries out, and all stop suddenly, staring at him on his deathbed. Vendee leaves Puissaye to go to La France but Puissaye kills her. The three kings regard this scene with bent arms, whereby it is clearly indicated that they regard with equanimity how France dismembers itself.

La France foutue is the full-grown flower of eroticism, the sadism of the *ancien régime* which completely expended itself on sexual perversions and was unable to enjoy anything other than vicious erotic experiences. According to Dr. Bloch this work derives from the Marquis de Sade, but this is unlikely since he was a thorough republican, while this writing must have had a royalist as its author.

Several additional theatrical pieces of importance will now be considered but no attention will be given to the merely erotic. Our purpose is to demonstrate the diverse erotic conditions which affected the social and historic life of France, and to eliminate any and everything obscene *per se*. If we have toned down many an erotic matter, it is because we wish to avoid all things unnecessary to students of French history and literature. We prefer to shoot below the mark rather than above it.

The piece *Les plaisirs du cloître*, though written for a theatre of high society, never was performed because no actors could be found for some of the parts. The rôles of Agathe and Marton were easy and desired by young women, but Clitandres and Jesuits required characters of robustness and these could not be found. The author believed that this dramatic piece would lose little in the reading and boasted that he had omitted every expression that might give offense. Was it such an incomprehensible boast which gave the book a tremendous vogue? In the first act Marton, a novice, is reading an obscene book in her cell and becomes greatly inflamed. Her friend Agathe who has been lying in wait comes to her aid, but the abbess surprises them, confiscates the book, and sentences Marton to chastisement.

In the second act the punishment is carried out and Marton gets forty strokes with the lash upon her bare body. After the flagellation, Agathe hurries to her friend and continues the discipline with her hand; then both friends give themselves over to sapphic love. Agathe promises Marton a still greater pleasure. In the third act, Agathe brings to her friend her lover Clitandre and a Jesuit father, whereupon a normal love scene ensues. But the Pater aroused by the sight of the lovers, Clitandre and Agathe, cannot resist the temptation of a pederastic exercise with Marton.

Another piece, *Vaste*, attributed to Piron, created a sensation at the time, but it is of such obscenity that we shall do no more than mention it. *Le Bourdel* set up the claim to moral effectiveness. What is better calculated to dissuade young people from going to brothels than a full depiction of all the disagreeable consequences likely to result from such a visit? To achieve this purpose the very words which are popular in such places must be used; and whoever writes in the style of whores cannot avoid such expressions. Then follows a list of words from the realm of pornology. After reading this piece it is hoped that those desiring to visit brothels will be scared away lest they lose their money, health and honor as a consequence. This piece contains many items of interest for the social historian. If one is to believe the following words, the contemporary moral police were in a pretty bad way. The police official is represented as speaking to a prostitute: "First one needs money. Don't trust friends. They may make it easier for you to leave the hospital but they certainly don't make it harder for you to enter. What you need above all are friends among the police. How can you have them? With money, Mme. Dru."

The piece closes in the most edifying way with an unexpected visit by the police patrol. The commissioner has all the exits guarded and asks everyone his business. Bel-air answers: "Sir, I am a soldier from Champign. I came to visit a sick jade just as you entered and I give you my word that I would not have come had I expected to find you here."

"I understand—a pimp?"

"Well now, commissioner, the king pays mighty little, so one must try to earn an extra penny."

At the conclusion several wenches are sent to Bicêtre and the moral purpose is achieved.

While many of these obscene compositions may have been intended for, and accessible to, the *hoi polloi*, the cavaliers of the court however had their own pornographers. The foremost of these worldlings was the Duke Henin who was born in 1744 and came into an enormous fortune at the age of twenty-six. Frivolous and passionate, he gave free rein to his lusts and to his affection for the theatre. With unlimited means at his disposal he had his own theatre and retained his contemporary, Delisle de Sales, to furnish erotic pieces which were collected into four volumes and were formerly in the possession of the bibliophile Alfred Begis. Henin is adduced as a typical case and his perverse tendencies were shared by many others who doted on obscene theatricals.

The foreword to these works testifies to the fact that these sketches were really acted out. Antiquity echoes with the dialogues concerning more than merely free love composed by Elephantis, for which professional artists drew pictures representing love in every attitude the coarsest fancy could imagine; and more recent times have contributed the dialogues of *Luisa Sigea* and the sonnets of Aretino. A nobleman and a fine fellow to boot, tired of normal pleasures, fitted out a private theatre to which only the roués of his circle were admitted and also those ladies of rank who were worthy of being courtesans. These were the saturnalia of the Regency. Here were enacted quite frankly the priapeia of Petronius and the orgies of Latouche. "On the occasion of one festival," de Sales says in the foreword, "I was asked how to make the last-mentioned daring play more interesting, and I had the weakness to explain that Socrates himself in this condition had surrendered himself to the folly of Alcibiades. Thereafter there were no secrets for me, and I was invited to refine the theatre so that even a sage in one of the lodges could give himself over to the pleasures of the play. Four pieces of this collection: *Juno and Ganymede, the Virgin of Babylon, Cæsar and the Vestals*, and *the Judgment of Paris* were played without change but some of the others were slightly altered for the performance. At least twenty times I thought of throwing into the flames the piece, *Ninette and Finette*, whose prototypes I knew but I have kept it here for a moral purpose to show the dangers of the little intimate theatre, where innocence is lost before the young person realizes the necessity of guarding it."

One may well ask what this *moral purpose* was, since all the

BOOK III: THE EIGHTEENTH CENTURY

pieces are swollen with a scabrousness so disgusting that we shall not even synopsize the contents. Furthermore, according to de Sales' own confession, there was no purity to be endangered since only roués and ladies of quality worthy of being courtesans, were admitted. In the first piece Juno seduces Ganymede, in the second there is represented the devirgination of a Babylonian girl by the high priest of the Temple. In the third, Cæsar first ravishes two vestals but later ends his performance like Onan. The last piece Myrza deals with a pair of lovers who go through a few amorous spats with orgiastic pantomime, at first in Sophie's bath, and later at the Opera Ball. The female rôle was acted by the celebrated Sophie Arnould, and her lover by Grammont, the famous author of the Memoirs. The dialogue was so shocking that the Chevalier was able to sing only the first six stanzas and those only under an assumed name. The dialogue unaccompanied by gestures left the erotic audience cold, but the situation was far different with Chevalier de Grammont and Sophie Arnould. Both finished their lines in the tensest heat, and less than an hour later the Chevalier rushed to the actress' lodgings where they repeated the performance with no omissions, and many repetitions.

These thespian debaucheries in the princely theatres soon began to exercise public opinion, and after 1779 the performances ceased. As long as the scandal remained behind four walls, everyone was permitted to seek happiness in his own fashion, but when the matter became a public concern the police had to interfere.

CHAPTER IX
VENEREAL VERSES

THROUGH undermining all ethical and religious sensibility, the last embers of shame and decency were extinguished. It came to a pass where the strongest type of brothel poetry, of which there was a veritable mass production, aroused hardly a ripple of criticism. Bachaumont relates that it was customary to bring the *filles d'Opera* couplets celebrating their venereal talents and gallantries. These couplets were collected and issued in form of almanacs: *Etrennes aux paillardes, etrennes gaillardes, etrennes aux fauteurs*. Only once, in 1763, were the *Tablettes de paillardes* suppressed, but soon these salacious products were afoot again.

It goes without saying that no gallant souper was without the spice of erotic verse, and frequently of the chansons that later went out into the world. These almanacs were usually small gilt-edged, coquettishly appointed volumes, provided with a tiny pencil and a few blank pages for memoranda. The titles of most give their lewd contents away, though some were much more lewd than others. A small *Almanach du Trou-Madames* which seemed fairly harmless gave rise to the most daring performances which were extremely popular about 1760 under the title of Trou-Trou.

In this poetry Priapus was king. Courtier and lowest of officials, poet and poetaster, all felt obligated to show their reverence for the sign of the grotesque god of the garden. It was good form to represent in smooth verse the normal process of copulation as something strange, as some special discovery of the century. When gallic wit was unable to transfigure this subject matter, the shamelessly prostituted fantasy could at least turn out quite ordinary brothel poetry. There was hardly a contemporary author who failed to place his votive offering upon the altar of the corporeal Venus, and almost every one that pretended to the name of poet composed *Œuvres badines*.

A very influential collection of these gallant songs and verse tales is the *Recueil de pièces choisies par les soins du cosmopolite* (1735). This was the first of these collections to be printed in the eighteenth century, and incidentally the only one of Jean Baptiste Grécourt's books to be published during his lifetime (1683-1743). The booklet was put together by Princess Conti and Pater Vinet at the castle of the Duke de Arguillon, and contains epigrams from many sources. Grécourt is the prototype of the gallant Abbé. At the tender age of thirteen he became a priest, but soon lost his living because his sermons, which described vice in the most natural colors, and his predilection for satire which he indulged unrestrainedly, aroused more evil than induced edification. He lived in the friendliest relationship with the Marshal d'Estrées and the Duke de Arguillon whom he kept amused with his peppery jokes. The first edition of Grécourt's fugitive works, none of which, except the above-mentioned collection, would have been preserved had it not been for the copies made by his friend de Lasseré shortly before the former's death, appeared in 1747 as the *Œuvres badines*.

It was a thankful and lucrative task, this compiling of erotic anthologies, and many famous figures occupied themselves with it including Count Caylus the renowned archæologist, Parny, and others. Related to this type of gay effort in name, but quite different in essence, is Sylvain Maréchal's *Almanach des sonnetes femmes de la Société Joyeuse*. In this wide-spread and frequently reprinted livret of but thirty-two pages, one hundred women are mercilessly censured.

Despite its eroticism it occupies so important a place in French literature because of its notorious influence, that it merits a brief examination. The "Joyous Society"—which by the way actually existed—is indignant because the almanacs have been appearing annually, had not paid sufficient and exclusive attention to the fair sex. This omission was now to be rectified. The saints are to be dethroned since no one pays any attention to them today; and in their stead shall be elevated the great heroines of love. January is henceforth the month of the Fricatrices. Not all ladies are fitted for this exercise. It requires a fine white hand and a long and narrow finger. The feast of circumcision on January first is to be the Festival of the Foreskin. Many nations observe the custom of removing something from the organ, but lovely womankind doesn't approve of that subtractive rite. February is dedicated to the Trictatrices. The second day of the month, Mary's purification, is to be known as the Festival of the Bidets. Cleanliness was law among the ancient Hebrews and the Romans. Why not follow this praiseworthy custom with the choice of bidets. March is to be the month of Fellatrices. Of all forms of passion, this is to be striven for most highly and consists of *sucer le gland de son amant*. Few women are able to bring themselves to this form of love; but such lovers are constant. March twenty-fifth, the Annunciation, is now to be the Festival of the Procurers. This change does no violence to our worthy religion because the whole world knows that the holy Gabriel was the love messenger of the holy spirit.

The almanac now mentions four mondaines who had given themselves to fellatio. April is reserved for Lesbians. In Lesbia girls were accounted virtuous when they bore no children. May is the month of the Corinthians. These lovely women multiply the delight

BOOK III: THE EIGHTEENTH CENTURY

of the men they love. Whatever way he caresses them he will always find new sensations. June belongs to the Samians renowned for their debaucheries. July to the Phœnicians, who refined the art of gamahucher. August is the month of Syphiasans (one of the Cyclades) who had very lazy men. In order to excite them their women inserted their little fingers into *la porte poste* of their men, the practice known today as *diligence* or *postilion*. September is reserved for the Phisidisseusans whose contention it was that men were not the only ones who had been created to give pleasure. They trembled at the approach of a vigorous man and much preferred the delicate tongue of a lapdog. October goes to the Chalcidians who employ young, innocent children. November is the month for tribady. December is assigned to the Hircineans (from *hircus*) who go in for peeping (voyeuses). December eighth is the Feast of lost Virginity; and December twenty-fifth, the Feast of the Cuckold, after the holy Joseph. The livret closes with the significant request that readers contribute suggestions for the improvement and completion of this calendar. Such were the worlds at the time!

Most notorious, because of its disgusting shamelessness and vile blasphemy, is Piron's Ode to Priapus in sixteen strophes which is found in almost all the contemporary anthologies. Alexis Piron (1689-1773) found fame at a very early age through this ode. Later his occasional verse, rhymed epistles, tales and epigrams, all distinguished by a caustic wit and amazing skill in discovering people's weaknesses, and last but not least by their shameless tone, brought him numerous admirers and friends. Piron who was "nothing, not even an Academician", failed to achieve a place in the French Pantheon through the disfavor of Louis XIV, and not because the other immortals didn't recognize his wit or objected to his Ode. Fontenelle, with characteristic impartiality, said: "Piron, having composed the Ode, we may be wroth with him; but Piron without the Ode—well, we would shut our doors against him." And President Bouhier said to the author: "If someone throws the authorship of this piece up to you, you should reply calmly, 'I was the author'" Yet all his life his Ode to Priapus hindered his progress. Protest as he might against the attacks of his enemies, point as he might to his blameless life and irreproachable morals, it was in vain. He was a malicious satirist and did not spare himself either.

The following anecdote is characteristic. One day Piron, an old man now blind, went for a stroll with his little niece. Men seeing them laughed, and the little girl informed her uncle that the laughter was due to a certain irregularity in his clothes. "Uncle," she whispered, "everyone is gaping at us. . . won't you please cover your. . . your history".

"Dear child," spoke the poet, "this history has long become fabulous".

His own characterization of himself is concise and telling. "The fury of an ape and the simplicity of the child; a wit-drenched spirit and a golden heart; that is Piron".

CHAPTER X
SECRET CLUBS AND PERVERSIONS

THERE has been no distinction drawn until now between those authors who luxuriated in the domain of normal love, and those whose minds and writings were obsessed by unnatural and perverse sexual activity. This would have led to difficulties and repetition, for hardly a single work confined itself to describing the natural act alone; rather did everyone of them drag in the accompanying expressions of the libido sexualis for their share of vivid expositions. Even the *Cloister porter* and its echoes, cannot be regarded as merely pederastic tales.

Voisenon wrote a book against bigotry and cant entitled: *The exercises of Devotion of M. Roch with Mme. Condor*, which, his contemporaries added, had better be entitled *The Devotion with Respect to the front and rump of Mme. C.* He wrote this story for the amusement of his young girl friend, whom he laid down beside him to warm him as King David had done of old. He always slept side by side with her and permitted her to remain virgin. In witty and caustic fashion hypocrisy and bigotry are flayed. There is a dialogue (in bed) between a Tartuffe and a young woman who has been married to an elderly husband. These worthy descendants of Tartuffe are always with us and under the pretext of combating the call of the flesh these hypocrites indulge in the vilest debaucheries. Here's an example. The good woman launches into the following edifying discourse to—her pious friend.

"When I have my attacks I am greatly to be pitied and without your generosity I would probably have died—and without sacraments too. God himself has brought me to you in order that you may help me with my devotional exercises today. He could not let me die before I've confessed. I thank Him and you for that. May I ask you for another favor, Mr. Roch? You see these attacks come upon me six or seven times and the last are always stronger than the first. Isn't there anything.... I am confident that I can get rid of them if..... Oh, if it isn't too much trouble may I ask you to give me the remedy, for the third time. In order to drive away every thought of sin and prohibited pleasure I shall do the following. I shall now imagine that my husband is doing the work of God in my garden, for the sake of my recovery. And when you have completed my cure we will renew our devotional exercises, we will read a second spiritual lecture and pray a while in silence.

While Madame was speaking, Mr. Roch had enveloped her and begun the work of God. As soon as it was ended Madame came to life again and asked: "Without appearing too curious, could you inform me what is the name of that which cures me".

"It's called my heart".

"What? That is your heart? I had never believed it. O dear sir, how surely your heart has been created for mine. I assure you that were our hearts forever united, I would never be ill...." etc.

This Abbé Claude Henri de Voisenon (1708-1775) had ability to treat the most trying themes with graceful charm, and composed numerous erotic works. His *Erotic Fairy Tales* are masterpieces of genial and piquant gallantry. His friend Favoit relates that his life was unexceptionable, and that he wrote these pieces to please his friends. As executrix of his will, he appointed the clever Countess Turpin de Crisse, chairwoman of the gallant society, *Société de la Table Ronde*, and directed her to publish his manuscripts. This task the gallant lady accepted and carried out without any prudishness or fear of scandal.

If it is true that the most popular erotic works gave equal attention to all types of sexual activity, natural or perverse, it is no less true that certain of these writings "specialized", i.e., gave particular attention and emphasis to certain types of abnormal sexual practises. Thus the vice of tribady was extolled by two works, *L'histoire de la secte anandryne* and the very popular *L'apologue de la secte anandryne*. The latter work is the story of a 15 year old girl who falls into the hands of the infamous panderess Mme. Gourdan and is conveyed to a lady of rank. Thus Mlle. Sappho is inducted into a circle of lesbians who celebrate their mysterious rites in a temple constructed for the purpose, and who at the same time satisfy their debauched desires. The book ends with a detailed address delivered by the actress Raucourt in praise of Lesbian love, an address replete with the most informative material on that theme. The society referred to in this novel actually existed and was one of the numerous clubs in contemporary Paris dedicated to the realization of erotic fantasies and the satisfaction of strange lusts. These clubs will be discussed presently.

It was quite natural that an age in which love really was or was only regarded as the foremost thing in life, should create manuals for the best possible use of this joy. It was really as Abbé Galiani said: one loved with the head not with the heart; and love for these people was the libertinage de la pensée. In it one realized the glowing dreams of an imagination artificially stimulated; hence love was debased to an exciting game. Ovid was master, and La Mettrie wrote his *L'Art de jouir* in conscious derivation. His essential thesis is that the highest that man can achieve is corporeal pleasure. Since the supposed spirituality of man is founded on the body, we can only strive after bodily happiness. It were infantile to forego pleasures or regret past joys because of the soul which is notoriously untrustworthy. Passionate desire stands in the first place not because it is the only one but because it is the most general; and spiritual desire must be subordinated to the corporeal. It is not reason which is antipathetic to happiness or lust, but prejudices. There is no absolute virtue; all is relative to society; the only difference between good and evil is that in one case the public interest predominates, and in the other the private interest has conquered the general.

The greatest success in this field of the manuals of love was scored by Gentil-Bernard (1710-1775) with his *L'art d'aimer*. For twenty years the salons of Paris heard his low and seductive voice read fragments of his poetry, and women listened with rapture to his orgiastic verse. Voltaire wrote him an enthusiastic letter. Pompadour invited him to her soupers and commissioned him to compose pieces for her amateur theatre. When his *Art of Love* was published in 1775 Bernard had already fallen prey to mental illness.

The art purveyed in these and other propædeutics of copulation was not to be merely book learning. Societies were formed to carry out the doctrines thus learnt; and if one desired consciously to cultivate "love" and ecstasy, one joined one of these clubs. The most famous *sociétés d'amour* were:

1). *L'Académie de ces Dames et de ces Messieurs*, founded by Count Caylus to bring before the public the facetiæ and serious works of the passionate muse. Among the members were Count Tressan, Duclos, Vadé and Count Maurepas. Their secretary, under the pseudonym of Vadé, has left us the constitution and history of the order. Although the literary products of this order are very frivolous and free, especially of the feminine members, they lack attic salt too utterly to be appropriate for our taste. Even the talented

BOOK III: THE EIGHTEENTH CENTURY

members somehow didn't do their best here, as for example, Crébillon *fils*. In 1776 the group died a quiet death.

2). Another society *La Paroisse*, met regularly at the home of Mme. Doublet de Persan who lived such a retired life after the death of her husband that for 40 years she never ventured outdoors. Into her home she received the most distinguished and witty great ones of her day, as well as the loveliest women. Bachaumont was the president. From this circle there first issued the *Nouvelles à la main*, so called because they could only be read with one hand. These tales were put on public sale, and contained such racy and wanton tales in verse and prose that they were prohibited in 1852. It was from this group that Bachaumont gathered the materials for his *Mémoires secrets*.

3). Certain societies like the *Order and Society of the Hose, the Bee, the Anacreontic Society of Rosate*, and the *Valmuse* were innocuous clubs devoted to the reverence of beauty, woman, and platonic love. *The Order of Felicity*, whose history was written by Voisenon, went in for much more realistic private pleasures.

4). The most famous of all these clubs is undoubtedly the *Les Aphrodites* whose history, constitution and feasts, Nerciat has voluminously recorded in his pornographic novel of the same title. If he is to be believed, the club lasted for 20 years, and during that time had 4959 members, about 260 a year. All classes were represented, from the grand seigneur to the simplest soldier, but the mode of reception was not so easy and quite costly. Every member paid an admission fee, of course, and gave the society a gift, in keeping with his circumstances. In addition he had to deposit 10,000 livres for himself and 5,000 for his female partner, since women were admitted without charge. This money was kept at 5% interest and if a member left the club, the principle was returned. At the time the club was dissolved, during the revolution, it had a fortune of 4,558,923 livres, which was removed from France. The purpose of the society was the cultivation of passion in every form—and about this Nerciat gives us very detailed information.

5). Certain clubs were devoted to particular perversions. Thus, lesbian love was the raison d'être of the club of the *Anandrynes* whereof Pidausat treats thoroughly in his *English Spy*. Pederasty was the specialty of the *Guebres* and the *Arracheurs de palissardes*, whose constitutions committed them to eschew women. There was also a society of hermaphrodites, to which Voisenon belonged, and many other types. Thus the Duchess of Gesvre was the head of the *Medusa* order whose membership was confined to high-born ladies. Their cult seats were decorated with statues of Priapus, Apollo and Sappho together, and other symbols of sexual pleasure. The ill-famed and horrible *Society of the friends of crime*, whose organization is treated in Sade's *Juliette*, had its own seraglio of boys and girls, and even its own zoological garden in order to do justice to all tastes.

These and many other clubs, devoted to the culture of the senses, were clearly portrayed by a contemporary, Vicomte de Varause, in his *Lewd Sisters*. The prospectus to a translation of this work published a quarter of a century ago, states that this writer was born in the country about 1750 to an impoverished nobleman. Thanks to the efforts of his aunt, one of the many mistresses of King Louis XIV, he became a page at court. The way seemed to be clear for advancement, but alas! he was caught with one of the young favorites of the king. All his dreams of happiness, wealth and fame were dispelled and he was sentenced, lightly enough, to a place in a line regiment. This was a very fortunate blow for it saved him from the storms of the revolution which sent so many of his friends to the guillotine, or compelled them to live in ignominious exile. He rose to the position of lieutenant but was severely wounded in

BOOK III: THE EIGHTEENTH CENTURY

the battle at Valmy, and one of his legs was shattered. After a protracted sickness he regained some measure of health, but emerged a cripple. He entered a Benedictine cloister at Rheims but his memories gave him no respite. Finally he had to write them down. He never loses his poise and at the wildest leaps of his imagination ever remains the elegant, clever man of hyper-refined culture. In the highest moments of happiness his lovers still use the polite address. Unfortunately he died in 1806. This whole account sounds very credible, and reproduces eighteenth-century club-life amazingly, but it seems unfortunately untrue. All the exhaustive French biographers and bibliographers report absolutely nothing about this writer, which would be strange indeed in the case of so important a work. Hence we are forced to the conclusion that we are dealing here with a hoax on the part of the publisher, or perhaps the author. Actually, the French original is not known before 1891 which is possibly the original date of publication.

CHAPTER XI
CELEBRATED PORNOLOGISTS

VIVANT DENON

OF WHAT grace the gallant age was able to write is witnessed by the delightful tale of Vivant Denon entitled *Point de Lendemain*. This tale, it is said, owes its rise to an interesting incident. In 1775, while the author was at the French court, it was asserted in his presence that no one could write an authentic love story without using smutty words. Denon was of a different opinion, and in a few days he read his story to them. It said everything and didn't offend good taste in any way. This anecdote need not be taken too seriously for the same story is related concerning Musset's *Gamiani* and Cleland's *Fanny Hill*. Denon's friend Dorat to whom he sent these poems and who published them in the year of his death, enjoyed some reputation as the author of a pedantic though frivolous work on kisses, which leaves us rather cold today. The same is somewhat true of Montesquieu's *Temple de Gnide* which, according to the author, was written in honor of the Princess de Clermont and after one of her ideas, without any further aim than to draw a poetic picture of passion. The direct causes of the composition were a heart affair and the reading of Fenelon's *Telemachus*. Montesquieu secured royal permission and in 1775 it was published anonymously in prose and purported to be a translation from the Greek. But the stuff is of such a nature that it can only be properly valued by powdered and curled heads. The Abbé

BOOK III: THE EIGHTEENTH CENTURY

Voisenon reported that the effusion brought its author numerous loves which he was wise enough to conceal.

Grimm, the friend of Diderot and of the philosophers, criticised these monotonous pastorals very unfavorably and perhaps he was thinking of Diderot's smart *Bijoux indiscrets* which was of an altogether different order than the insipid poetry of shepherds. Diderot felt impelled to deny his authorship of the *Bijoux* but no one else could have written this masterwork, which no less a personage than Lessing had translated into German. The book owes its origin to a chat held by the author with Mme. de Puisieux. The scabrous novels of Crébillon *fils* were being discussed when Diderot asserted that this stuff was easy, for once one had a pleasing foundation, everything else depended on the execution. The others doubted his opinion, so Diderot went home and set to work. In a fortnight the *Bijoux* were done and he had won 50 louis d'or. It is not impossible that Diderot was strongly influenced by a panurgic work which had appeared as early as 1747 under the amazing title: *The cavalier who could make vulvæ speak*.

The contents may be briefly summarized thus. In the kingdom of the Congo lives the Sultan, Mongogul, in the friendliest relations with his favorite wife, Mirzopa. But despite his success in love, ennui overcomes him and he turns to the demon, Kukufa, who has often been of help to his house. From him he obtains a ring which possesses the extraordinary quality that it can make the jewel of every woman speak as soon as a stone inserted into the ring is turned upon it. At the same time the ring makes the bearer invisible. Mongogul finds great pleasure in the ring for a whole series of women surrender their secrets to him. The Sultan duly reports this to his Mirzopa, and both use the knowledge thus won to criticize contemporary morals, which are sad enough. None of the solicited women has ever stood the test, and all their jewels have been tarnished. The Sultan promises his favorite a castle and a little baboon that she desires very strongly, if only he will be able to find one faithful woman at the court. Soon he has the opportunity of testing his theories. His beloved falls into a severe fit of cramps and the sultan in great curiosity hastens to turn his stone upon her jewel, but this remains silent. Whereupon the Sultan realizes with immense glee that she is the only faithful woman at the court.

One can see from this brief synopsis that the *Bijoux* is not really a novel but a loose enchainment of realistic tales, a gallery of the most diverse varieties of the female nature. The chill, fiery, gallant, coquettish, passionate, tender, moody, and constant are drawn with psychological exactness. The hypocrisy, intrigue, cunning, dissimulation, wantonness, and insatiability of women are illustrated in a thousand piquant lives. We can read between the lines that women can be moved by self-seeking, pleasure and vanity, but not a word can be said in defense of her love and fidelity. Diderot did not forget to satirize Platonic love and could not desist from touching on the aberrations of the sexual libido. The sapphic love of Fricamone to Acaris, the inclination of Haria to her dogs, the sodomy of a Pasha, cast their murky and repulsive shadow over the comic lights which generally play in these cynical anecdotes. Diderot seeks to satisfy bourgeois justice by having marital infidelity in the Congo punishable by the forcible subtraction from the sinner of the sinful member, which generally brings death in its wake.

Diderot's work was impelled by the Horatian *ridendo dicere verum*, and for this purpose he employs comic and fantastic elements as well as humor. But his satire leaves the modern reader unmoved; for Diderot possesses neither the force of an Aristophanes nor the healthy joy of Rabelais, nor the seductive frivolity of Crébillon. One recognizes the thinker and the savant through many pedantic and doctrinaire undertones. Diderot never abandons a certain standard of decency, save in the confession of the travelling jewel of Cypria. Strong as the work is in imaginary power, it is very poor poetry. Diderot later denied this child of his muse, and regretted having composed it.

In 1796 there appeared *La Religieuse* (the Nun) based on an actual event. A nun was coerced into breaking her vows. The Marquis de Croismare of the Encyclopædist's circle interested himself in her welfare. Later owing to family circumstances he retired to his country seat. His friends desiring his return, cooked up the story that the nun had escaped from the cloister and stood in need of his help.

What has given the book its odium is its representation of tribadic scenes between the nun and the mother superior. But with what tenderness has Diderot approached his task! Nothing lewd or obscene is contained in it. Diderot ever remembers that it is a girl, in whose name he is writing, one who has only a vague premonition of the vice that is threatening to engulf her. He only permits her to go far enough to make us realize the extent of the danger. One feels that his whole interest is on the side of the persecuted nun, whose whole sin lay in her being nothing more than a woman. This, however, she is prevented from being; and Diderot depicts with high gusto and disgust the infamy of the attempts to divert the natural sexual life of the girl into unnatural channels.

The third of Diderot's stories belonging to this class is *Jacques the Fatalist*, written about 1772, a collection of tales contained and held together by the story of the narrator. A master and his servant tell each other of their love adventures, which are frivolous but not in the sense of libertinage. Nevertheless, the book was declared lewd. Diderot defended himself against this charge of obscenity and took a fling at the practise of permitting to the ancients what is forbidden to the moderns. But in this apologia his expression became more offensive than the story had been.

VOLTAIRE

IT WAS the *Maid of Orleans* which made Voltaire's name known to every pious churchman. The work was composed in sections and at first the early poems circulated only among his friends, in more or less complete copies. The wider public was introduced to the work in 1751. While Voltaire was staying at Rome the manuscript was stolen and came into the wrong hands, for in the same year there appeared the first unauthorized edition. Another unauthorized edition followed and Voltaire made vociferous denial of his authorship. However, in 1762 he authorized an edition provided with 20 copper plates and in it he toned down the most improper passages; for instance, he now had the maid keep her *pucelage* until the capture of Orleans, and only then offer it up on the altar of victory.

The poem opens with a very intimate description of the erotic connection between King Charles and Agnes Sorel. While both are living in their idyl of love, France is being devastated by England who has already arrived at the gates of Orleans. Now the patron saint of France, Saint Dionysus waxes indignant over the sloth of Charles and riding upon a sunbeam enters the terror-stricken municipal council, as they are considering plans to cope with the imminent dangers. He assures them that just as France had been brought into the present plight by a woman, so they will be saved by a virgin; but they are incredulous and laugh him out of countenance. In high dudgeon he departs on his sunbeam.

Voltaire now introduces us to Jeanne d'Arc, the fruit of an idyllic hour between a monk and a peasant woman. An English

BOOK III: THE EIGHTEENTH CENTURY

itinerant friar, Dom Grisbourdon, who was an adept at magic, and learnt from Sybilline books that France's destiny depended on Jeanne's virginity. Hence he immediately decides to obtain this precious prize, and his decision is shared by his rival, an ass driver. To this end he causes Jeanne to fall asleep, uncovers her, and prepares to snatch her prize; but while the rivals are bickering about priority, St. Dionysus comes ariding and they flee. The girl awakes, covers herself again, and is provided by the saint with historic weapons and launched upon her historic mission. To complete matters Dionysus bewitches a winged donkey which she is to bring to King Charles. They come upon the English first, and get to the tent of the enemy general, Hans Chandos, whose sword and trousers she steals, not before making a few drawings on the exposed hind parts of a handsome page. To Charles she comes and the Saint spurs him on so that he becomes very bellicose when he hears what sort of treasure Jeanne owns. The latter is examined by the king's physicians and her reputation sustained. Now the battle can begin.

After a few sorties against philosophy and the clergy, Voltaire describes Agnes' grief at her lover's desertion. She sets out in the company of Bonneau to pursue Charles, and in the meantime stops off at the inn where Jeanne is tarrying. Here she steals Charles' trousers and Jeanne's armor. Bedizened in this heavy armor she is captured by the Britons and led before Chandos, who strips her of his trousers and wants to ravish her naked, when Jeanne storms into the hostile camp. The Englishmen suffer a crushing defeat, but Jeanne and the hero Dunois in their martial fury become separated from the rest, and find themselves alone. Suddenly a little dog appears and leads them to a fairy place inhabited by a monster who is man by day and woman by night. Conculix, for that is his name, lives only for passion and he seeks in vain to have his dual lusts gratified by either or both his guests. Out of revenge he attempts to burn his guests. When they are both standing naked upon the stake, Dom Grisbourdon enters through the air upon his ass and persuades Conculix to spare them, promising that they would share the wench. Presently we find Dom Grisbourdon in Hell, again in the circle of devils, and the satanic monk reports his last exploit. Naturally this scene is just made for Voltaire—and he deals hefty blows to the church. Dom Grisbourdon meets Constantine, the holy Dominicus, and others. The monk tells how he and the ass driver had been on the point of forcing Jeanne, when Jeanne's ass had come through the air and taken her away to Dunois. Whereupon he had disguised himself as a seductive girl by whom Dunois was thoroughly ravished. The ass driver now turned his attention to this stunning girl, whereupon Jeanne in ire and jealousy had run him through with her sword.

Agnes, who regards herself as having been very shabbily treated by Chandos who had rejected her, turns her back upon the camp of the English still wearing the clothes of their leader. But the page of the latter observes her flight and pursues her. Agnes has a fall and he treats her wounds and later escorts her to an hostelry where he leaves her alone. But a friar knows how to take advantage of opportunities and shares Agnes' bed and body. In the meantime Dunois rescues a young witch from the stake. She informs him of her love story and her rescuer fights for her and wins. King Charles now learns with grief of the disappearance of his Agnes who all this while was being made happy by the friar. Thereafter the page became recipient of her favors, but both are apprehended by the English in the midst of their copulatory activity. Agnes succeeds in escaping to a convent where she desires to expiate her sins, but alas for her good intentions, the acting mother superior is a disguised youth. Now the English break into the nunnery and hold

BOOK III: THE EIGHTEENTH CENTURY

foul orgies with the nuns. St. Dionysus sees all and hastens to the scene with Jeanne to dam the torrent of passion. But St. George also arrives and both holy ones fall to with their swords until they are forcibly reconciled by Gabriel. Charles with Bonneau and his confessor arrive at the castle of Cutendres where the young page, who has just slain the lecherous monk that had done violence to Agnes, was now enjoying her again after a long absence. Full of desire the king hurries to Agnes and the page scurries into hiding but throws over a night table and is discovered by the king. However, Agnes is able to hoodwink the nit-wit monarch.

In the meantime luck favors the English. Jeanne fights with Chandos and loses, whereupon the sensual Briton seeks to rob her virginity but Dionysus succeeds in preventing this. In the church Dorothea is oppressed by the all too free attentions of Chandos. Her lover Trimouille arrives on the scene and measures swords with the latter but is worsted. However, Dunois takes up her cause and slays the Briton. Charles is victorious at Orleans but loses his Agnes when the earth opens and swallows all the pretty girls plus the page Montros, to deposit them in the magic palace of Conculix. Jeanne's ass makes an avowal of love to its mistress but is driven off by Dunois. In the meantime, our heroes are with Conculix who will release them from that captivity when one of the captives will give himself in love. Since all shrink back, Paul Tirconel decides to sacrifice himself for the others. The ass comes to the castle, takes Agnes off to her Charles, and rushes to Jeanne who finally surrenders to him.

From every line there is wafted to us the love with which Voltaire wrote the *Pucelle d'Orléans*, and his delight in the erotic situations which are interspersed through the epic. Voltaire wouldn't really have been himself had he not utilized every opportunity to hurl his darts of satire against the court, Louis, his mistresses and the clergy. If we who read it today are apt to set it down with meagre delight or perhaps even with some disgust, it is because the book no longer contains truth for us. Our world view is no longer a frivolous one; but we must remember how and why it could be so then. It came about as the practical reaction against Christian spiritualism. In Christianity, the sensual in man is fundamentally denied in theory, and only tolerated in practice. Continence and virginity are the higher, the true ideals, which should be fulfilled and established in the lives of men and women if only they could be compassed; and occasionally in some few individuals these virtues are realized, which sets them off as the very paragons of our species. On the other hand, the enlightenment in the sensualist form which it assumed in France asserted, and to that extent at least justly, that man was not essentially spirit. But now it went further, and became just as one-sided as the church, by proclaiming further that he is only flesh and nothing more than sensuality. Hence, the poet endeavors to discover a series of pictures in which the flesh always brings the spirit to ruin, in which ostensible purity is always revealed in the end as hypocrisy, and the most unsuspected saints, as the most dissolute of men. It may be said that in Voltaire's *Maid of Orleans*, the eighteenth century took delight in its frivolity, which in itself is certainly not praiseworthy, but which cannot be separated from its other characteristics.

CREBILLON JUNIOR

THE frivolous literature of France reached its high point in Claude Prosper Jolyot de Crébillon (1707-1777), and who as the most radical representative of this class of writers, worked his field with resolution and perspicacity. His works thoroughly convey the tone and spirit of his society and evince an unexampled candor. Crébillon's novels are always sparkling and frivolous to the point of folly, and yet always (with some few exceptions) stopping before the ultimate revelation, always halting before the naked representation of the final climax. His desire to mirror life as it really is, is aided by his utter lack of piety, and his mercilessly clear powers of observation. Crébillon had no more illusions. Wherever he looked he saw lechery and rottenness, and these conditions are truthfully mirrored in his works. If despite this we accuse him of lewdness, we are forgetting that an author who wishes to be read must ever be the slave of his reading public. Crébillon wished to be read and his public deified frivolity. This subservience to the taste of his time explains, in part, the immorality of his novels which found their admirers even in England. British men of the world frequently came to Paris to become better acquainted with the refined art of loving, to provide themselves with clothes, and to purchase a dozen of Crébillon's novels to present to their friends upon their return.

His best known work is undoubtedly *The Sofa*. When this novel appeared it aroused great discussion. The very title reveals the essential tendency of the work. In 1741 he received a command to exile himself from Paris because the king and his courtiers believed themselves to be portrayed in this tale. Crébillon fled to England and confessed that he had written *Le Sopha* at the wish of Fredrick II, that it had not been intended for publication but that the manuscript had been stolen from him. After some time, he received permission to return to France.

As in Sade, so also in Crébillon, the wars of love are fought not upon the bed, but upon the sofa. The story takes the form of an oriental tale, in which Almanzai, a nobleman in the court of a certain Shah, Baham, becomes transmogrified into a sofa for punishment. The conditions of the enchantment and the subsequent release are that he may choose any form, any material, any color, which he wishes, and serve whom he will; only that he must remain a sofa until there will be enacted upon him or in his immediate vicinity a scene which is of extreme rarity: namely, innocence meeting innocence, and both being mutually conquered. We may wish to remember that Crébillon drew the framework of his story from another novel of his time; *The Metempsychosis of the Mandarin Fum Hom*, in which the latter experiences the most intimate details in his various incarnations. When Crébillon cast about for some object which would be compelled to observe the most suggestive and lascivious scenes, his first thought was the sofa, but it goes without saying that Crébillon was altogether original in the erotic situations. The success that greeted this book was so immense that many imitations were found. Even England produced echoes of this novel, but instead of the sofa to observe and report the amorous tidbits such diverse objects were introduced as lap dogs, drawers, bank notes, and formal coats.

An example of a typically French *causerie* with fine pointed psychological graces is offered us by Crébillon in his unusual *Sextravaganza*. It is a faithful mirror of the naughty life at the court of Louis xv, where women give themselves as naturally as the men who take them. In *Sextravaganza* there are but two characters, Countess Cidalise and Count Clitandre. The scene is a country palace at night, more exactly, the room of the countess, who has retired but forgotten to bolt the door. Clitandre, walking about in his nightshirt, sees an open door and walks in. Is he expected? We are not informed, for Crébillon is master of the half-tone, who leaves much more to our surmise than he tells us definitely. Conversation becomes more and more lively and more intimate. The Countess wishes to hear more of his love adventures. He is rather reluctant to continue his tale, because he is quite frozen, but by and by, he obtains the Countess' permission to finish the tale in her bed. Now he relates his meeting with Julie on one hot summer's day, during

BOOK III: THE EIGHTEENTH CENTURY

which the influence of heat on virility was discussed and in which, finally he gave her proof that in his case at least, no diminution was to be marked. After this the two bed-mates huddle closer to each other, and each makes sexual confessions to the other, and declare themselves attracted one to the other. Clitandre now lays siege to her, according to all the rules of the art, until the citadel capitulates. This performance is followed by the vivid narration of other amorous relations, and when morning grays, Clitandre has exhausted his report and his power.

Next in importance is Crébillon's Chinese story, *The Parasite*, which pretends to be a translation from the land of lotus blossoms. The story is prolix and involved and the conclusion is rather dull. In all it is a rather painful task for the modern reader. The thread of the story is constantly torn by unnecessary details—and there are frequent intrusions of philosophic and gallant details. The sale of the book was strictly prohibited and as a result it enjoyed a large underground distribution and even court ladies are reported as having been "crazy" for it. The reason for the prohibition was that in this book there could be discerned a satire against Cardinal Rohan, with the result that Crébillon had to spend some time in the Bastille.

If Crébillon here has retained some traces of decency he dropped all the veils in the work now to be mentioned, the famed *Dialogue Tableaux of Morals in Different Ages*. Both this volume and *Sextravaganza* have recently been published in this country. In seventeen chapters a veritable master paints the gallant life of the old empire. Seventeen pictures out of life, caught by the inexorable eye and limned with a delicate impressionistic pencil, joined together to form a total portrait of the most ostentatious era of French history—glowing with ardent sensuality. In the midst of this kaleidoscope of passions stands Mlle. Therese, a society girl of enchanting beauty and grace. We make her acquaintance when she is just a young girl being educated in the cloister and already here, within the holy walls, her hot blood simmers. Her senses cry out for fulfillment and a stormy need for love draws her to her friends and associates. How these young girls at the cloister engage in numerous, deeply erotic practices, how the awakening of spring finds expression in the most daring of games and adventures, constitute one of the most effective and exquisite parts. Later we see the girl in full bloom as bride and young matron. Very soon, however, the marriage partners go their own way.

This remarkable book has a very interesting history. Crébillon wrote it at the request of the enormously wealthy farmer-general of taxes, Popelinière, who was famous for his grand style, his luxury, his lavishness and his wenching. In addition he had an itch to write poetry, which hasn't survived. But two of his novels have come down to us, and the *Histoire de Zairette* has been preserved because its author affixed it to Crébillon's *Tableaux of Morals*, to rescue it from oblivion. Zairette, born in Paris, is after many venereal adventures brought to the kingdom of Karaktay where she must serve the sensual desires of the ruler Moufhack, which love scenes are represented with sextravagant imaginativeness. According to Marquis de Paulmy's account, this book of Crébillon was printed with the utmost care in just one copy, in the house and under the eye of Popelenière. After printing, the plates were destroyed. The work contained twenty large but handsome miniatures which showed Popelenière in various positions. After the latter's death this volume was found in a sealed packet so that at first Popelenière was suspected of being the author of both books, both *Zairette* and the *Tableaux*. As soon as it was unwrapped and examined, the great monetary value of the book became obvious because of its rarity and the beauty of its pictures. Mlle. de Vandi, one of the heiresses to the Popelenière estate cried out aloud when she saw this find and insisted that the work of the devil be burnt immediately. But the officer in charge explained that this procedure would have to be sanctioned by all the heirs; whereupon he sealed the package again and informed the chief of police who in turn communicated with the minister, Saint-Florentin. The minister ordered that the book be obtained for His Majesty, and so it was. Later the book changed hands many times, and in 1891 it was sold to a bibliophile for over 20,000 francs. There have been numerous reprints and Rops once contributed a frontispiece to one of these. The French government has always confiscated these reprints so that copies are exceedingly rare.

Crébillon wrote numerous other works and all were widely read in his day. His writings fitted the taste of the times perfectly—to portray the most amatory situations with the most moral words. Sensual pleasure has but little charm without spirited talk. The witty preludes are the ornaments and the excuse for these immoral carryings on. The fairy tale form and the Oriental framework were also part of the contemporary mode which Crébillon adopted.

Peculiar to Crébillon is the extraordinary combination or moralizing tone with scabrous reporting of love relationships. No one can fail to appreciate his desire to give a faithful mirror of his time. At moments the satirist in him makes his appearance when he takes aim at theological and political abuses—but he does it guardedly and makes these reconnoitres appear quite accidental. His influence on the literature of his time was tremendous and can easily be demonstrated.

THE EROTIC HISTORY OF FRANCE

CHODERLOS DE LACLOS

SINCE love was everything in this century, the gallant ladies and gentlemen of the day became systematic and reduced seduction to a system. The mere surrender of a woman was no great achievement. One had tasted so much, and so frequently, that one could find pleasure only when one gained one's goal by craft or force. "First enjoy, then destroy" went the slogan. With unsurpassable mastery Choderlos de Laclos (1741-1803), in his *Liaisons Dangereuses*, reproduced with the fidelity of a photographer, all the details of courtly depravity which degraded love to sly deceit. A young and innocent girl is seduced by two genial criminals and made into the meanest whore. A young and religious matron is systematically driven to infidelity by this pair and finally to death. And the motive of it all is not love, not even sensuality, but the exquisite lust for psychological experimentation which will stop at no crime. Seduction is not the motive but corruption. But the satirist was hardly so much in earnest about his theme that he forgot his Gallic smile and frivolity. He was impelled by literary ambition, and to achieve a widely-read book he would have to employ the loudest colors possible in the depiction of vice. De Laclos cannot be accused of depicting crime with great expansiveness and providing the "heroes" of corruption with such brilliant accoutrement. If his work was to be complete and effective it would have to be done in the finest and most circumstantial manner.

De Laclos's contemporary, Count Tilly, makes a very interesting comment. The author expended much art upon Mme. de Mertuil. He purposely represented her as being so corrupt that he might the better contrast the angelic purity of Mme. de Tourvel. And he is even justified in making the former lady outdo in evil Valmont

BOOK III: THE EIGHTEENTH CENTURY

himself, for he is a student of men and knows that generally women are better than men and worthier than us; but once they have left the path of virtue and womanliness, they proceed downhill into the mire at an alarmingly fast clip. For the rest he has drawn pictures more reprehensible than Aretino; but most of them are elegant, some true, others exaggerated, and their colors laid on with a trowel. By those who knew the great men only from hearsay this work was accepted as a splendid representation of the general morality of the higher classes; and in this sense it can be regarded, as one of the thousand billows of the revolutionary ocean which swallowed up the court, one of the thousand lightning flashes in the storm that razed the throne. In a word, his work is the product of a head of the first rank, a heart given over to rottenness and the genius of evil. So well was he able to get the proper note that people actually asked whether the correspondence was genuine or fanciful; and Laclos, in a naïve and philistine introduction, sought to maintain the belief in the genuineness of the letters.

De Laclos told his friend Tilly that the work originated while he was stationed in a garrison on the island of Ré where he was perishing of boredom. He had already tried composing some elegies and had also gotten into scrapes. But now he yearned to achieve something that would bring him lasting fame, even after his death. One of his friends, a literary man who had also made his mark in the sciences, had had a host of adventures in his life which lacked only a frame and a stage since they had plenty of glory and éclat. This friend was really born for woman, and was thoroughly versed in the falsehoods and infidelities in which the female species has accomplished so much. Indeed, had he been born at court he would have been a lovelace and would even have surpassed the latter in form. This friend chose Laclos for his confidant who laughed at his pranks and occasionally helped out with advice.

The latter knew one of his mistresses who stood near to Mme. de Mertuil, and in Grenoble he found the lady who was the prototype of the Mertuil woman in the story. It was a certain Marquise concerning whom the whole city knew and told things related only of the most notorious empresses of ancient Rome. He wrote down the most noteworthy of these reports with an eye to using them later, and added to these erotic episodes that had become bywords, and certain passages from his own life. Then he melted it all into one precious metal, invited the rest and created particularly the character of Mme. de Tourvel who meant very much to him and whom he regarded as being too virtuous for this earth. After expending a number of months of diligent labor to perfect the style he sent it into the world and achieved his purpose. Fame was his in large measure. During his own life the book was reprinted fifty times. Stendhal (Beyle) sought to make his acquaintance and was so impressed by the Laclos reputation that he acted like a diffident schoolboy in the presence of the famous author.

LOUVET DE COUVRAY

IN STRICT contrast to the *Dangerous Connections* of Choderlos stands another, hardly less famous work, *The Adventures of Chevalier Faublas* by Jean Baptiste Louvet de Couvray. In 1772 he was taken into the convent where he joined the party of the Girondists and was not afraid to rise against Robespierre. In 1793 he had to flee but after the death of the latter he returned and was readmitted into the convent, joined the Council of 500 and died in 1797. But his work will live for all time as the creation of a great poet. This work permits us to see yet once more in roseate hues all that the old society had fitted out with so much pomp and circumstance. If the *Dangerous Liaisons* had exposed its contempo-

BOOK III: THE EIGHTEENTH CENTURY

raries with cynical candor, the other book waxed enthusiastic about the handsome lie—its lovely grace, its exquisite frivolity, which the society flattered itself it lived under.

In contrast to Casanova's experienced reports, Faublas's is an imaginary account, and may be accounted as the moral balance of the time. The whole is a web of lubricity and passionate boudoir scenes where people love, converse wittily, debate about love; where night and day there is nothing else but carnal pleasure; where folk smilingly deceive and are deceived; where despite all this nothingness, no tedium is experienced. Everything remains superficial and neither lust nor grief goes very deep; and above all, these idlers fear a genuine passion which is not compatible with their trivialism. Faublas sums up all these hundreds of individual details in his wonderful pictures of the times. The contents of this book are too well known to need repetition here. Besides, a compressed narrative account will give no notion of the attractive and vividly warm paintings, for it is just this mass of little mischievous and lascivious details which afford it its true splendor. Louvet comprehended the ideal of rakishness with almost remarkable talents. His inventiveness is happy, his devices which set it in motion are nimble, swift and effective. One marvels at the heap of aids and combinations the author has at his disposal. The situations he invents are comical and original and his dramatic talent teaches him how to handle characters properly. The action is full of fire. The movement of scenes abounds in vital warmth which never harms the probability or impedes the unfolding. Twenty characters and a half dozen intrigues are going at one time and nothing gets in the way of anything else. On the contrary they illuminate each other with pure and tender love and patriotic enthusiasm resting the mind, for everything fatigues, even vice. His style is elegant and light; and if panurgic in places, thoroughly pleasant. It has more of grace than wit, more wit than passion, more passion than observation and more of frivolity than anything else. To sum up, the queer amalgam of inconstant tenderness, sensual intoxication and merry comedy produces a remarkable but dangerous book.

Extremely praiseworthy is the naturalness with which emotion is represented and motivated. Here is no affected sentimentality, ostentatious with artifiicial sensations, but pure truth, even when it goes hand in hand with the greatest frivolity. As an illustration of the spirit of the work and its language, a scene will be quoted in which the Marquise apparently makes the discovery that the young Faublas who is lying beside her, dressed as a girl, is really of masculine gender.

> DEEP silence reigned for a few breaths, then the Marquise asked me in a wonderfully changed voice.
> "Are you asleep already, pretty child?"
> "No, I am still awake."
> She opened her arms rapidly and pressed me to her bosom.
> "Heavens!" she then cried out with a surprise that was excellently simulated, "A man." And pushing me from her quickly she added, "How, sir, is this possible?"
> "Madame, I told you expressly..." I answered trembling.
> "Quite right, sir, but it was incredible. You shouldn't have remained here or you should at least not have prevented them from preparing another bed for you."
> "But it wasn't I who did it, madame, but the Marquis himself."
> "Please speak quietly, sir. I repeat you must not remain here. You must go."
> "Good, madame, I go."
> But she seized me by my sleeve and cried, "Go? where to—and what for? To wake my maids so that we will surely be apprehended? So that all will be able to say that a man has been in my bed?"
> "Gracious madame, do not be angry. I shall spend the night

BOOK III: THE EIGHTEENTH CENTURY

in an armchair. This will be the best way out of an awkward situation."

But she still held on to my arm and went on, "Now that's an idea for you. *Tired as he is, a night in this cold room would certainly give him a cold—if not some more serious illness.* As a matter of fact you deserve some such fate, but I will permit you to remain here if you promise to be good."

"Then you forgive me?"

"No. I don't forgive you. I am merely looking out for myself, much more than for you. *But dear—what a cold hand he has.*"

Full of pity she put it upon her ivory neck, but guided by natural impulse and love, the fortunate hand soon slid down; an incomprehensible excitation set my blood aboiling.

"Has ever woman been in such a pickle as the one he has put me into?" the Marquise complained petulantly.

"Forgive me, forgive me, dearest mama."

"You are really considerate of your mama, you little wretch." Then her arms drew me to her again, oh so gently. And soon we were so close that our lips met and I had the temerity to press a hot kiss upon hers.

"Fanblas, is this what you promised me?" she said almost voicelessly. Her hand suddenly strayed, and a consuming fire raced through my veins.

"Gracious lady, forgive me, I die!"

"My dear Faublas, my friend!"

I became motionless. The Marquise had pity with my helplessness which she rather enjoyed and helped along my timid awkwardness. I underwent with as much wonder as pleasure a lesson which I repeated more than once.

CHAPTER XII
OTHER CELEBRATED PORNOLOGISTS

COMTE DE MIRABEAU

IN 1749 Honoré Gabriel Riquette, Comte de Mirabeau was born at the castle of Bignon. He died in 1791. His biography is known to all. Because he had seduced Sophie Ruffey, the Marquise of Monnier, both were persecuted by the furious husband. Mirabeau was sentenced to the jail at Vincennes, and Sophie was immured in a cloister. But the motives which impelled the aging Count Ruffey to these acts of punishment did not spring from any exalted motives. Repeatedly, Mirabeau accuses Monnier unequivocally of the ignominious design to get a child from his wife at any price, which he himself could not hope for from his own efforts. He wanted a child so badly because he wished to avenge himself against his married daughter and her husband. He would be able to disinherit them only if he could have a child by his second marriage which in the eyes of the world could be considered as his own. When these calculations were destroyed by Mirabeau and Sophie he became extremely embittered and engineered the persecutions of the lovers.

While Mirabeau was in prison the Marquis de Sade was brought there, and there were many subsequent encounters between these two writers. In the 1780's the latter came to pay his respects to Mirabeau, who later wrote the following account of this visit to Police Chief Boucher, whom Mirabeau called his guardian angel:

BOOK III: THE EIGHTEENTH CENTURY

"Yesterday M. de Sade fired his cell. He did me the honor of introducing himself to me and without the slightest provocation on my part he made me the butt of his infamous attack. He accused me of being the favorite of the inspector of prisons—M. de Rougemont—who accorded me the privilege of a daily stroll which was denied him. Finally he asked for my name so that he might have the pleasure of cutting my ears off after he would again be at liberty. Then I lost patience and replied: 'My name is that of a gentleman who has never cut women up, and poisoned them, and who will spell the name out on your back if you won't shut up, for which business I shan't have much regret.' Whereupon he kept still and he hasn't dared to open his mouth since. If you are inclined to bear me some ill-will about it I might answer that it is easy enough to exercise patience at a distance, but mighty sad to live under one roof with such a monster."

The incarceration of the lovers, Mirabeau and Sophie, did not have the effect of extinguishing their love. They languished each for the other and their letters bear witness to their passionate temperament. Sophie is delighted to read the description of Mirabeau's love affairs with the highest ladies of the court.

His letters are momentary inspirations of the most personal art, not really meant for the external world. When rumors came to him that some one was planning to publish them he was shocked and vowed that if he could survive the blow he would live only for revenge. Unfortunately, he had no way of hindering the realizations of these rumors, for all the letters had gotten into the Paris police archives. During the revolution the whole department came under the control of the municipal council whose syndic in 1792 was the convent deputy Manuel. The latter used his position to obtain the letters for himself and to publish them despite the opposition of the family.

Mirabeau also corresponded in a very free manner indeed with another lady whom he did not know at all. The suppressed desires of the lovers found partial expression in this erotic correspondence which is an important source for the life of Mirabeau. Thus we learn that Mirabeau is the author of the notorious *My Conversion*, frequently known as *The Libertine of Quality*. Some have suggested that it was the father of Mirabeau who wrote the book but attributed it to the son that the latter's name might be discredited, but several of these letters to Julie contain explicit and indubitable testimony that Mirabeau himself wrote the book. Thus he writes to her:

> "I am not enclosing a quite insane book that I have written and called *My Conversion*. The following extract may give you an idea of the contents, and show you at the same time how faithful to you I still am. (There now follows a quotation from the above book.) 'Until now, my friend, I was a ne'er-do-well. I pursued skirts and was only a rotter and a ——. But now youth returns to my heart. Hereafter I shall love only for gold. I will advertise myself as a sworn stallion for women whose summer is almost gone, and so will teach them to hop with their posteriors every month.'
>
> "You can't believe how many figures and amusing contrasts fit into this frame. All types of women, and all ages pass before the eye. The idea is quite mad but the details are rollicking and some day I'm going to read it all to you, although I fear that you'll be scratching my eyes out. I've already finished the woman of means, the prude, the nun, the president, the business woman, the court lady, the old one, and now I'm doing the young woman. This is one grand work and a correct manual of morals."

In a later letter he writes Sophie that he is preparing engravings for the book which if he were its bookseller and not its author, would be making his fortune. He promises to leave enough time for hours of dalliance with her, even if he is giving most of his present time to the completion of this book. If she will promise to

BOOK III: THE EIGHTEENTH CENTURY

be tolerant to free words and loose portraiture, which is, however, nothing but the reflection of current immorality, he will send her the book which is less frivolous than would appear at first glance. He has already thoroughly analyzed the court ladies and finished anatomizing the nuns and the opera girls. Now he is treating the monks but is planning to make a short excursion to the underworld where he will fornicate with Prosperina and dig up some droll news. In short, he regards his book as an extraordinary piece of madness which no one can read without laughter. A month later he sent her the first part of the book. The second he was afraid to entrust to the mails. A melancholy note is sounded in the brief note accompanying the book as he speaks of the dismalness of the prison environment where one must beat one's thigh to induce laughter: "For if one doesn't laugh one loses all courage, or reason, or even life."

The novel is entirely concerned with a man who sells his potency. In order to pay for his luxurious indulgences a cavalier belonging to French court circles distributes his favors for suitable remuneration to a whole series of women, more or less old and more or less ugly, but always rich. Mirabeau published the book because he just had to pay off some debts. Hence we cannot assume that we are dealing with an absolutely faithful reflection of the social life of the times. The lascivious life of that epoch appears caricatured; but the book has an abiding human value.

Later Mirabeau wrote his little pussy, Sophie, that he had composed a new and very original work entitled *Erotica Biblion* treating the most roguish themes in a grotesque but none the less serious fashion. He asks her whether she can believe that in the Bible and classical times investigations were instituted concerning onanism, tribadism, and on all indelicate matter treated by the casuists. These matters were treated in the Bible in such a way that they were readable by even the most squeamish, and incidentally they were interlarded with philosophical ideas. Here Mirabeau treats all manner of passion and perversity in a fairly unexceptionable style and shows that among the ancient peoples, particularly the Jews, there existed the same degree of sexual excitability as in his time. The work is cleverly erotic but by no means pornographic. In many respects it is one of the strangest books ever written. Here are some of his chapter headings—with their paraphrased meanings:

ISCHA, *or the creation of man and his superiority to woman.*
TROPOIDE, *or about incest.*
THALABE, *or concerning masturbation.*
ANANDRINE, *or concerning tribadism.*
AKRIPOIDIE, *or concerning circumcision.*
KADESCH, *or concerning unnatural unchastity.*
BEHEMAO, *or concerning unchastity with animals.*
LEGUANMANIE, *or views about orgasm and divers notes anent prostitution.*

The whole edition of this work was confiscated immediately so that only fourteen copies of it are extant today. It was naturally placed on the Index, too, under the title of *Amatoria Bibliorum*. Subsequent editions met the same fate but the book has reproduced itself.

If Mirabeau's authorship of these books is fairly certain, this is not the case with *Hic a Hec*, dealing with the adventures of a young pupil of the Avignon Jesuits who becomes a tutor in a wealthy home after the dissolution of the order. The characters are recruited from the clergy and nobility; and the action leaves nothing to be desired in the way of caprice and lasciviousness.

Another work of uncertain authorship that has been attributed to Mirabeau without justification is *The Raised Curtain*, probably a work of the Marquis de Sentilly. It purports to be an apology for incest but the task is not carried out, perhaps because of a sudden

BOOK III: THE EIGHTEENTH CENTURY

access of scruple; and the story as we have it today has been worked over by another pen. Little Laura whose education is completely in the hands of her father, gets a new governess who spends an unaccountably long time in her father's room. To allay her curiosity Laura ties a thread to the curtain in this room and leads it through the keyhole into her own room next door. One day she pulls this thread gently and as the curtain rises, discovers her father in a tight situation with her governess. But her deed has been noticed and she must be witness to the performance. Later she receives the information that no natural bond ties her to her *father*. Since she is too young for the tussle of love and since her *father* is aware of her fiery temperament, he has her fitted with a chastity belt which she must wear until she becomes ripe. When little Laura reaches puberty, it is removed and there follow orgies with the *father*, youths, etc., which are broadly depicted with philosophic discussions and justifications.

A number of other works are attributed to Mirabeau, some justly but others wrongly. His works found wide recognition even outside of France, and were greedily read by women, too. Pauline Wiesel, the lover of Prince Louis Ferdinand, was greatly enthusiastic about them as we know from a letter of von Benz which characterizes Mirabeau's writing as cold libertinism and urges her friend to read cognate productions of Voltaire, Crébillon and Grécourt if she would know the best that has been achieved in this field.

NERCIAT

ANDRE Robert Andréa de Nerciat was born in 1739, led a fairly adventurous life and died in 1800. He began to travel very early in order to perfect himself in languages, then entered the service of the king of Denmark and finally returned to France where he rose to chief lieutenant. After being pensioned he journeyed through Belgium and became assistant librarian to the Landgrave of Hessen-Cassel, but after the newspapers accused him of disorganizing the public library he resigned, and became director of construction to the Duke of Hessen-Rothenburg, and finally returned to France. During the revolution he emigrated and served the Duke of Braunschweig. In 1798 he was sent to the pope on a special mission by the queen of Naples but was captured by French troops and jailed. Shortly after his release, he died.

As a writer Nerciat is distinguished by his spirit and style. His dialogues are brilliant and evince strong dramatic skill. Even in erotic scenes he knows how to introduce relief. He never offends with coarse speech but even in the freest scenes he knows how to divert attention from carnal reality by the aid of proper sentiment. But despite all these virtues, his writings leave the reader untouched for they lack the chief desideratum—emotion. He belongs to that type of rococo individual to whom Choderlos de Laclos erected such a lasting monument in his immortal story.

Nerciat's chief work is *Felicia*. The person of Felicia is no creation of the author's fancy but a real individual, a friend of his, and we meet her again in *Montrose* and *Aphrodite*. The heroine opens her eyes upon the world on a pirate ship. She is adopted by an Italian who gives her an excellent education. Her libido is aroused when she is still very young and at fourteen a little dancing instructor turns her head. At nineteen she falls in love with the Chevalier d'Aiglemont. Then a prelate is added to the series. Her lust for adventure draws her to Paris. On the way she is attacked by robbers but freed by a young, knightly hero, Montrose. Her love adventures with him fill the first half of the second volume. Despite their great love for each other neither hesitates to stray off into other pastures. Felicia falls in with a rich Briton who is a slave to a peculiar whim.

BOOK III: THE EIGHTEENTH CENTURY

He invites young couples and pretty girls to his castle and eavesdrops upon them quite invisibly, for the castle has double walls. There are numerous episodes and many characters appear. All the love scenes give way to a mass wedding. Sidney marries Zeila whom he had once lost. Aiglemont takes a little flapper home with him and only Montrose escapes the matrimonial chains. He finds his family, joins the army and is promoted to the rank of captain.

A subsequent novel, *Montrose*, carries on this story, although there isn't really an integral plot. Many new characters are introduced and all have but one function besides the inevitable sexual debauchery; they are all actuated by the caprice of play-acting. Nerciat boasts that his characters are not the usual simple creations, utterly clear, calculable and of one cloth, but are rare mixtures of virtues and infirmities. They make swift and constant transitions from sorrow to joy, from lust to regret, from wrath to tenderness. They are half chastity and half corruption, of the sort that it is a unique achievement to escape in the metropolis, especially if one has the inclination and the means of gratifying it. In this tale Felicia has already been advanced to the presidency of the *profligate love society*. An added point of interest in this book is that the hermaphrodite, Nicelte, probably served as the model for Zambinella, in Balzac's short story *Sarrazine*.

In *My Novitiate*, the author describes the experiences of a daughter of joy in his own peculiar compound of clever sophistry and licentiousness. Better known is the book with the amazing title *The Devil in Him*. This story, like all of Nerciat's work, is strongly interwoven with dialogues and contains some pretty broad expressions. A pair of dissolute women who engage in monstrous practices: the Marquise and her friend, Countess Motte-en-feu; a German prelate whose life work consists in purveying most unequivocal knightly services to pretty women; the lovely Mme.

Couplet, the most refined brothel mistress in all Paris. The worthy abbot and his monks all of whom must bring sacrifices to the love altar of the little Countess; Nicola, the earnest and jealous; and Phillipine, the soft and amorous servant of the Marquise—both of whom emulate the example of their mistress; the always faithful Hector, alias Bel-amour; and the boy Felix who has long since ceased being a boy. There is also the amusing phenomenon of the Capuchin who fears nothing and is able to cure the Marquise afflicted with a fever; the negro Zamer; and finally, the ass. This concludes the enumeration of the characters who go through their merry pranks in this book.

This novel portrays the moral coloring of the French society that he saw and there are very few invented or imagined elements in this work. The same is true of the next book to be considered, which is not quite as accurate, but nevertheless based upon contemporary facts. It is *Les Aphrodites*. The *Aphrodites*, also known as *Morosophs*, were a society of men and women current in the reign of Phillip of Orleans. At first they met in Paris on the slope of the valley of Montmorency under the chairmanship of a certain Marquis de Person. The purpose of the society was simply the gratification of sensual lusts. These actual circumstances formed the skeleton of Nerciat's novel. He added some fictitious material to the plot and embroidered everything with fragments of his own eclectic sophistries.

A summary of *Les Aphrodites* follows:

The chevalier dismounts from his horse and enters a villa before the gates of Paris. Two servitors, one dumb and the other deaf, lead him to the landlady of this house of joy. Mme. Durut receives the guest joyfully; for it was she who had inducted him into the mysteries of love four years ago, and since that time she has not seen him. Durut lets him examine and adore every one of her charms, for

BOOK III: THE EIGHTEENTH CENTURY

despite her thirty-six years she still knows how to captivate men. Then she brings him to a boudoir where a negress washes him and a maid soothes him with chocolate. In the meantime the proud and high-spirited Duchess de Enginieres enters to keep a rendezvous with a certain count. She is disgruntled at being kept waiting and orders a bath prepared in the meantime, to be accompanied by appropriate reading. Mme. Durut brings her Mirabeau's *My Conversion* and *Le Fils d'Hercule*; the first is rejected by the noblewoman because its author, himself a nobleman, had taken active part in the revolution. Durut now weaves a new intrigue. She arouses interest of the duchess in the chevalier whom she speaks of as her nephew and calls him in on the pretext that the duchess is a famous actress who can help him get a place in her company. Durut presently leaves the two alone and the chevalier acts the chambermaid when the duchess leaves her bath. She now suggests that the young man who has pleased her shall enter the bath; the chevalier plays the part of a real lover despite her struggles, which arouses her fury since she regards the love of any but a nobleman as an abomination. In the meantime, the expected count, the real lover of the duchess, arrives but Durut receives him and knows how to detain him from disturbing the pastime of the duchess. She sends him Celestine, her supposed step-sister, who arouses the count to a double sacrifice. During this love episode Durut hurries to the duchess and the chevalier and informs the lady that he is really a nobleman. Whereupon the latter is relieved and overjoyed. Meanwhile the count, who has tired of waiting, comes in and is witness to his defeat. A duel appears unavoidable, but the cunning Durut knows how to mollify the rivals. At a sumptuous repast to which Celestine is also invited, the roles are exchanged. The duchess chooses the count and the chevalier, Celestine, so that general satisfaction is achieved. After the guests have gone, Durut remains alone with Celestine and they go over their account to discover that this month has brought them a surplus of 1200 livres. The outstanding debts are discussed and the perverse erotic practices of certain members come in for full discussion.

The next visitor is the Marquise Fieremotte who is looking for a travelling companion. Durut has suggested M. de Limecœur and while they are waiting for him, the marquise spends her time with Bel-amour in reading the eroticon *Matinée Libertine*. Limecœur arrives punctually, but the post doesn't suit him and he declines the offer. The disappointed panderess notifies the marquise of his decision; she desires to speak with him herself, only they must both be masked. Limecœur is given a comfortable sleeping outfit and is led to the marquise. Her voice captivates him at once and he ravishes her. However, to punish him for his initial reluctance the marquise slips away with the help of Durut. They inform him that she has already journeyed to Paris in her chariot and that she is ugly as night but he will not renounce his passion.

The next chapter introduces us to M. de Trottignac who, because he is such a swaggerer, has been hurled into a cage. A physician examines him to see whether he is infected. Then Celestine tests his virility by hanging a 150-lb. weight upon his tumescent organ, which the athlete easily carries for three minutes. At the recommendation of another member he is accepted. Next morning madame looks up the marquise and discovers that she has come to an agreement with Limecœur. Now Durut plays the panderess and instead of Bel-amour she sends her the Chevalier Alfons whom we've met above, disguised as a servitor. The latter succeeds in achieving his goal which is eternally one. In the meantime Limecœur has gone off to Paris.

The early scenes of the second volume are enacted at a country house near Paris. Mme. de Montchaud confesses to her cousin,

BOOK III: THE EIGHTEENTH CENTURY

on actually experienced incidents, the example of a corrupt society always before the eye, a society whose members sought to surpass each other only in profligacy, who clamored for the sweet poison of pornography in all the relationships of life and hailed every one that could purvey a new variation of pleasure, one cannot be surprised that the revolution came and indeed had to come... The corrupting influence of an imagination operating with the most unthinkable cruelties had to make itself felt finally. This condition spread from so-called society down to the people and after cruelty had been praised as the stimulant of passion and practiced to a small degree, then the blood-shedding of the reign of terror was only a magnification of the same doctrine by the larger group that had become infected by it. If the former had had to see suffering and blood in order to be merry, then Robespierre and his associates found no less joy and passion when the heads clattered down by the dozens from the sharp knife of the guillotine.

De Sade fitted into such an age and was its typical representative. You may recall Flaubert's forceful judgment about him, that he was the last word of the medieval and Renaissance Church for in him spake the spirit of the inquisition, of punishment by torture, of aversion to nature. In 1791 there appeared his *Justine* which in the first edition is only obscene and does not contain the blood-drenched incidents of subsequent editions. The year 1797 saw the edition of *Justine* and *Juliette*—with 104 horrible illustrations both as regards subject and execution. De Sade was well aware of his destructive contribution and in his foreword he remarks that virtue might well forget to wipe her tears in pride that France should possess such a significant work, one that combines the most cynical language with the strongest and most daring system of immoral and blasphemous ideas. The tendency of his infamous book is meager enough. In *Justine* virtue, represented by Justine is very unfortunate, falls into evil and crime. The good fortune of vice is portrayed in horrible pictures. The basic thought is that either there is no God or else He is not concerned with the welfare of man, else virtue would not suffer so much here on earth, nor would vice have such triumphs. He adds iniquitously: "Will not men say that when virtue is followed by misfortune and vice by prosperity that it is better to go with the scoundrels who are favored by nature than with the virtuous who meet with ruin? In order to bolster up this point of view —there is no point in concealing it—we wish to give to the world the story of Justine. Maybe this will induce those fools to quit praying to that ridiculous idol of virtue which will only reward them with ingratitude; and will strengthen in the opposite belief those sensible folk who always see the amazing examples of happiness and fortune which crime and debauchery almost invariably bring in their wake." And how much monstrous evil there is in this grimace. "It is undoubtedly painful to have to recount the dreadful misfortunes that pour upon the gentle and sensitive woman who hearkens entirely to the voice of virtue; and on the other hand to demonstrate that those who persecute this very woman and drive her to death, enjoy great happiness. But the author who is enough of a philosopher to be able to tell the truth stands above these unpleasantnesses. Coerced by necessity, to cruelty, he tears down with merciless hands the superstitious veils with which stupidity seeks to beautify virtue, and shows to the ignorant man, who has been gulled until now, vice with all the charms and joys that follow from it uninterruptedly. For these reasons we shall describe crime in the most cynical language and with the most immoral and godless ideas, crime as it is, triumphant, always satisfied and always happy; whereas virtue shall be seen as eternally unhappy, and persecuted."

In the same style as Sade's larger work is his *Philosophy in the Boudoir*. It is not unlikely that Mirabeau's *Education of Laura* gave

BOOK III: THE EIGHTEENTH CENTURY

Sade the impetus and perhaps the idea to compose this work. The education of a young girl to vice is represented in the form of dialogues and long quasi-academic speeches, only punctuated every so often by the practical demonstration and application of the theoretic principle so discussed. A few words about the contents may not be irrelevant. In the first conversation there appears Mme. de St. Ange and her brother, Chevalier de Mirvel. The lady is a Juliette type who poisons everything she touches and her brother is far inferior to her. The scene is dominated by Dolmance, a thoroughbred in vice, cynic, pederast and atheist. Eugénie de Mistval, a young girl, is being expected. Mme. St. Ange had corrupted her so far theoretically that only a bit of practice is necessary for her to be a real prostitute. In the course of a single afternoon she is duly initiated into all the mysteries of sex life. Later others are added to the corps of instructors in the applied art, the Chevalier, a gardener boy, and the idiot Augustin, so that Eugénie learns the arrangement of obscene groups. Towards evening, when Eugénie has already become a ferocious erotic monster, her mother comes in. In the sight of her exulting daughter she is monstrously raped, infected with syphilis by the slave Lapierre, and before they go to the table, Eugénie must carry out the operation of infibulation upon her mother.

Another of his books, *Aline and Valcour* reminds one very strongly of the *Justine*. Valcour, a virtuous young man loves Aline, the lovely daughter of the gentle wife of the cruel President de Blamont. The latter desires his daughter to marry the old debauché Dalbourg, to which old man he had already given the virtuous Sophie whom he regarded as his own daughter, for a mistress. He yearns to have his plan succeed for a vile reason. After the marriage he intends to give his own wife, Mme. de Blamont, to Dalbourg for a lover, and in return he wants to get the latter's wife, namely his own daughter Aline, as his lover. The plan fails. Aline kills herself and her mother is poisoned at the command of her husband. Valcour enters a monastery. Dalbourg becomes virtuous and the President must flee. In *Rosa and Leonore* there are represented two foul hussies. The latter especially is always in luck and is a sort of pendant to Juliette.

Sade also wrote a pamphlet against Napoleon which earned for him the enmity of the mighty Corsican. It is *Zoloe and her Acolytes* and deals with the debaucheries of Napoleon and his circle. Zoloe represents Josephine and the two acolytes, Lameda and Volsange, symbolize Mesdames Tallien and Visconti. In very sluttish style, Sade relates the orgies of these three women with three male partners. So far as obscenity goes, Sade does not surpass any of his contemporaries. It was not immorality, but the satirical sallies against Napoleon and his circle that aroused the ire of the ruler. When the story appeared in 1800, a tremendous scandal ensued. Practically all the characters were easily recognizable. Thus d'Orsac, *anagram* for de Corse, was Napoleon. Sabar stood for Barras, etc. In 1801, while Sade was visiting his publisher and discussing the rewritten *Juliette* which he had brought with him, he was arrested. He was kept prisoner in the Hospital of Charenton where he died on December 2, 1814 at the age of 75. It is very interesting to note that Sade sent a de luxe copy of *Justine* to the consul and his two foremost assistants in the state, and that Napoleon had no other punishment for this immense boldness than to consign the work to the fire.

About thirty years ago, Dr. Iwan Bloch, the world's foremost authority on Sade, found another work of Sade's which had been preserved in MS. only: *The 120 days of Sodom*. This MS. has a rich history. Although it was well known that Sade had written such a work, it was held to be lost because in 1832 the MS. of an unedited

BOOK III: THE EIGHTEENTH CENTURY

work of Sade's was burnt in the presence of the latter's son, and this was presumed to be *Les 120 Journées de Sodome*. However, it must have been another, for Bloch was able to find this MS. Sade wrote it while he was in the Bastille, in 36 days between October 22 to November 27, 1785. He worked at it three hours daily between 7 and 10 in the evening and wrote in loose papers which he pasted end to end until he had a roll 12 meters long. Inasmuch as he lacked paper, he wrote on the reverse side of the roll as well. Thus the MS. in its final form is a roll of strips written on both sides. When the Marquis left the Bastille in 1789 this MS., together with other of his works, remained there. It finally came into the possession of the family Villeneuve-Trans where it stayed for three generations until Bloch found it. But no customer was found for it. A young German novelist succeeded in deciphering the almost microscopic writing, now almost illegible through age. The book seems undoubtedly to be the one referred to by Restif de la Bretonne, and the internal evidence is almost irrefutable. The peculiarities of his sentence structure, tropes of speech, and narrative manner are perfectly in evidence here. And above all there is the peculiar defense of the most profligate passion so idiopathic of Sade, which comes to clearer expression here than in any other work. The plan of this book has come down to us and although only a part of it lies completed in the *120 Days*, we can see that this book was conceived on a far larger scale than even the comprehensive *Justine*. All conceivable perversions were to be illustrated through 600 examples. The plan of the story is the following. Four wealthy rakes, too blasé to find any joy in the ordinary pleasures of life, join forces in a most unusual and passionate undertaking. They have panders and panderesses journey all through France to abduct the handsomest boys and prettiest girls from the richest and most distinguished families. From this collection the most attractive are chosen and with other objects of lust are brought to an inaccessible mountain castle belonging to one of the voluptuaries. In this castle they immure themselves with their victims. All entrances are walled up and the only bridge that connects the castle with the outside world is broken down. And now, secure from any surprise or interruption in this marvellously constructed castle, appointed with every luxury and every thinkable necessity, they are ready for the beginning of the most extraordinary orgies. Four of the most experienced brothel mistresses of Paris have the duty of relating in assigned order and in full detail, the experiences of their life. In the course of a month each woman will have told 150 stories of the most interesting cases of sexual perversions in her experience. In all, then, there were to be 600 different tales of sexual profligacy, systematically ordered, and proceeding in the direction of ever greater and rarer perversions. In this way the whole great realm of Psychopathia sexualis is unrolled before us, clearly and thoroughly. During these narratives the human objects, of the debauchées' lust of both sexes and every age, are kept on hand so that whatever sex urge is roused in them by any of the stories, may immediately be gratified.

RESTIF DE LA BRETONNE

SADE's antipode and yet like him in many ways, except in the cruelty typical of Sade, is Restif de la Bretonne, whose printed works number two hundred and twelve volumes. He is as much of a graphomaniac as Sade. He writes about his life, his experiences from day to day without inventing much. He doesn't see anything objectionable in using his own correspondence and does not even halt at giving the names of people. He desires to portray the truth: "*Je dois et je ne dois rien dire que la vérité, fut-elle impertinente.*" And impertinent it certainly was on innumerable occasions, for Restif was also an erotomaniac. Women had to give content to his life and without them life was empty. Hence his whole existence revolved about them, the bringers of joy and the sources of happiness; in short, his life was fixed by the sexual. Eulenberg's judgment about him was that he was goaded by the wildest sensuality and driven by the idolatrous worship of his own self to a sort of exhibitionism. For that reason he was able as no other to analyze the origin and distinctiveness and demoniac force of sexual love and to devote to his ego a most refined cultivation.

Thus he relates the story of his life in sixteen volumes, entitled *Monsieur Nicolas*, which is nothing more than the narrative of his erotic achievements. In the thirteenth volume he keeps a diary of all the women whose acquaintance he had made, had seduced and impregnated. Very likely anecdotes and experiences of others are woven into it, for Count Tilly once mentioned that Restif, who had never met him, had once requested the story of certain of the count's amorous exploits, which the latter very decidedly refused to impart. Despite the not infrequent obscenities and the free scenes, a very definite value attaches to the work. Schiller held it in high regard, and in 1789 wrote to Goethe to inquire whether the latter had ever read the unusual work of Restif.

> "I have already read it and despite much that is flat, distasteful or even revolting, have nevertheless greatly enjoyed it. For I have never come across a nature so sensual; and one must also be interested in the multitude of characters, particularly female, the vitality and contemporaneity of the writing, and the depiction of the moral life of certain classes of the French people. For one who has so little opportunity to draw from outside sources and to study men in real life, such a book has incalculable value."

Another work of Restif is also well known, *The Contemporaries*, in seventeen volumes. These are a series of tales based on experiences and pictures of moral conditions. According to the established formula, Restif wishes to employ Catullus' phrase upon himself: *Lasciva nobis pagina, vita proba.* In the preface he says: "If science is deserving of respect, the same can certainly not be asserted of false modesty. *The Contemporaries* is a piece of moral medicine. Should the details appear ribald, it is in its essentials deserving of respect and is destined for a career of great moral usefulness. For what is a novelist? The painter of moral conditions. Now morals are corrupt. Shall I then depict the morals of an ideal creature? You respectable ladies, hold your nose against this thoroughly hypocritical public morality, those infamous double entendres, those free gestures, those shameless expressions that men permit themselves to say in your presences and before your daughters as well. But do not account it a crime if a courageous writer who, serving a moral purpose, dares to hold a mirror to vice in order to bring you knowledge, uses perforce revolting matters, in order ultimately to improve them." But, despite these emphatic words, we feel in every line what utter joy he finds in tarrying over the most intimate things, and what expansiveness must be his as he indulges himself in the broadest drawing of the most immoral incidents and situations. The end is supposed to sanctify the means, but the end is no whit better than the means employed.

In succeeding works, *The Ruined Swain* and *The Ruined Lass*, he intendes to demonstrate that even the most exalted goodness must necessarily go to the dogs when touched by vice. Here is the most bizarre collection of adventures and characters possible; and in addition the *milieu* is constantly changing. Restif leads us to public houses, churches, free spirits, salons of worldly ladies, boudoirs of prostitutes and, with most delight, to the brothel. The book is written in the form of letters and consists of scenes but loosely joined together. The characters are well drawn and we feel that he has modelled them from life. These books he considered his best, written not only for his own time but for subsequent generations as well. But it was just these two novels that got him into difficulties with the police and especially with the censor, who delayed their publication for two years. It required continued efforts and the enormous persistency of Restif, to free his book. He himself tells of seventy-two fruitless visits to the police. The animosity against these novels appears strange in view of the fact that so many other scandals of far worse and reprehensible quality were passed without a murmur.

The next book to be mentioned took Restif 20 years to write. *The Nights of Paris* occupied every morning of these years. Herein, were inscribed that which he had seen and lived through the night before. Hence these eight volumes constitute an excellent account of the moral situation of the time.

In the *Ingénue Saxancous*, he worked in the style of Sade. The book is supposed to tell the story of his daughter who had made a very unhappy marriage. After the wedding she has to give herself to the most profligate whims of her husband, a rake of the worst order, and suffers the most incredible cruelties. Naturally the material is such that there is no lack of obscenity, cynicism or cruelty; but none the less Dumas borrowed very much from this story for his own *Ingénue*.

If Restif follows Sade here, he took up arms against him in another work where he scored Sade's horrible imagination. This erotic polemical tract was entitled *Anti-Justine*. This work was mapped out on a very large scale but of eight sections planned, only one and a fraction were completed. It is said that Restif finished six copies in his own underground press, of which number the secret division of the Paris National Library has about a half. La Bedoyère was the first to possess an original. Another was in the possession of Cigognes who sold it to the Duke of Aumale, whence it went to Frederick Hankey for 2000 francs. All the books of the latter later came into the possession of Pisanus Fraxi, who left his library to the British Museum, where there is probably a copy of the original. As in all his works, Restif represents himself in such a stupid fashion that the reader is at once repelled. There is no development of character, no serious thought, only a piling up of erotic situations, pure pornology, only so improbable and so horribly tiresome! The very titles are so vile that we forbear to mention them. Suffice it to say that incestuous relations between father and daughter as well as between mother and son occupy a large place here.

The obscenities with which the *Anti-Justine* is swollen were supposed to have been written for a moral purpose! Restif remarks in the preface to this book: "No one has been more irritated than I by the dirty works of the hideous Marquis de Sade—that is, the *Justine, Boudoir,* and *Theory of Passion*—which I read while in prison. This devil has represented the delights of love forever accompanied by torture and murder. My purpose is to write a book that will be juicier than the others, one that women can confidently put into the hands of their husbands in order the better to be served by them; a book in which the heart will have its place by the side of the senses, in which passion knows no cruelty; in which love conceived naturally without any affection or hesitation conjures up only gay and joyous pictures. When one has read it one will worship woman, and after one has enjoyed her, one will deify her. It is to be hoped that when that manslaughterer, Sade, will be dragged from jail on July 14, 1789 a whitebearded old man, he will be detested according to his deserts. May my charming work which I am herewith publishing annihilate his own; it is a bad book, perhaps, but written with a good purpose. Thus, I have only introduced

BOOK III: THE EIGHTEENTH CENTURY

incest in order to supplant those cruelties with which Sade galvanizes the senses of the enervated roués."

Restif followed this intention and purveyed the coarsest and foulest depictions of passion possible. He was not by any means content with following the established custom of the time of the erotic writer, who has the tyro inaugurate his sex life by witnessing an erotic scene between his parents, or a pair of lovers. Oh, no, that will never do. He starts right off with perversities. First, his eight sisters are the objects of his youthful lust; then, he accidentally cohabits with his mother; and finally, the father seduces his own daughter; but "seducing" is hardly the word, for they give themselves gladly and are as profligate as the narrator. In addition to his love for beautiful feet and shoes, Restif seems to have had a special predilection for *cunnilingus*, for this form of sex satisfaction comes in for much attention. What is worse, he even has a scene after the fashion of the degenerated Sade. A rascal by the name of Vit-Négre sells his wife to a monk for 60,000 francs. The latter rapes her in such a brutal and bestial fashion that she dies of the consequences. Whereupon the latter draws and quarters his victim and finally consumes the pieces. Such horrible productions flowed from human minds! What a price to pay for the gift of language and thought!

✠
CHAPTER XIII
PORNOGRAPHIA RAMPANT

To what purpose these writings served is obvious at first sight. It is true that in a certain number the erotic elements were subordinate to satire, panurgics or libel—be it political, anti-clerical or personal. Some few others had undeniably artistic aims and actually achieved their ends. But by far the greatest portion of these works were written only to inflame erotic desires and amatory hunger or to enrich sex lust. And since the French of the rococo period were artists in pleasure, its ladies and gentlemen of the pen knew how to sound the proper chords perfectly calculated to achieve the desired effects. They are entirely free from Germanic heaviness. There is a good deal of chat and play and laughter, and love; but the latter is graceful and seductive, yet entirely without passion and having no connection with the inner spirit and the deeper emotion. One must be truthful to give the effect of truth, but this truth is born of the time. These erotica which permitted their purpose, viz., to seduce, to be clearly discerned, fluttered out into the world in little insignificant volumes, and were bought, read and discussed avidly.

By the side of these stood the hypocrites who assumed a mask in order to remain unknown and the better to engage in their nefarious business. Is vice abominable? Certainly! Must one then be frightened away from it? Undoubtedly! But how can this occur without a thoroughly faithful reproduction of it? The more one unveils it,

BOOK III: THE EIGHTEENTH CENTURY

the greater will be the revulsion from vice. Virtue has real value only when it is based upon experience. Aside from this, all laws set penalties for crime. But how can one avoid that which one does not know thoroughly? Thus we have a second cogent reason for representing it in the most terrifying aspect and maximum clarity. But it is just the sins of a sex nature which are of greatly diverse character; hence they require diverse treatment. It is admitted, oddly enough, that the unchaste are stimulated by such reading to greater lust; but for them nothing is holy. The good, on the other hand, are strengthened in their virtue. *Quod erat demonstrandum.*

It is striking how many works are directed against the clergy, monks and nuns. The reason is that the immoral conduct of the clergy, induced by their enforced "celibacy", had assumed the proportions of a national plague, so that nunneries were virtually disguised brothels. In these practises the nuns followed the comforting dictum that much would be forgiven to whoever had loved much, and successfully forgot their vows. But the erotic writer doubted this intrepretation of their conduct, and has a different view of these matters altogether. To start with poverty, says he, can a girl documentate her lack of all needs better than when she removes everything till her skin? Can she show a more ravishing chastity in any words or deeds comparable to that of her gleaming natural nakedness? Can a nun show greater token of her obedience than when at the command of her priestly adviser she hikes her dress up to her navel, offers up her virginity or submits to flagellation? This interpretation has at least the virtue of originality.

But one gets a very unpleasant impression when the preacher of morals, still wearing the mantle of morality, begins to revel in foul obscenities. Here an ethically degenerate Capuchin is lashing the vice of his time but he uses such expressions and images to leave no doubt that he is not at all in earnest about his preaching.

Then too there was no dearth of manuals for worldings which contain much that is of interest to cultural history. They afford us an insight into the life of Parisian prostitutes, the affairs of the profligates of both sexes, and the chronicles of scandal. And because debauchery is the rule, and virginity is to be found only in the cradle, another philanthropic author renders counsel how lovers can obtain even this rare delight, and how they are to guard themselves against second-hand goods being fubbed off on them as virgins. But it isn't only the males that are looked after and provided with advice. The females are taught ways and means, whose application is gone over in practice, how to palm off upon their unsuspecting bridegrooms, their abused and marred virginal honor as intact.

It is obvious that the entire imaginations of these readers were utterly obsessed with eroticism. But the life of the normal person contains many other aims than sexual pleasure. Hence only those people were chosen as chief bearers of the erotic action who devoted their whole life to "love", that is, brothel mistresses and celebrated whores. And it is remarkable how much these dames from the half- or quarter-world can accumulate in the way of experience as related in many novels or memoirs written by them. Their whole deportment is based upon the experience accumulated on the capture of men, on a knowledge of the male psyche. And in the "pleasure" itself they must accommodate themselves to the wish of any of their fares, and submit to any of his lusts, however perverse or disgusting. Their business calls for it.

Now if the prostitute lives through so much, especially in her love life, how much more is this true of the panderess. For no matter how energetic the strumpet is in her trade, she can after all know the taste of men only, and even then, of but a small group, for generally her clientel will be recruited from but one class

BOOK III: THE EIGHTEENTH CENTURY

of society. Hence her experience is always one-sided. But the panderess is differently situated since her vocation brings her into connection with all classes of the populace. Her clientel comprises women as well as men, and she knows how to appease the desire for sex partners of the opposite or the same sex. She purveys stout and vigorous navvies and farmhands of overflowing strength with the same ease that she supplies full-bloomed beauties and young girls barely in their teens. She procures for the lascivious rake the prostitute versed in all the arts of whoredom, and knows how to hunt up the virginity of a scarcely developed adolescent. She aids the powerfully natural instincts of the farmhand to find satisfaction and accommodates herself to the desires of a taste refined by "culture". She comes into contact with the dregs of the people and at the same time counts among her customers the notables of the kingdom and the ladies in waiting to the queen. In short, she can certainly claim for herself that nothing human is alien to her. Hence, such a worldly person who seems to know everybody and everything can certainly reveal a great deal when she has begun to display the riches of her experience. That is why we find so many of these Memoirs, Confessions, Diaries, etc. of panderesses, in the erotic literature of this time. The calling of such a brokeress was not so despised and marked with the badge of shame as it is today. After all, Pompadour belonged to this profession, and Madame La Comtesse certainly had no negligible influence. Their activities were conducted publicly and were fairly well-known. One could really expect something from such confessions, and one was usually not disappointed. It scarcely needs to be mentioned that many of these memoirs were invented and that they were attributed to notorious loose women, opera girls and brothel mistresses, in order to make possible greater sales. These works had a perfectly tremendous success; and many a poor wretch who still had some shame left excused his conduct by pointing to the public's taste which he was compelled to gratify or else starve.

In another set of works, the results of a careless pleasure were set forth in the form of a confession. To the gallant diseases, such works as *Foutromanie* and *Cacamonade* erected a very questionable monument. Thus in *The Mortifications of Pleasure*, the author unfolds his tale of woe. He had fallen in love with a married woman, given her presents and finally had won her favor but got a present from her that he hadn't anticipated. He has to undergo a long treatment, and while waiting for the cure, he makes the acquaintance of Auguste, an opera girl. She tells him her life story, and he lets himself be carried away; whereupon luck being against him, he becomes infected a second time. They both look forward to their cure; but he forever forswears love and women, whom he now despises.

After all, that is the natural result of every pleasure driven to the extent and enjoyed to the utmost, the insidious payment that lurks behind every intoxication. Before fulfillment, no price is too high to pay for the object of pleasure whose possession is considered of indispensable value. Afterwards, he (or she) who has been diseased by passion cannot find invective strong enough. Such works as Sade's can only arouse regret, surfeit and disgust.

As far as the technique of the average erotic work is concerned there is a regularly recurrent scheme. Very typical is the increasing tempo with which these erotic scenes are portrayed. Starting from the gentle awakening of sensuality we are introduced to all the stages that a libidinous fantasy can imagine. A motif that is very popular is that of the keyhole. The young girl in her puberty once observes through the keyhole the antics of her parents or a pair of lovers as they perform the act, and from that time on her sexual imaginings, subconscious until now, take on tangible form. A very

BOOK III: THE EIGHTEENTH CENTURY

common device is the gradual initiation of the inexperienced into the arcana of sex, whereby the rôle of teacher or enlightener is usually played by an older and experienced girl friend. For this purpose the naïve one must be made as naïve as possible in order that the friend versed in all the procedures of "love" may be able to display her wares to best advantage. Usually she is married and reports to her astounded listener all the lurid and gory details of her defloration with the preliminary scenes and the ensuing orgies of delight. The naïve one must ask questions if the narrative is not to become dull. Or a young man talks of his successes in the realm of Venus, tarrying at first in the realm of probability, and the first sortie into sex is graphically drawn. But after this peak has been passed, the narrator usually loses power and cannot invent anything new. His whole art now consists of multiplying erotic scenes, progressively more improbable and revolting. All too rarely do we find cases where the author limits himself to single erotic incidents which are drawn with refinement of invention and wit. Of course, such excellence is the privilege of only extraordinary writers, who were not too common in eighteenth-century France.

We have already seen that the rococo can be regarded as the classic age of erotic literature. This tremendous productivity which could appease every appetite must naturally have coexisted with a correspondingly great demand. If this had already reached an exorbitant figure, according to our present conceptions, it grew to enormous dimensions the nearer the Revolution came, and even after this world-shaking event. Thus, in 1796 Mercier reports that the only books displayed were the obscene ones, those whose titles and engravings outraged modesty and good taste alike. These porneia were sold everywhere, at restaurants, near bridges, at the gates of the theatres and on the boulevards. They were sold cheaply enough from 10 sous a piece and up. They outdid each other in lust, and undermined public morals without a vestige of scruple. The peddlers of these brochures were to a certain degree privileged dispensers of obscenities, for every title that wasn't filthy was very obtrusively kept out of their display. From these defiled sources, youth drank up the essential elements of all vice, without hindrance or difficulty. What one would read on the title-pages of these pamphlets was alas! too true: "this pamphlet is always to be found in the pockets of even those who condemn it." The horrible *Justine* of the Marquis de Sade with its equally impossible and vicious engravings lay open in all shop windows. For our present-day, none too prudish notions such protected vice is criminal. Mercier de Compiegne (1763-1800) private secretary, marine official and finally book-seller, published a host of pornographic and scatological works, and even wrote some of them himself. Even in the very Bastille there was a secret press which printed the most obscene books, with which the police did a thriving business.

The best erotic writers of this period found an intelligent and sympathetic publisher in Cazin, who combined the business of printing with publishing. Born at Rheims in 1724, he took up the lucrative trade of bookselling and the still more lucrative one of publishing erotic works. His relations with Mercier de St. Leger and Merard de Saint-Just made matters easier for him and brought him to the idea of issuing a handsome collection of erotica, in line with his own taste. These works have been rewarded by the respect of book-collectors so that the merit of a Cazin edition is recognized even today. Until 1792 his business flourished but then came the revolution which brought him ruin and death. He was killed by a cannon ball as he left a café.

Many examples have come down to us of striking and shocking productions of the erotic imagination. Carriage doors were decorated with pornographic drawings, and women surpassed men in this ribaldry. The latter, not to be outdone, sought to score in another way by decorating their clothes with obscene pictures, namely their *vestes de petits-soupers*. According to the prevalent mode, the jackets were worn buttoned up and the upper portion of the vests could not be seen. The rich debauchees used to have their vests embroidered with obscene figures and at certain moments they would unbutton their jackets and display their "art".

It goes without saying that by the side of the cheap stuff designed by the masses, there were bibliophilic tidbits, illustrated by contemporary artists, for the greater delectation of the elegant and rich. Pompadour possessed a library of such porneia, and in letters to her friends admits that she frequently experienced with pleasure the stimulating effect of such writings.

When Sade speaks of obscene books and libraries, this rests on the foundation of facts. There is the characteristic scene in *Juliette* where she and Clairmil are browsing about in the home of the Carmelite Claude and come upon his excellent pornographic library. Juliette remarks: "You can have no idea what obscene books and pictures we found there." Among the books were the *Porter of Chartreux*, more of a prankish than a passionate book; the conversations of *Luisa Sigea*, well planned but poorly carried out; Mirabeau's *Laura*, a poor scrawl with little passion and much murder; and *Thérèse philosophe*, about which Juliette is enthusiastic because here passion is combined in full harmony with atheism. A devastating glance is cast at the horrid little brochures which are found in every café and brothel. In another place, too, at Délibène's, Juliette finds a large collection of erotic works, some of which she is to read during mass, in order to alleviate the monotony of having to sit through such a horrible ceremony.

Two more important witnesses to the wide distribution of these works are Casanova and Gœthe, though numerous others report the fact. In his memoirs, the former relates the following: "When the hour came I went to the Temple of Love. While I was waiting for my goddess I amused myself by examining the books of the small library which the boudoir contained. There weren't many books, but well chosen and worthy of their place. Here were all the books against religion, and all that passionate pens had written about the joys of love, seductive books whose style sets the reader on fire and compels him to seek the living reality of that whose incendiary depiction he has just read. Many richly bound folio volumes contained lascivious copper plate engravings whose great merit consisted much more in the purity of their drawing than in the lewdness of their representations. The English engravings to the *Porter*, the pictures to *Aloysia*, and others, all were of rare beauty. Innumerable masterpieces covered the walls of the room, all masterworks of the same sort as the copper plates. I spent an hour in examining these things, which aroused such an excitement in me that I could scarcely await the arrival of my mistress who presently entered bedizened in men's clothes." From the account of our second chronicler Gœthe, we learn that raw warriors carried such stimulants about with them. In *Wahrheit und Dichtung*, he reports how he found erotic paintings in the room of the lieutenant Thorane. Seeing a black box behind the oven he drew it forth little suspecting what it might contain. To his great surprise he found a collection of paintings which very rarely come to one's eye, and which sent the blood tingling through his body with a great excitement and heat.

It is hardly worthy of notice that the brothels were richly furnished with such articles for the stimulation of the impotent. So, we are told the famous house of Mme. Gourdan had a small chamber called the *Infirmerie* in which the light fell from above. On the walls hung passionate paintings and engravings, in the corners stood obscene plastic figures and groups, and on the tables reposed obscene books. In the autobiography of Clairon (about 1750), whom the brothers Goncourt have called the most delicate *artiste* in love that the eighteenth century possessed, we are informed that to make herself more desirable she educated her spirit through educative and piquant reading. "Brantome and Aloysia delighted me with a thousand beauties. The attractive pictures found therein were a feast to the eye and mind and I could hardly await with impatience when I could transmute these pictures into reality". The library of the Maréchale de Luxembourg consisted of the *Thirty-six Postures of Aretino*, *Philosophical Theresa*, and *Luisa Sigea*. Short but significant is her comment apropos of a *livre polisson* of Count Besenval: "It can be read with one hand only".

Interestingly enough, it was women who supplied the greatest contingent of readers. In fact, their hypocrisy went so far that they bound obscene pictures and brochures into their prayer books so that by this means they could drive away boredom during mass and yet retain the reputation of piety. Here is what the Duke de Choiseul says in his memoirs: "The nobles of Hautefontaine and their guests would not have missed a Sunday mass for the world. Everyone went to church very proudly, but it was not considered remarkable to see a smile playing around the lips of a worshipper, here and there. Everyone had a book in his or her hand out of which they read greedily. According to the covers it is a prayerbook, but its contents are really a collection of indecent, scandalous tales. This is known to all, and all week these books remain in the chapel for the delectation of the servitors and watchmen."

In the *Voyage through the Boudoir of Pauline* (1800) in which La Libordiére depicts how the girls of his time lived, he praises his mistresses for lacking those obscene engravings which were being exhibited as openly as pious paintings had been in days gone by. His own chosen one, he relates with pride, had in her chamber no passionate pictures, no voluptuous paintings which are calculated to seduce. But so saying he continues the report with the statement that he had advised her to visit certain literary rooms where she would find the choicest collection of the best novels produced in France during the previous four years. No one hesitated to present such panurgics to women; indeed it was quite the thing. The books were produced in pocket editions, and every dress was made with a special pocket for this purpose.

Sade praised his own works as models of obscene reading matter and reports that in the execution chamber of the Archbishop of Grenoble an Abbé read the *Philosophy in the Boudoir*. In bookshops these books were displayed opened up so that their contents might be sampled by all; and they were everywhere to be had. They were listed in all catalogues and sold without any hindrance. A great capitalist supported the distribution both domestic and foreign with ample means, and reaped a pretty return from his investment. Sade even dared to send a de luxe edition of his *Justine* to the members of the Directory, and even when Napoleon became consul the distribution of these pornographics was not interfered with. But all this was suddenly changed in 1801. In the previous year Sade had been thoughtless enough to launch his *Zoloe* with its denigration of Napoleon and its anti-religious fulminations. These factors, and not its overweening immorality, were responsible for the ensuing persecution of Sade's work which soon extended to most other erotic works. At the command of Napoleon all compositions of this category in the possession of his soldiers or their prostitutes were confiscated and destroyed. Only two copies of every work were kept and secreted in the National Library at Paris, as reported by Penchet, erstwhile archivist of police under Napoleon. Parent-Duchatelet, author of the *Immorality of Women in Paris* got a glimpse of this collection and actually saw them on the

BOOK III: THE EIGHTEENTH CENTURY

ground floor. This collection is still extant today and it has been greatly augmented by many new acquisitions. It is very strongly guarded and one can gain access to it only by permission of the local police.

A collection of such works, almost comparable to the one just mentioned, is that contained in the Palais Bourbon at Paris. This library also dates from the time of the revolution and was the property of the famed law teacher and politician, Gaston Camus. In 1793 he was sent by the convent to disarm Dumouriez but was turned over by the latter to the Austrians who kept him prisoner for two years, until he was exchanged for the daughter of Louis XVI. When he returned to Paris, he succumbed to the book-collecting fever. At that time the gallant libraries of emigrated nobles were thrown upon the market for sale, in mass quantities, and Camus bought up everything pertaining to Jesuits, theology, and above all else, pornography. Later he presented his collection to the Palais Bourbon, where the Council of Five Hundred met, and where the Chamber of Deputies now has its seat. Today this library is patronized more than any other.

BOOK IV
THE NINETEENTH CENTURY

CHAPTER XIV
THE NAPOLEONIC REGIME

THE French Revolution with its reign of terror was able to clean up the French love of life for a little while especially since that portion of society which before the revolution had been most set on such pleasures, viz., the nobility, was now out of France; but even so, this restriction could last only awhile. The type of love which had reigned in the pre-revolutionary salon did not soon return, for at present the field was held by the plebeian coarse manners of the parvenu speculators and usurers who had battened on the misery of the people. What there remained of the old society did not dare to resume its old life out of fear of the new wielders of power, but by that much more did the mob and the bourgeoisie throw itself into the enjoyment of its new freedom. Never was there so much immorality as in the years following the revolution. Presently there came into being the society balls to which every man had access, for there were no differences of rank and position. To these came the grand ladies of the former society, rich profiteers, officers of the revolution, and many, many prostitutes; and each vied with the other in constrained merriment, in order to forget the worries of the time.

As a consequence of the colossal changes, the people lost all understanding of spiritual interests and set up the belly for its god. The place of spirituality now came to be occupied by the adoration of crude power. Post-revolutionary France made a cult of athleticism: boxing, wrestling, etc. The men of brawn who participated in these tournaments and matches feasted like Homer's heroes. To be a big eater was a grand thing and these fellows enacted the most incredible eating bouts. Thus there was one titan who once put away 100 dozen oysters for breakfast. It is understood that such gluttony was accompanied by equally tremendous guzzling. The other amusements of the time were on the same level. The crudest jokes were in order and there was no prank too coarse. At this time clowns and mysticateurs were very popular at parties. And after these had set the tone and enough wine had been consumed, there came the recitation of bawdy stories and the most revolting ditties.

What could one expect of this crowd which had grown rich overnight? Everything could be bought for money and even the members of the Directory were accessible to bribery. From their residence, the Palais Luxembourg, the pestilential vapors of their moral corruption rose up and poisoned their surroundings. Barras, the lazy passionate glutton, needed a great deal of money for his feasts and orgies. Hence he had to let himself be bought, as did the other directors. Women threw themselves upon Barras, greaseball that he was, and he didn't pass up any one of them, not Josephine Beauharnais, who was later to become empress, nor Madame Tallien who was open to anyone who could pay for her, nor the mulatto Hamelin, who would publicly expose her nakedness through its "moral" covering of muslin, nor Madame Récamier who knew modesty only above the waist, nor dozens of other citizenesses who gave themselves to this voluptuary without a struggle. If they could gain something by their surrender to this omnivorous roué they regarded their physical surrender as worthwhile. Napoleon realized that there must be certain ordered conditions of life if his rule were to be maintained. Hence he made the strongest

BOOK IV: THE NINETEENTH CENTURY

efforts to check this immorality but without much success. He did however succeed in increasing public safety and reducing brigandage. The salons reappeared and the rawness of the immorality of the years immediately preceding was mitigated. At these parties the émigrés would be in attendance and would reintroduce the vices of pre-revolutionary times. Yet Napoleon countenanced these parties and even encouraged and subsidized some of them for through them his spies were able to keep tabs on certain people. The chief of the secret service Fouché went to great expense to have numerous purveyors of information. Many unsuspected ladies of society stood in his pay and were expected to overhear the conversation of their guests and to ascertain their various reactions. Many a soirée ended with an arrest—a tribute to the faithful work of these spies. When Napoleon was in the field one of his faithful ones, Madame de Genlis, had the obligation of keeping him informed about opinions current in Paris, at an annual salary of 6,000 francs and free residence in the arsenal. Even the domestic servants of the Corsican were not seldom paid to keep him informed about what was going on at home.

All efforts were directed at keeping the revolutionary spirits in check in order to safeguard the hardly won imperial power. The best and easiest way to achieve this goal was to permit all sexual impulses to be satisfied. In this way those restive spirits who were dissatisfied with his regime were silenced. Indeed, he himself set a good example in this direction. He who in all his actions showed the despot did not belie this character in sexual matters. When he wanted a woman he made no pretense about charming deportment or winning conduct. He wasn't at all concerned about captivating the lady with the charms of his personality. An order to his valet or his privileged pander was held to be sufficient to supply the desired object. And if his fame was not sufficient to attract the lady, she was brought by force. His impulses are best illuminated by the concealed fact that he would sometimes in the midst of the most bloody battle dash into his tent and order a woman *toute de suite*.

His relatives were lashed by the same fierce impulses. One need only think of Jerome who didn't permit anything to stand in the way of his epicurean life; or of Lucien who, when his mistress no longer satisfied him, shared her with his friend. He finally got so enmeshed in the snares of the notorious whoremonger Mme. Jouberthon, that he made her his lawful spouse. As compared to Jerome, Lucien was an ideal personality, for this caricature of a human being regarded the court of Cassel as a harem, and many women dazzled by his royal status fell victim to him. His physicians were constantly engaged in restoring his expended vitality of which in truth he had none too much, and they believed that wine baths would be the best remedy for his malady. The wine thus used would, after the bath, be bottled up by the courtiers and secretly sold to the innkeepers of Cassel. One remembers his lovely and dissolute sister Pauline, of whom one of her erstwhile lovers, Frederick, wrote in his memoirs; *Forty Years out of the Life of a Dead One*, that at twelve she had already had lovers; and the malicious world had it, though without justice, that Napoleon himself had been one of them. Very well known are the adventures which under the name of Amélie she enjoyed with a young man with whom she had many rendezvous at 188, Rue du Bac. One day he went to the theatre and was struck dumb with amazement to see his Amélie bedecked with brilliants in the imperial box and learned that she was Princess Borghèse, Napoleon's sister. The next morning he was ordered to appear at the ministry of the Interior and a very lucrative post was assigned him some fifty leagues away from Paris; but he had to leave for his new situation within 48 hours. Everyone knows her amourettes with the actor Lafont

BOOK IV: THE NINETEENTH CENTURY

Forbin, the Prince Cononville, etc., whose horse (and rider) Napoleon during an inspection found too wild and hence sent hundreds of miles away from Paris. For the most part however the great number of Pauline's adventures as well as those of her sisters remained unknown to their royal brother for no one was eager to bring them to his notice. Even the chief of spies Fouché was unwilling to bring his master into bad humor.

Nor were the other members of the royal family any better. Not the step-daughter Hortense, the former mistress of her royal step-father who, when she was pregnant, attached her to his brother Ludwig; nor Joseph who was intimate with the most infamous courtesans, such as Mme. Regnault, a veritable nymphomaniac, probably one of the most immoral women of her time, whose husband calmly regarded his notorious wife's sexcapades and capitalized on them. Concerning the latter there are many piquant anecdotes. These conditions were very widespread. Even Talleyrand, Napoleon's most influential minister, who lived with a demi-mondaine of very low grade, (and had to marry her later at the direction of his master) once expressed his regret at the death of one of his trollop's intimates: "He was an honorable man and gave her good counsel which she certainly needed. Who knows into what hands she will fall next?"

The memory of the gallant pre-revolutionary times in which the designation of "whore" was regarded as a title of honor was still too green for giving too much honor to chastity; but the former remembrance was distant enough to give some rein to the puritanism demanded by the heroes of the revolution. Gluttony and epicureanism came to the fore again. The famous dinners of the Minister Cambaceres could have taught Lucullus plenty. His table was decorated by the rarest delicacies and this at a time when the endless wars of Napoleon had brought extreme poverty to the land.

THE EROTIC HISTORY OF FRANCE

In a government which depended exclusively upon the might of bayonets it is obvious that the army would occupy the first place in the life of the nation. The officers, the backbone of the army, were distinguished for nothing more than a good figure and smart uniform. They carried over into civilian life the rude manners which characterized them in the roughness of martial existence, and their excessive combativeness and cruelty were a great burden for the public. Play, women and gossip were the chief amusements of garrison life. When the warriors went off to the wars their womenfolk amused themselves very agreeably indeed, and to such an extent that many disliked the approach of peace, with the consequent return of the husband and the end of their delightful days.

The marshals and the generals set the worst possible example to their subordinates in cruelty, dishonesty and lust. Wherever these fellows pitched their tent they indulged in orgies whose pomp and prodigality shame description. During his six months' stay at Lisbon, Junot had such an open table that 300,000 francs were insufficient to cover expenses, and of course his mistresses cost him no less than his table. These tremendous expenses, of course, were squeezed from the conquered land.

All these upstarts sought to establish their reputation by surpassing pre-revolutionary nobles in lavishness and extravagance. The aforementioned Junot paid a certain actress 12,000 francs for an hour of love. Napoleon never went beyond 4,000. Murat would never spend less than 500 francs for drinks. The women of these military leaders didn't lag behind in crazy prodigality. Thus 200,000 francs for a toilette was not an infrequent expense. Duchess de Junot spent 10,000 francs for needle and thread. All these ladies accoutred in little more than a title and free of the weight of spirit or heart, were strong adherents to one moral principle: live and let live. There was no such thing as an open, deep and honest

BOOK IV: THE NINETEENTH CENTURY

love for these folks. One seized the opportunity whenever it came, and then shook oneself free without much concern on either side.

This was the society which owed much of its being to the Corsican and one can't say that he was proud of it. He realized that he could not hope for power and consolidated rule until he had succeeded in winning over all the royalist groups. But despite all his efforts the latter remained on one side and met his efforts, to create a new nobility, with nothing but scorn. Napoleon was furious but did not show his wrath. Instead, he tried to appear grateful and drew the ladies of the old regime into his circle as court ladies. But he only succeeded in making of them witnesses to the scandalous practises of his family which contributed not a little to increasing the aversion of these elegant groups to him, who showed himself all too much in the manners of an upstart when he put on the glory of his imperialship. Thus he contributed to his own downfall.

CHAPTER XV
BABYLON ON THE SEINE

AFTER the revolution, and in the first third of the nineteenth century, moral conditions in France were not a bit better than they had been in pre-revolutionary days. The ladies of the demimonde still set the pace for the rest of the world. There was, to be sure, a police regulation ordering the confiscation of all publicly-exhibited indecent pictures of women, but so great was the number of prostitutes that this regulation was unenforceable. There were at least one thousand houses in Paris where public balls were held and where the half-world sought its victims. Since the court proceedings took place quite publicly even when the most delicate and shameful matters were being discussed, "for only unworthy females would be present at that sort of thing," old and young ran to these hearings as though they were the most spicy theatre performances. Efforts were made in the theatres to restore morals and propriety. In 1794 the former French theatre was reopened under the name of the *Equality* theatre, in which the actors were pledged to maintain the sanctity of morality and modesty. But it went no further than the pledge, and people flocked to the theatre if only to save light and heat at home.

Prostitution could not be restrained although it did not perhaps flaunt itself as openly as before. How well appointed and politely conducted were the good Parisian brothels of that time can be learned from the memoirs of Castelli. There were servants in livery

BOOK IV: THE NINETEENTH CENTURY

and the ladies and gentlemen wore formal clothes. There was no rude note, no conversation or amusement that would offend outward decency or honor. But after the souper every gentleman would withdraw with the fair one of his choice into her room.

Such houses catered only to the public of means. But poverty was widespread and had to buy its joys cheaply; and in the country too they did without any veneer. The same Castelli relates that at Dijon little boys between seven and fourteen would act as panders. Every one praised his wares to the traveller and sought to underbid his competitor.

In such circumstances there was naturally no lack of secret subterranean literature. The old and well-known erotica continued to be published and there were always new and eager purchasers. One moral advance can be noted during the revolutionary period. This merchandise was no longer sold so openly; ever since 1815 the police kept surveillance over dealers in these products. A most interesting sidelight as to how the distribution was effected is given us by the same Castelli who was an eye witness of so many erotic scenes. "At the Palais Royal I was frequently amused by an old fat rascal who stood right at the entrance, with many large and small books resting on his head, reposing under his arms, and stuck into his pockets, bosom and even boots. He looked like a walking bookstall. And how curiously he hawked his wares. All that he could offer for sale publicly, he shouted in a penetrating raucous voice, and all that pertained to the prohibited articles, he whispered quietly into the ears of passersby."

The restoration received a difficult inheritance indeed, and it was necessary to sweep clean with an iron broom. Napoleon would not have a nominal censorship but actually it was practised; and after his downfall it was again officially instituted. But it was extremely difficult to force the disappearance of these erotica which flooded the market and were available at every stall. The authors were not to be reached since they had taken refuge in other lands during the political storm. Hence it was decided to dam up the circulation of the anti-religious and erotic writings at the consumer's end. In 1825 the government issued an order to all police inspectors laying down the general procedure for the suppression of this corrupt and corrupting reading matter. But alas! the success of these manœuvres was contrary to original expectations, as is evidenced by the continuous confiscations and litigations in which long prison and money sentences were imposed upon the guilty. There could not be any thoroughgoing success in these endeavors if only for the reason that all the wheels of the organization did not click together. Thus, the dealers and publishers in order to forestall objections, might obtain a permit direct from the minister to publish a certain somewhat free but valuable work of literature; but the courts would reverse the decision and condemn the book anew when public opinion demanded the suppression of such writings. These prosecutions frequently fell to the lot of books which belong to the best type of erotic French literature, as La Fontaine's tales, for example.

In the first third of the nineteenth century there came into fashion the transparent obscene cards which, for the poorer public, was a substitute for erotic literature, since the latter had become costly as a result of the suppression. On one side of the card one saw only a smooth surface, and the obscenity of the representation only became visible when the card was held up to bright light, as to a burning lamp. Booksellers didn't bother as much with these smutty articles as did pedlers, which indeed is almost as true today in Paris.

Now people began to look back with admiration and yearning to the great love artists, masculine and feminine, of bygone times.

BOOK IV: THE NINETEENTH CENTURY

Hence there was a great market for the memoirs of such personalities, which were now proliferated in immense quantities. Now the panurgics of famous libertines like the Duke of Lauzun were reprinted, or entirely new books were issued to satisfy the hunger for these *piquanteries*. Some versifiers seized upon the old idea of working up the lives of the hetairai in poetical fashion. Thus Ninon de Lenclos, Marquise de Montespan, and Sophie Arnould were some of the subjects chosen for these poetized autobiographies. But there was a type of writing much more popular at this time, the so-called secret memoirs which usually appeared anonymously under fictitious names, since the contents were very definitely objectionable. To a considerable extent these memoirs of piquant details derived from the private lives of the French kings, from the families of Orleans, of the queen Hortense and the royal family, the Duke of Normandy, son of Louis xvi, etc. The authorities took drastic measures against these writings, and many, which were issued with impunity in German translations, brought their publishers in France long prison terms or high monetary penalties.

There were enough novels appearing at this time in addition to the types just mentioned. Perhaps one of the most popular was *Madame Potiphar*. In this story Pompadour is the heroine of the title; and the author depicts the amorous adventures of an ambitious solicitor with two nuns. Because the book contains about sixteen free situations it was confiscated. The same fate was shared by others. Nor was France poor in collections of erotic songs. These went the whole hog and chattered volubly and unconcernedly about everything connected with sex, hesitating at nothing at all. Hence we cannot be surprised that many of them were confiscated, and those responsible, severely punished. Thus, in 1844 a hawker who had sold the *Songster of the Daughters of Love* was sentenced to pay 6,000 francs and in addition to serve five years in jail. This collection contained forty-five *chansons* of Beranger in addition to Piron's *Ode to Priapus*, and was tame in comparison with others. Much filthier are the collections like the *Broad Songs of Priapus* or the *Satirical Parnassus* of the nineteenth century, which in obscenity rival the most lascivious products of the eighteenth century.

We have already mentioned that memoirs were directed against the royal families no less than against other humans. The typical Frenchman is not excessively oppressed by feelings of awful respect. Many dozens of scandalosa could be mentioned here, but we shall give only one specific illustration. That Napoleon I was no paragon of virtue, needs no exposition to the student of history. He had his recognized mistresses, and gladly strayed to foreign pastures to boot. But a much more welcome butt for erotic jests was found later in the person of his namesake, Napoleon III, and his marriage to the fiery Spaniard Eugenie de Montijo. The chauvinistic French people turned up their noses at this *mesalliance*, much as their grandfathers had done when Louis XVI had brought the Austrian Marie Antoinette home with him. But the broad satiric verses of this time which were quickly and continually being born, also disappeared quickly, and were not filled with that drivelling hate which made so many cognate effusions of the eighteenth century so unpalatable. An example is the *Wife of Cæsar*, a biography of Eugenie de Montijo, Queen of France, by Mme. U. R. (M. de S.). These initials were designed to give the impression that Madame Urbain Rattazzi (Marie de Solins) was the author of this pamphlet. However, it was soon discovered that a certain Vesinier was the author, whereupon he was sentenced to eighteen months of jail, and 1,000 francs fine. This book tells the supposed loves of Eugenie with three princes of the house of Orleans, General Navarez, Rothschild, etc.

After the Franco-Prussian War, Paris was inundated by the so-

BOOK IV: THE NINETEENTH CENTURY

called Bodinguettes, which were printed in just a few sheets, in all formats, and occasionally with illustrations. They were characterized by the grossest license and displayed none of that customary Gallic grace and gallantry. Even the famous opponent of Napoleon, Henri Rochefort, also contributed to this fad. After the destruction of the Commune, the restored government went at these foul things hammer and tong, and it succeeded in checking the abuse.

In the preceding century, the clergy was continually being represented as "loving", and tons of rubbish had been emptied out of pots over the heads of the unfortunate servants of the church who had sunk quite low, it must be admitted. The revolution deprived many of them of their privileges, displaced them from the center of interest and the restoration appointed them to a very modest place indeed. Hence the number of pamphlets directed against them at this time did not compare with the swarm of the earlier period. Most of these scandal stories were written in the form of love stories. *The Child of a Jesuit* by Laumer (1822) described the immoral life of a Jesuit's pupil, rich in licentious and shameful deeds, until his sentence to the gallows. Other stories like *The Woman of the Jesuit* (1826) and the *Mysteries of a Bishopric* (1872) contain vigorous attacks lit with glowing sensuality against the church and its servitors. Two books sought to give actual source materials for a history of the infamies of the church and the clergy, erotic and otherwise, and thus to have an educative influence; they were *Crimes, Delinquencies and Scandals in the Bosom of the Church*, by Villeneuve and Casenade (1861), and *Morals of Convents, Abbeys, and Monasteries* (1843). The broad descriptions of intimate scenes and the ostensible generalizations, rendered the latter work objectionable; and it soon became the object of continuous reprints and suppressions.

In our times we have experienced a tremendous growth of Sexology, the science of sex. In the nineteenth century we can see the beginnings of the application of the scientific all-conquering viewpoint and method to the study of this most important realm, and the compilation of the first fruits of this method as garnered in various introductory researches. The first place should be assigned to a book of Jacques-Antoine Dulaure (1805) in which he treats of phallic worship under the title: *The Gods of Generation*, the first English translation of which has recently appeared in the United States. Like Dupuis before him, Dulaure derives the phallic cult from solar worship; but he gives an excellent description of the ceremonies among the Egyptians, Syrians, Jews, Phœnicians, Phrygians, Persians, and Assyrians. In addition, he presents a detailed exposition of lingam worship among the Hindus, treats briefly of the related cult among the Mexicans, and then, turning to the Greeks and Romans, he considers the cult of Venus in relation to phallic worship. After considering these rites among the early European peoples, he gives a highly interesting and instructive account of this worship among the medieval Christians who in certain respects surpassed the immoral orgies of antiquity.

The noted bibliophile Paul Lacroix composed his complete *History of Prostitution* in 1851-3. This is the first comprehensive work written on this important subject, and it remained decisive until the appearance of Bloch's monumental work. Unfortunately, it remained a torso, for Lacroix, weary of perpetual legal persecutions, lost all desire to complete his task. One seeks in vain for sources or exact quotations of contemporary material, so that scientific verification is extremely difficult and the usefulness of the work is thereby impaired. Despite the subject matter there isn't a loose allusion in the book. Quite on the contrary, so often do angry protests occur, that one gains the impression that the author was a prudish moralist; but other scientific writings by Lacroix prove that he had a fine understanding of erotic and pornographic literature.

The literature of popularization also found many representatives. Among the numerous *guides for lovers* there should be mentioned the *Physiology of the First Night of Marriage* by Octave de Saint-Ernest (1842). Warnings against venereal disease were sounded by the *Protector against the Disease of Venus* of Rubempre (1826) and the very widely known treatise of the physician Tardieu, *Medico-Legal Moral Offences*.

There were any number of writers who saw to it that those who derived pleasure from reading books on sex should not go unappeased. In 1870 Jean Richepin issued his poetry collection *La Chanson de Gucux*. The eroticism of these songs, however extreme, is just gibed with the taste of the time, and in a month the first edition was exhausted. Richepin paid for his success by spending the next month in jail. It is unfortunate that such a gifted writer did not turn his talents to better tasks.

Paul de Kock (1794-1871) found numerous readers for his ribald stories of sex sins in modern French society which he crammed into his fifty-five volumes. His namesake Henry did not lag far behind in lasciviousness. He sought to gain the favor of his readers with his saucy, scandalous work, *History of Celebrated Libertines* (1870), and wrote numerous other risque stories. The best known is *The Murder in the Chestnut Forest*, in which the bloodthirsty and lubric achieve a unique amalgam.

The foremost representative of the gallant novel in the last quarter of the nineteenth century and the cleverest, was indisputably Marcel Prévost. In most of his works he depicted the intimate relations between men and women with rare magic of language and a wonderful comprehension of the physiological and psychological motives behind them. His pictures are almost oppressive in their fidelity to truth.

The importance of these and other unnamed writers lies in their natural representation of contemporary circumstances which they portray without disguise. In the third empire the cocotte again came to power and set her seal upon French life. She drew everything under her sway and dictated all laws. The morality of the cocotte was decisive in all realms of sexual morality. The spirit of the cocotte dictated the mode, and controlled the forms of expression in the realm of the spirit and of language. Of course, her field of action has always been in the domain of sexuality, and she remains true to her own class when she reduces all relations to the common denominator of her coarse taste. With her polyplike arms she tears everything to herself with irresistible force, and the victims who can no longer envisage redemption from her embraces, finally surrender completely to her with body and soul and deem themselves fortunate when they are permitted to sing the praises of their mistress. In an age when the cocotte is supreme, there can be no more inward cult than that of the female body, no theme of conversation more important than the description of adventures and chances in the service of Venus. There could be no greater praise for a woman than when her praises were sung in everyone's mouth.

The real beginning of the supremacy of the prostitute in literature and drama began in 1840 with the *Lady of the Camelias* by Dumas *fils*. A strumpet falls in love with a young man of distinguished family who is naturally not in agreement with his choice. After his family remonstrates with her by appealing to her love for him and pointing out the dire consequences of such a union, she decides to give him up. She pretends to her betrothed that she really loves another, leaves him, and finally dies of tuberculosis.

BOOK IV: THE NINETEENTH CENTURY

The question that immediately occurs to us is this: Are the characters of prostitutes and such, capable of poetic or dramatic development at all? The answer would seem to be an affirmative one. A false step or a breach of marital fidelity very frequently has consequences of a tragic nature. Surely no one will be intolerant enough to insist that one error is enough to seal the fate of a woman and to be taken as the index of her worth. Sin demands repentance, and this is found sufficiently in regret and sorrow. Such regret is an inward process, a protracted psychological process, and presupposes lengthy analysis of changing impulses and reactions. This is difficult to achieve within the narrow limits of a drama, destined for representation on the stage, and which must reckon with the relatively short time available for its production. The problem thus posed would seem to be much more amenable to epic, than dramatic treatment.

But the nineteenth century French dramatists did not aim at creating a logically constructed theatrical piece corresponding to the laws of internal probability; for in their plays of adultery it is not the results of waywardness that are represented.. Not at all. This situation is used in all possible piquant permutations and combinations in order to amuse the public for the greater enrichment of the author's purse. The French believe that it is permissible in the theatre to live somewhat in the fashion of the demi-monde, to violate the marriage vow, if only the dramatist and public can get a satisfactory ending for the whole mess.

If one asks why these pieces of adultery, with their undressing scenes, became so enormously popular, the answer is not difficult to find. Nineteenth century life was exciting and nerve-wracking in its mad pursuit of success, and in most people it helped to destroy the normal uses of composure. The average Frenchman, of an evening, sought in the theatre refreshment and entertainment. He respected esprit, and if the dialogue was witty and interspersed with erotic allusions, the author or dramatist had fulfilled his duty and deserved approbation.

The material of these comic writers and dramatists were usually taken from life. Venal love is found among men and women alike. Thus Poritzky relates that many of the poor students in Paris were able to keep their heads above water only because they were erotically potent. The demand, by insatiable licentious women, was very great. Students whom nature had especially favored were ardently desired and besought—and well recompensed for their labor.

The novel stood on the same low plane with the theatre during the third kingdom. The ordinary feuilleton story prettified vice and fitted it out with all the splendor of romance. The adulterous woman was an angel, the courtesan always a delightful creature, and her profession a fascinating fault. Lovers and seducers were always handsome, generous, extremely masculine, irresistible. The deceived husbands on the other hand were always ill-mannered, dumb or simply ridiculous. And every intrigue trailed a cloud of musk and rice powder. Intimacies! That was the shibboleth of the novel and the theatre alike. In their diary, the brothers Goncourt have an entry under February 14, 1866, in which they quote a dictum of Dumas the elder. "What do you wish," he called out, "when you can only make money in the theatre by making girls' tights rip. These constantly ripping tights made the fortune of Directeur Holstein. He ordered his dancers to wear tights that had a ripped seam, always on the same spot. Those were the days for opera glasses. But finally the censor interfered and with his interference, most dealers in opera glasses went out of business."

Two citations may be adduced here to characterize the morality of that period. In the excellent novel drawn from life by a German author, and entitled the *Tale of a Clerk*, we find the following statement: "Lucian deeply enjoyed this lounging in Paris, utterly idle, purely a spectator, and was richer in pleasures than he had been five days before. In Montmartre he had become acquainted with the caverns of luxurious vice; with orgies which left one cold because they were ordered and paid for, and did not proceed from genuine emotion but were enacted by actors and actresses; naked dancing and living illustrations of Aretino's sonnets and the dialogues of Luisa Sigea, and scenes from the life of *The Philosophical Theresa* and the Marquise of Montrevers. Now Lucian learnt what real vice was, and it is so cheap in Paris. He came to opium dives and to lascivious balls in the quarter of St. Michel, in the atelier region of Montparnasse. He visited the Roman baths where amid clouds of steam there were arranged the erotic figures found on Greek pottery and vases, where the invention of Nero did not appear at all shameful in this Olympian atmosphere, in the circle of enraptured spectators, but rather beautiful, since it was handsome youths who were acting out the pantomime."

It will very likely be objected that this is only a novel in which no limits are fixed to the author's fantasy. But in real life however there are bounds set to profligacy. Yet this *captatio benevolentiæ* is here being employed on an unworthy cause. Let us hear what an author like Alexander Moszkowski says, who speaks out of his own experience and who is wholly reliable: "A flood of nudity inundated the whole of Paris. With the exception of the Elite theatre which found a natural dike in its fixed repertoire, no stage was able to withstand the wild flood, and other show places grew up like mushrooms which varied the theme of nakedness either stupidly or wittily, as the case may be. In the Horloge Theatre on the Champs Elysées, Prévost's *Half Virgins* was enacted in travestied society scenes. The young ladies of this piece were dressed very correctly in front, but when they turned their backs they revealed a wide split extending from the neck to the calves, so that every half virgin could be either an elegant lady of the salon, or a Venus Kallipygos, depending on her position. The Olympia Theatre in the Boulevard acted out a pantomimic drama which represented all the phases of a bridal night with painful accuracy. In Paris it was no longer worth the trouble of mobilizing the censor and the police against the living enactment of these details.

"In the Cigale, an attractive suburban temple of the nude muse, nakedness overflowed to the other side of the footlights among the spectators. After there was no more clothing left for the actors to take off, the orchestra leader and musicians began to remove everything dispensable, and soon the public began to participate in the orgy of disrobing. In many establishments of the Pigalle district this stark nakedness took on allegorical forms. The seven deadly sins or the cardinal virtues were shown as animated moving pictures without any subterfuges of tights; and the effect was heightened by the introduction of optical aids, especially mirror reflections which still left something to guess about, even when one saw everything clearly with one's eyes. In addition there were parties which did not differ in any way from the scenes represented in the erotic theatres of the revolutionary period. The way was led by the artists' guild of Montmartre with its sensational arrangements of the *Bal des quatrez-arts* and the *Bal du Courier* which were carried on in the wide spaces of the Moulin Rouge. These balls were under the dictatorship of a strictly enforced regulation concerning costume which was constantly changed, sometimes ancient Greek or Oriental or Renaissance, etc. Everyone had to come before a whole set of authorities who would pass on the authenticity and correctness of one's costume before one could be admitted. Any one who was unfortunate enough to wear a costume not absolutely in keeping with the decreed style was kept out. Until midnight the festivities were a delight to the eyes, with its recreation of a past epoch. Everything was utterly decorous, and not a gesture or allusion would betray the real purpose of the ball. Then a single woman would suddenly appear in the gallery, bathed in a flood of light. This one was the bearer of good tidings and the living semaphore of the festivities. With one little tug her dress fell from her and this was the signal; in a moment every woman had cast off her every bit of covering. Clothes were now off and flesh was on. With clothes hurled off, shame was exorcised and wild passionate orgies were now begun. The chronicler deems it necessary to draw the curtain on the herd exhibits of these scenes worse than bestiality."

But these were private performances. What was the situation with regard to those in public? Zola protested indignantly against the applause which would always greet one of these so-called actresses whenever she would emphasize some obscene expression by some bodily motion or contortion. "What a disgrace!" he exclaimed, "on the day when some woman will come to the exalted idea of playing the whore *au naturel*. All Paris will be beside itself with enthusiasm. And how can it be otherwise? We have fallen into shame and ignominy, we are the bastard offspring of an accursed age. We have only got so far as revealing the breasts, and showing the thighs, but we shall certainly fall into the gutter unless we arouse ourselves and become free men."

Zola's call died unheard. Marcel Prévost shows us with inexorable sharpness the utterly immoral life of his time and nation, and the reflected image is anything but pleasing. An example of the worst moral dissoluteness combined with corporeal intactness, i. e., hymeneal imperforation, is given in the *Half Virgins*. Here everything is permitted the educated girl of the better classes provided only that she enters marriage with an unimpaired maidenhead. It is perfectly evident that under such circumstances a morally pure marriage is impossible, as well as that this type of parent cannot be a model for her children.

Most of the works of the other writers of entertainment literature touch the borders of the pornographic. One of these deserves brief notice, he who wrote under the pseudonym of Willy. His real name was Henry Gauthier-Villars and he never wrote about anything other than sex life, of which he treated all the possible forms of adultery and perversion. The representation and choice of language is so unrestrained that he is only one little step from the morass of pornography. His writings are dangerous because of their gracious and vivid depictions which say almost everything in half-concealed word-plays, or at least manage to hint at everything so that no doubts are left. The reader's imagination is compelled to collaborate and to spin further the thought begun by the author. Willy draws his sexual pictures with naturalness, but he is far inferior to Zola in objectivity.

Paris still remains the model city of *Venus vulgivaga*, and only Brussels offers really serious competition. The stranger just come to Babylon on the Seine generally seeks erotic pleasures. Very early therefore there were to be found printed directories of guides to women's flesh marts. These brothel directories were already in vogue during the eighteenth century and, as an example, one may be cited. It bears the remarkable title *Funeral Oration of the very High and Mighty Mme. Justine* (1786); it is said to have had a very prominent personage as its author. In the nineteenth century, as population grew and means of transportation brought more visitors to the great capital of pleasure, these directories became more numerous and obtrusive. In every little bookshop and dance hall these *Guides to the Stranger in Paris* were sold, either as collections

BOOK IV: THE NINETEENTH CENTURY

of obscene pictures, or more usually as printed manuals to the pleasure-seeking provincial or stranger. The address of the brothel and the jades, their prices, and the catalogue of their sexual practices and perversities were described with breath-taking frankness and exhaustive detail. One of these manuals bore the amusing title: *Les cocottes, biches et lorettes*. Naturally such guides had only a short lease of life for they soon were out of date or were rapidly confiscated. Nevertheless, this was a very profitable business for the unscrupulous individuals who engaged in it, as we can judge from the enormous number of these guides.

The horrible mixture of cruelty and passion, so peculiar to Marquis de Sade, as well as the predilection for philosophical excursions in defence of his perversities, did not remain without influence in the nineteenth century. A work was published about 1830 which was so full of the spirit of Sade that for a while it was attributed to the latter. Only a careful examination reveals that the book could not have been written in 1803, as the title page declares, since it deals with characters who lived under Louis-Philippe. The book is *The Dominican*. At that time, too, a mass of obscene political pamphlets was thrown upon the market. *My Cousin Matthew* by Rabau is one of the most important of this class. Another is *The Pranks of the High Ladies*, containing a wealth of gossip and scandals concerning actresses and well-known society women.

The first important erotic type character who bobbed up about 1830 was that of *Mayeux* by Traviès. He is the born cynic, practically always erotic if not directly obscene. His bodily malformation made him desirable only to insatiable women, who knew how to appreciate his extraordinary potency. Hence quite apart from his pictorial representation, he figures as the panurgic hero of erotic novels, such as *The Secret Loves of Mayeux*; *The Twelve Labors of Hercules*; *The Twelve (erotic) Days' Work*; etc.

THE EROTIC HISTORY OF FRANCE

Louis Protat was the author of the notorious and grotesque erotic tale *Serrefesse*. Some notion of its contents may be gained from inspecting the characters. Pinecul, whoremonger and thief; Cuillardin, chief sewer cleaner; Cruche, supposedly a eunuch, seller of condoms; Pinolie, Cruche's wife; and Serrefesse. The whole plot hinges on the fact that Cuillardin had raped Serrefesse and after she has shot herself, her betrayer is put out of the way by Cruche and his gang. The language is foul though there are traces of wit in the volume. Another book of Protat's, *The Examination of Flora*, eclipses all its contemporaries both in erotic license and, in this one case, in literary value as well.

A few more of erotic writers in the last quarter of the nineteenth century must be mentioned. Le Nismois wrote many pieces, mostly for the theatre but no director in the world would be found to produce any of his works. One of the most fruitful French erotic writers is the pornographer who hid himself behind the initials E. D. This Dumoulin had a certain amount of literary skill. He was a flagellant, but was also able to appreciate other types of sex activity, for orgies of natural indulgence are plentifully littered throughout his books. Some of the titles: *Procession of the Bare Buttocks*, *Turned-Up Skirts*, *Schoolmistress*, indicate sufficiently the type of porneia that they contain. He is the foremost representative of flagellational eroticism. In the last named novel, the adventures are related with honesty and a luxuriousness of detail which argues for personal knowledge and participation. There are also numerous tribadic scenes in this girls' school. In *The Animated Marble* he treats a variant of the Pygmalion and Galatea theme. The hero of the romance enkindles passion in the living but marble-cold statue of a princess. In numerous other books the author never forgets to indicate that he is also the author of other smut.

The best tribadic novel of the time undoubtedly was *A Summer*

BOOK IV: THE NINETEENTH CENTURY

in the Country (1868), long attributed to Gustave Droz, who nevertheless was able to obtain the legal right to have his name removed from the title page. This novel contains the correspondence of two young ladies, a governess and her former pupil, who inform each other of the emotions rising in their young souls, of their erotic observations and experiences, and finally their first introductions to love.

CHAPTER XVI
THE HEYDAY OF OBSCENE ART

THERE has been but one great age of erotic literature in France, namely the eighteenth. No previous period, nor any subsequent one, can be compared to those halcyon days of the seventeen hundreds. Nevertheless we shall find some great writers in this field during the nineteenth century, men who made signal contributions to the understanding of erotic problems and their representation in letters.

The first great name to be considered is Honoré de Balzac (1799-1850). In his *Droll Stories*, he endeavored to revive the fresh sensuality of the old fabliaux and the roughness of Rabelais in modern combination. In the language of the old French he tells stories of the most suggestive sort after the manner of the Italian novelists, and perpetrates many a jolly jest on the way. The work contains thirty-six stories, each one gayer than the preceding, and all going as far as possible in daring and suggestiveness. Who can refrain from laughter at the monk Amader who possesses the best instrument for winning the suit of the abbey? Or who will not be amused at the cuckold who can no longer recognize a certain thing? The panurgics of the good king Louis XI really belong to the realm of scatology. The king arranges a peculiar sort of entertainment. At the instigation of his paramour he mixes a purgative with the food and when the effects begin to show themselves he hinders every one from visiting the toilet. The resultant scenes are of overwhelming comedy.

In poetry there was a bard who stood out considerably above the remainder of contemporary singers both because of the contents and the influence of his work. Béranger (1780-1857) was the real creator of the French *chanson*, and is still today famed as the national poet. He sang for the people and captured their native notes as perhaps no other. The singing quality of his songs captivated all hearts. He knew how to live himself into the soul of those who were tried and rejected by fate, and this capacity of sympathy and understanding won him the affection of all. Curiously enough, Béranger is almost as great in political satire as in simple songs. But his chief strength lies in his erotic *chanson*. He does not represent the overwhelming passion, or sentimental love; he knows only the dalliance with love which he celebrates and decorates with true gallic wit and jest. One must laugh at the worthy philistine who boasts of the transparent friendship of the senator; or at the epithalamion to the lovers who have been living out of wedlock for the past twenty years. By the side of these there are the glorifications of adultery, of carnal lust, of the *carpe diem*, which has sometimes a depressing and even harmful effect. Everything occurs cheek by jowl in these collections. The moving farewell of Mary Stuart near a bawdy street song, and a song of King Yvetot near that of an uncontrolled grisette.

In addition to these songs, which all too often violate the dictates of good taste, Béranger composed poems entirely in the demesne of powerful eroticism, which are, to be sure, not found in the official collections. They were first published in 1815 under the title: *Songs, Moral and Otherwise*; when the edition was reprinted a few years later, it was confiscated. Béranger was sentenced to pay 50 francs and spend three months in jail for insulting morality and religion. In 1832, all these obscene songs introduced by Piron's *Ode to Priapus* and a few miscellaneous pieces were published in the previously mentioned *Le Chansonnier des filles d'amour*. Two years later a complete edition of Béranger's work was issued in four volumes; a fifth volume containing all the erotic poetry was printed secretly, but was confiscated in the same year. Thirty years later these forty-four pieces were issued under the title, *The Gayeties of Béranger*, and this constitutes the most complete collection.

If the field of erotic literature was relatively sterile at this time, the realm of art was very fertile and French erotic art continued to lead the world. From the year 1825 France was mistress of the market of erotic pictures, and it still remains the chief producer. The artists Bouchot, Poitevin, Deveria, Maurin, Gavarni, Johannot and Monnier were in their heyday and at their maximum productivity. Only Portevin and Monnier had any breath of greatness in their work, especially the *Diablerie* series of the former which are to be accounted as among the boldest, most fantastic and perhaps the most memorable productions in all erotic painting. Johannot and Monnier, on the other hand, are merely the vicious, cynical depicters of lower middle-class salacity. The same is true of Gavarni's erotic lithographs. Bouchot again has something that reminds us of Poitevin.

What some of the others lacked in greatness they made up in quantity. Maurin and Deveria were virtually inexhaustible in their production of lithographs which they brought to the market in series. These two and others of their ilk, glorified obscenity without manifesting any trace of a higher idea. Although they gave themselves out for anti-philistines, everything they produced lacks any idealization of sensuality. The representation of the sexual act in hundreds of variations was their chief theme, and only at their very best do they show an occasional gracefulness or refinement in their tasks. They are the most enthusiastic eulogists of the mechanics of love, and they can suggest nothing more than the physical delights which masculine potency brings to the woman, and which female wantonness and sophistication afford the man. In fine, it is a glowing cult of the individual erotic charms of the female body. Numerous gallant lithographs that appeared publicly in the 30's of the last century were obscenely varied and touched up for those who liked their eroticism undiluted. With the spread of photography, this flood reached its ebb, and a new period of activity began.

One of these artists was also by way of being an author. Indeed, Henry Monnier (1799-1875) was also an actor of repute. When he was still a subordinate official in the ministry of justice, he revealed a native gift of observation, a sharp and inexorable eye for idiosyncrasies, the weak and ridiculous features of his environment, which he endeavored to perpetuate with his drawing pencil. In 1820 appeared his little booklet, *Administrative Customs*; and at the same time he created the figure of Joseph Prudhomme, that worthy smug bourgeois who has become as much a figure in French literature as Molière's Tartuffe. Soon Monnier was admitted to the circle which included Musset, Paul de Koch, Gautier, Gavarni, and he gave free reign to his abilities. His erotic compositions were developed with swift strokes and were originally composed just for his friends, without any thought of publication. When the erotic theatre was established on the Rue de la Santé in 1862 he contributed a small piece entitled *The Strumpet and the Student*. The playlet has no action to speak of. It is a series of love scenes between the two characters, punctuated by quarrels and reconciliations, but the charm of the writing and the capricious wit are what give it power. Here is an example.

The student is sitting alone and reading a letter. "Tuesday at noon I shall come to you rather earlier than later. Love me always as I love you. Be clever and understanding but not too wanton. If you wish, we shall kick over the traces a bit." (He speaks: "It is 11:10. She will not come.") Reading again: "Tuesday at noon") (To himself: "She surely won't be late. I will arrange the seat.") 11:30. He reads again: "I shall come rather earlier than later." A knock is heard: "Who is there?"

A light voice: "I."

The student pretends not to recognize: "Who is 'I'? Is that you?"

"Yes, of course, it's me."

He opens the door, the grisette enters red as a beet. (Remember, it's six flights up). "Good day, my little pup. How goes it? My lord, you live high up. I'm all out of breath. And your housekeeper, below—what a bitch she is! She asked me again and again whom I wanted. You understand? She made me repeat it many times over in order that I might become worried. I despise these damned female tricks. Don't I get a kiss? Let me remove my hat first."

The student, ready: "Come here my angel."

The entertainment grows more exciting, passionate, and finally winds up in groans and snorts. The grisette pants: "Oh, how wonderful you love! Kill me!...oh, kill me!"

Whereupon a deep bass voice from the adjoining room booms out warningly: "No murder in this house, please." But this does not disturb the lovers and they continue their activities undisturbed.

Monnier has another little work, *The Lesbians*, which can be compared to Crébillon in its supple narrative skill. Two women of Paris, young, handsome, elegant, pleasure seeking, visit a mutual friend in the latter's country home. The two visitors who have never met before, are given a bedroom in common. At first the conversation flows in quite conventional channels. They chatter about social events, about their husbands. Both feel themselves misunder-

BOOK IV: THE NINETEENTH CENTURY

stood. Each flatters the other, and makes pretty little speeches to the other. Their speech becomes freer and more intimate. They draw closer to each other in the wide double bed, and gradually each attempts certain tender manipulations which the other reciprocates. The talk becomes more ardent and more intense, and their digitation more ecstatic, until both give themselves over to their desires. The charm of the work lies in its manner of treatment, in the witty and clever wantonness which never forgets the canons of good taste.

CHAPTER XVII
THE REIGN OF THE PROSTITUTE

IT WAS with perfect consummate planning, and cleverness that Louis Napoleon was able to maneuver his election to the presidency of the French Republic in 1849. His term of office was to be only four years but already there were a sufficient number of signs to indicate that he intended to remain in the saddle very much longer. When his efforts in this direction became too obvious he dealt a *coup d'etat* and in 1859 he dissolved the Assembly, sent sixty of the hostile delegates into exile, and caused the arrest of about 26,000 malcontents. But this brutal exercise of force did not guarantee any sort of safety or certainty. There were many attempts on his life which showed how great the disaffection of the people really was. From the very start he had numerous powerful enemies, chiefly the great horde of Orleanists who had representatives in commerce, in officialdom and among the bourgeoisie. Here were such men as Thiers, Guizot, Remusat and others. Then there was the party of legitimists of the Faubourg St. Germain, descendants of the *ancien régime* with numerous connections throughout France. This party possessed but few capable brains and practically their only weapon was gossip but this they knew how to use masterfully. The whole mass of scandalous stories circulated at this time concerning the emperor and his spouse, the beautiful Spaniard, Eugenie, springs from this source. And although most of them bear the stamp of falsehood their importance must not be underestimated. They knew well how to uncover the nakedness of the emperor so skillfully that their fictions achieved the semblance of verity.

Even more than in the gallant period the prostitute now ruled. She played the first fiddle in life, literature, the theatre and the arts, and Napoleon himself bore the blame for this state of affairs. The *coup d'etat* had pressed the clamp down on the press. Any one who now wished to found a new newspaper had to deposit a security of 50,000 francs, which made virtually impossible the growth of a press. Misdemeanors of the press were no longer permitted jury hearings but had to be tried before criminal courts and were threatened with Draconian penalties. After two warnings a newspaper was suspended and after two convictions it was abolished. Since the press was gagged and prevented from discussing political matters, it turned to realms less dangerous: social satire and scandal, financial operations, and journalistic wit. How successful such cultivation of new pastures was may be judged from the fact that the circulation of the *Constitutionel* jumped from 3,000 to 45,00; and Villemessant who edited *Figaro* after 1854 made his paper the favorite of the capital. What did it matter that those attacked and libelled in his sheet sought redress in the courts and that he had to pay out considerable money in fines? The growing popularity of his paper with its consequent financial gain was more than enough to balance his losses.

But once the tiger has licked blood he is insatiable. The public naturally fond of gossip and saucy details, took delight in the steaming ordure served up to them, and found it difficult to live without such slop. In no realm can gossip be as enjoyable as in the sexual, and in this respect no class of bourgeoisie society offers more material than the half-world. Their whole life is one chain of scandalous episodes. Particularly did the cocottes of the second empire offer considerable material. And what a gap separates these prostitutes who peddle their flesh from the grisette under Louis Philippe! Murger in his *La Boheme* has represented them as creatures of lovely frivolity who do not shrink from giving themselves as long as they have the illusion of love, however momentary. But the cocotte of this time has gone far beyond such considerations. When she sells herself she uses her opportunity well and chooses only the highest bidder. She is not overburdened with an excess of spirit, nor is this what the business men and knights of happiness seek in her. The only thing of value is her capacity to purvey sexual satisfaction.

Many of these creatures boasted a rare beauty but they did not always exercise the greatest fascination. Thus Cora Pearl, one of the most famous denizens of the half-world, was actually repulsive, what with her coarse features, coachman's voice and vulgar manners. Yet she had twelve horses in her stall, charged 10,000 francs for a night and, it is said, received from a grand duke the gift of a massive silver bidet filled with jewels and gold pieces. Exploitation of their lovers and senseless squandering of money were the occupations with which these hussies busied themselves and instead of repelling men, this unconcealed pursuit of gain drew them on. It was a source of popularity to be seen with a strumpet and to squander one's money upon her. The Duke of Grammont-Caderousse, wasted money and health until he died of tuberculosis. Arthur de Lauriston lost everything, and one day ran off to Algiers where he entered the army. Prince Achille Murat shot himself when he was left penniless. Moreover, it was not only the Parisians but also foreigners who fell into the nets of these modern hetæræ, for Paris had gradually established itself as the Babylon of the Seine. Visitors from every land came here to find pleasure at all costs, and not infrequently lost their shirts in the process. In

BOOK IV: THE NINETEENTH CENTURY

two or three years Khalil Bey ran through 15 millions and returned home impoverished. The Princes Narischkin, Paul Demidoff, and Lord Hamilton threw money away with open hands though they did not exactly employ the method of their contemporary, the mysterious Prince Possos, who amused himself by dropping gold pieces upon the heads of the passersby from the balcony of the *Maison Dorée*.

Although merely tolerated by the state at first, the prostitute soon became recognized by society. It was no longer necessary for them to crawl in the darkest corners, like pariahs. They could now ply their seductive occupations in full publicity, rob the man from his consort, and through him inoculate his family with the vice. Soon the most honorable woman assumed the manners of the demi-mondaine and sought to emulate her fallen sister's immorality. It came to the pass where the boundaries became indistinguishable and one could no longer tell cocotte from honorable woman.

The great world occupied itself only with her. Art and literature brought her undisguised praise and the theatre lay at her feet. She dominated everything, no matter whether an artist drew a mythological divinity; a Phryne, a Leda with the Swan, or whatever other mythological name he immortalized upon the canvas, it is always the sensuality incorporated in the cocotte that served to inspire him. Journalism too, stood in the service of the demi-monde. For an hour of love the fortunate scribbler would sing the praises of his love in his sheet; and for similar favors the hopeless mediocre creatures of the stage could expect glowing dramatic panegyrics upon their deathless art. If this method failed these ladies would buy favorable critical notices by counting out good gold. Even the famous critic Jules Janin never showed any aversion to a certain sort of erotic handclasp, and people knew that after every première he could enter upon his books between six and eight thousand francs from unspecified sources.

THE EROTIC HISTORY OF FRANCE

The prostitute made her triumphal entry into literature when the younger Dumas brought upon the stage in his *Lady of the Camelias*, a prostitute dripping with sentimentality. Through five long acts says Vieil-Castel in his notebook, this woman hawks out before an educated public all the disgusting details of her prostituted life. Nothing is missing in the representation, and scenes are borrowed from the most corrupt places. And this wench with camelias is supposed to represent true love, she who accepts alternately the embraces of customers and the kisses of her heart's own friend, who permits the rich one to pay in order to support the poor one. Nor do the other details of her sordid existence improve the picture at all, culminating in the apologia for her life, at her grave where it is said: "Much will be forgiven her for she has loved much."

Although this writer designated the exaltation of the strumpet as the shame of his age, this drama corresponded so well with the instincts of the populace that in a short while it became one of the most popular pieces of the Parisian theatre, whence it made its way throughout France. In addition, it also created the type which hereafter was to be quite at home on the stage. Soon there were many models and copies of this. Barriére's *Girl of Marble* appeared a year later; and Augier wrote *The Marriage of Olympia* in 1855 and *Poor Lionesses* in 1859. The rudest and crudest sort of realism dominated the theatre and the novel and amounted to nothing more than a servile copying of the dirtiest patches of life. In both fiction and drama the period revelled in the depiction of filthy scenes and in the eulogy of vice.

When prostitutes realized that they occupied the chief interests of even serious writers, they themselves came forward as authoresses and sought to depict their own experiences. One of the most whorish of them created a tremendous stir with her memoirs which underwent one edition after another. This was Marguerite Badel,

BOOK IV: THE NINETEENTH CENTURY

called Rigolboche, who was too unlettered to be able to write even one sensible sentence. Hence her memoirs were really composed by two unscupulous writers, Blum and Huart. The same circumstances were true of the memoirs of Céleste Vainard, called Mogador, who could neither read nor write but none the less demanded the spotlight of literature. People knew all this, knew the utter ignorance of this cocotte, but were somehow crazy about her lewd confessions. Indeed, her lurid past did not prevent her from climbing up the social ladder for she later married Count Lionel de Moreton Chabrillan. Similar marriages into the nobility were effected by other notorious whores like Rosalie Léon, Marguerite Bellanger, another known as Madonna, and Paiva who captured respectively Prince Peter Wittgenstein, Lord Coulback, Prince Soltikoff and Count Henckel von Donnersmarck. Since such incredible success attended these daughters of joy, it is no wonder that women of society began to copy the loose allurements of their weaker sisters in order to try for similar prizes. Bœhn gives a number of names, for example, that of the lovely Countess Castiglione who is said to have received for one night from Lord Hertford the sum of one million francs. In Dieppe during 1854 the Marquise de Belbœuf and the Countess Gouy competed with the cocottes in their scandalous dancing and daring clothes. In Paris the ladies looked to the stars of the operettas, Lise Tautain, Hortense Schneider, Zulma Bouffar, Blanch d'Antigny and copied their clothing and gestures, and made their own the repertoire of a Theresia.

A most powerful and masterful delineation of the demoralizing influence of the prostitute and the poisoning of public and private life through her was given by Emile Zola in his *Nana*; this effort was abetted by the drama of Augier, *Infection*, and by Sardou's *The Family Benoiton*. The only goal of the cocotte is money and her greed is nourished in the pursuit of unscrupulous transactions. Only money offers the key to power and happiness, and hence everyone pursues it. France swam in gold and this profusion developed a fever of speculation. Everyone desired to multiply his possessions quickly and without effort. The newly created stock banks, after the model of the brothers Péreire which was founded for this purpose in order to finance great enterprises through accumulation of small holdings, led to risky enterprises. Commerce and business expanded and the income of the middle classes skyrocketed. Napoleon understood very well how to use good suggestions for the gain of France and particularly of Paris. In 1855 there took place in Paris a world fair after the model of the one in England which brought over five million visitors to the French metropolis. This influx naturally purveyed a very numerous and elaborate clientele for prostitutes. The world exposition of 1867 went it much better with fourteen million visitors who came not only for business but also, in good part, for pleasure. The devotees of Cimmerian love thus had their hands full, and their purses too, for these bulged with gold. The prostitutes swarmed in all streets and places of amusement. In full consciousness of their importance they pressed ever further into the foreground.

Soon this rottenness, this disintegrative process of society found its analyzers and depictors. But an interesting contradiction is to be observed at this point. While the cult of the prostitute was being celebrated as never before, the artists who merely copied nature saw themselves continually exposed to the chicaneries of police and authorities. Flaubert, Edmond de Goncourt, Zola, Maupassant, and others, had to practise the most artful wiles in order to avoid being all too forcibly reminded of the existence of a harsh censorship. That was thoroughly logical. When an artist represents the morals of his time in his serious work, he should sit in judgment upon such conditions. Judges and other officials who had permitted themselves to be carried along by the stream of foulness and corruption saw themselves represented in their true and quite unflattering light in these writings. In these works those who should have been guardians of morality saw themselves accused. Accordingly the personal animosities of these outraged officials found vent in the imposition of indiscriminate punishments upon serious writers. On the other hand, pornography, the outright panegyric of vice and the real herald of prostitution against which the real opposition of justice should have been directed, found wide distribution and flowered in gallic profusion.

Venality—wherever the eye fell. Besides the actual sale and purchase of flesh, there was the degradation of spirit and attitude. Bribery triumphed over justice which never let her left hand know what her right hand was doing; and placed itself squarely on the side of the large capital that was defending these foul-smelling transactions with brutal cynicism. The press influenced public opinion in favor of those who showed themselves most willing to pay. For the journalists it was a seductive and profitable business to make themselves the unscrupulous organ of speculation on the Exchange. Most of the greatest Parisian newspapers were the possession of the speculators who set the tone, and didn't hesitate a moment to expend huge sums when they saw the possibility of realizing their aims. The newspapers merely served to draw the public into the swindling business of the publishers or the bankers who stood behind them. That thousands of well-meaning readers had been brought to beggardom by their foolish trusts in the honesty of the press, meant nothing to the latter.

Similarly the jurists were accused of venality and other officials as well. Napoleon himself and his family were accused of being purchasable for a sufficient price, a charge surely untrue in the case of Napoleon himself. But this charge was certainly true of his stepson, the Duke de Morny, the first cavalier of his time. A certain voracious swindler, the banker Jecker, had lent one and a half millions to Mexico and wanted sixty-five millions in return. To help this swindler realize his usurious demands, Morny was won over to advise Napoleon to go in for the disastrous Mexican expedition, which cost Maximilian and his followers their lives, and Napoleon a goodly share of his imperial splendor. This he sought to counteract through a renewed call to arms against Germany. Thus indirectly, a swindler was the real cause of Napoleon's downfall.

CHAPTER XVIII
MASTERS OF EROTIC LITERATURE

THE second half of the nineteenth century is more fruitful than the first regarding the composition of erotica. It is as though the erotic imagination had exhausted itself in the period of the Enlightenment and the Revolution, and required a long breathing space to recruit its constitution; or to vary the metaphor, the much-worked field had to lie fallow for almost half a century, or be only partially and lightly cultivated, so that in the second half of the century energetic and ambitious cultivators might again reap plenteous harvest from it. There were a very considerable number of writers and only the most important will be considered. We will first consider the Symbolist novelists D'Aurévilly and Huysmans. After that we shall cast a glance at Musset, Gautier, Stendhal and Hugo. We shall then tarry a moment with Flaubert and his school, Maupassant and Zola. And the chapter will close with a statement concerning the symbolist poets, Verlaine and Baudelaire.

The *Diaboliques* of Barbey d'Aurévilly (1874) still remains one of the masterpieces of modern French literature, but it is only known in castrated editions. At the time of its appearance it aroused great interest and opposition. Aurévilly is a very remarkable writer, one of the most powerful representatives of late French romanticism. His work is characterized by dazzling wit, psychological observation, a wonderful flow of talk, and a panurgic joy in the coarsely physical, erotically mysterious and perverse. In these stories he let himself go all the way. The six tales were so open and unvarnished that they could not be distributed, but were immediately confiscated because of immorality and blasphemy. When Aurévilly was taken to task, he naturally declared that he had not wished to profit by the ribaldry of his readers, but that he had on the contrary, desired to exert a moral effect. He had desired to lash vice, he asserted, and had therefore, been compelled to remain true to life. His story was believed, but the remaining 480 copies of his work were none the less confiscated, with his approval.

It is difficult to transmit the flavor of these devilish stories which are fiendish in their cruelty, their horrible ingenuity, in their overtones of the demonic world which swathes about us, and of which we hear echoes in the ecstasies of sex. When the senses are afire with sex, we are somehow brought near to the elemental flames of the universe, blazing murkily in the primeval chaos and flaring with undiminished heat and unmitigated destructiveness beneath the thin layer of cosmic, orderly coolness. It is this weird apprehension of eternal depths and flames in eternity, and in its tiny cinders, which are the children of men, that Aurévilly scores his greatest victories. Who can ever forget that monstrous story of that beautiful woman of inextinguishable lusts, who burns perpetually with the diabolical flame? She is the wife of a general and accompanies him upon his military expeditions and while battles are being fought or campaigns planned, she hurls one man after another upon her flame. One night she is apprehended in an assignation with an old lover who has come with a formal message but has remained for an altogether different business. The general berates his spouse for her wantonness, and hints that he has heard rumors of her incessant and promiscuous venereal practices. Stung to fury, she informs him that the child she had born him and which

BOOK IV: THE NINETEENTH CENTURY

had but recently met its death, even that was not the general's, but the fruit of her lust with the lover just departed. She informs him too that when the child had died she had cut out its heart and kept it in a beautiful casket as a perpetual memento. In demoniac rage, she now rushes to this casket and hurls her child's heart at the general, the supposed father. What a frightful scene! Two partially demented figures, a woman charred by many lusts and a man blinded by elemental furies, hurling at each other the heart of a child! But the end is even more demoniac. The crazed general in an orgy of berserker rage beats his wife down with his feet, and despite her terrible shrieks, melts wax upon her, burning her to death. Thus the hellish fire in her is quenched forever.

In this connection we should also mention Joris Karl Huysmans. In his novel *Là-bas* (*Down There*) he scores the emotional poverty of our time and his imagination looks hungrily at the religious and satanic ecstasies of the middle ages. He creates Gilles de Rais, a problematic nature who dissatisfied with the even monotony of daily life, brings emotional content into his life with murder and sexual excesses. There are many crass scenes in this novel and Huysmans gives a stark characterization of his hero persecuted by erotic spectres, obsessed by satyriasis. "It appeared as though nature grew sick in his presence and that his mere proximity corrupted her. For the first time he understood the uncleanness of the immoble existence of forests, and discovered the priapic festivals in the life of deep dark woods. Here the tree appeared to him as a living being, head down dug into the earth with tufts of its roots, feet on high, straddled and branched out onto ever new thighs, which are continually opening up and getting smaller the further away they are from the stem. Now it appears that another bough is rammed in between these legs in an immoble orgiastic writhing which is transmitted from branch to branch until the very top. There the shaft seems to be a phallus which has become erect and which disappears into a skirt of foliage; or on the contrary shoots out from a green coat into the over-stuffed abdomen of the earth. Images confuse him. In the pale and smooth bark of the long-stemmed beech trees, he saw again the skin of boys, alit with their parchment-like whiteness. In the black and grooved barks of the old oaks he discerned the deeply fissured elephantine skin of beggars. At the knots where the branch forked out, little openings yawned in which the bark rolled up in ovals, these apertures reminded him of filthy rectums or the small gaping genitals of female animals. Everywhere obscene forms arose out of the earth and shot up madly toward the heavenly vault. That too became satanic. Clouds swell to huge breasts, split into buttocks, swell into immense penes, which disseminate their contents in wide showers of milky seeds. These all correspond to the sultry revelries of the forest, where nothing remains but the images of giant or branched thighs, the feminine deltas, the form of the great V, sodomite mouths, gaping wounds, moist excretory orifices."

And here is a later excerpt: "By and large, everything here below, runs into the act which you refuse. The heart which has the reputation of being the most noble constituent of man, has the same form as the penis which is supposed to be a lower organ. And it is extremely symbolic, for all love of the heart culminates in that organ which resembles it. When the human imagination seeks to vitalize artificial creatures, it has to take models from the motions of living creatures in the act of procreation. Look at machines, at the play of pistons in cylinders; what are these but steel Romeos in cast-iron Juliettes. The varieties of human expression are in no wise different from the motions of our machines. This is a law which one must do homage to, if one is to be neither impotent nor holy."

BOOK IV: THE NINETEENTH CENTURY

What a feeling for nature and a living of oneself into her moods! What a contiguity with, and strange comprehension of, apparently inorganic matter! And what philosophical absorption in the vague mysteries of sexual impulses and instincts even in the domain of the non-living. It needs only a development of these thoughts to make an eroticon par excellence, but Huysmans' work was strictly limited for he was a psychopathic case, with the peculiar visions and obsessions characteristic of such types.

ALFRED DE MUSSET

WE HAVE already remarked about Alfred de Musset's (1810-1856) erotic story, *Gamiani*, to the effect that while in the company of a number of Bohemians, the conversation turned to the inferiority of current erotic literature. It was maintained that no one could write that sort of work without using obscenities in profuse quantities. Musset disputed this and offered to prove the contrary. Three days later he read his *Gamiani* before his friends, a book which describes everything without employing a single indecent word. A truer explanation of the genesis of this work holds it to be a pamphlet directed against Musset's erstwhile mistress, George Sand. In 1834 the lovers had undertaken a trip to Venice, where poor Musset became sick with brain fever. During his illness Sand is said to have been unfaithful to him with a certain Italian, for which reason Musset left her. The abandoned woman now began to circulate the report that he was impotent. To revenge this, Musset represented Sand as Gamiani, the tribadist. This version of the story is also found in the *Memoirs of a Singer*. But the first one is much more likely to be true since the first edition of *Gamiani* bears the date 1833, one year before the journey to Venice. Not only is there a dispute about the real motive for the writing of this novel, but a number of distinguished authorities have expressed the doubt that Musset was the author of the book, which is absurd. The work exhibits all the peculiarities of Musset's style. Secondly, he himself showed it off to a number of his friends, and even provided lascivious drawings for it. And finally, as long as he lived the book was attributed to him, and he never once denied this attribution. Through an indiscretion the manuscript fell into the hands of a publisher at Brussels who issued it with colored lithographs. Today there are countless translations and reprints of the work, one of the high spots of French pornographic literature.

Here is a brief summary of the plot. At a house ball Baron Alcide, becoming suspicious of Gamiani, the mistress of the house, discovers that she is a lesbian. He determines to eavesdrop on her, and hides himself in an alcove behind some clothes. Presently Gamiani enters with Fanny, a young girl of seventeen. The latter doesn't know how to get home in the pouring rain since no coach is in sight. Hence she accepts Gamiani's hospitality for the night. The latter overcomes Fanny's opposition with flattery and tenderness, and proceeds to undress her hastily. When both are completely undressed Gamiani can no longer restrain her lust. Her tribadic desires break through. Fanny is at first frightened, but at length in her sensual excitement surrenders to the fierce manipulations of her hostess. Alcide, who has observed everything from his concealment now springs out and hurls himself on Fanny, despite the attack of Gamiani. After he has had his fill, they are reconciled amid a lot of erotic playing. Now Gamiani narrates how she has come by her abnormal tendencies. As a girl she had been placed in a nunnery by her aunt. Once, after a frightful flagellation, all the monks had taken their desire of her; and since that time she has had an antipathy to men. Then the others tell the stories of their earliest love adventures, which motivate the most erotic scenes of normal love and abnormal perversions. Finally, Gamiani mixes a poisonous love potion for herself and Fanny, and ends their lives in a mad embrace before Alcide can come to their help.

THEOPHILE GAUTIER

IN HIS *Mlle. de Maupin*, Gautier (1811-1872) sought to ape *Gamiani*. Maupin is too well-known to require any description here. Gautier's little novel, *This One and That*, aroused so much opposition among the strait-laced, with its open-hearted representation of erotic scenes, that it was confiscated. Furthermore, Gautier was recognized as the author of a primitively powerful eroticon in the form of a travel diary which he wrote to a woman friend in Paris, a certain Madame Sabatier to whom Baudelaire also dedicated a cycle of his poems. Madame Sabatier, who lived in the Rue Frochot, received only artists, and every Saturday most of her friends would foregather at dinner. Gautier, Flaubert, Baudelaire and Henry Monnier were her regular guests. She would have none of gallantries and desired that the most abstract and serious subjects be discussed in her company. For this reason they gave her the nickname of president which she wore with all possible grace and inimitable charm. Gautier called his travel diary: *Lettre à la Présidente*.

Gautier's son-in-law who edited this *Lettre* says in his foreword, "with regard to the tone of the letter which I confess I have endeavored to tone down, it must be remembered that its author was twenty-four years old when he wrote it; that it was directed to a friend who belonged to the same romantic storm and stress period with himself; and that he was accustomed to the ribald tone of the atelier. Furthermore, the letter was not written for publication, which it seems almost superfluous to point out. Theophile Gautier wrote two or three letters in his life, more to gain practice in Rabelaisian coarseness that was native to him, and in the use of forbidden words, than out of base motives which might perhaps be suspected by some. Gautier sought to master the language of the older Gallic narrators and dreamed of being able to use it with lavish eloquence. One of the letters I have referred to, a record of a trip to Italy, is entirely in the style of Rabelais, and the artists of our circle who have read it, speak with great enthusiasm about it." These and other works of his which because of their erotic content could not be published in official collections, were issued separately in a very limited edition.

STENDHAL and VICTOR HUGO

STENDHAL-BEYLE was also an erotic writer. There are a number of grounds leading us to conclude that he did engage in such activity but none is quite conclusive. When he was but twelve years old he read erotic works, particularly Nerciat's *Felicia*, and *Dangerous Liaisons*. He tells all this in his *Vie de Brulard*. "I found ways and means to get into my father's library where there was a precious collection of Elzevir editions, but alas! I understood no Latin. I tried to read a few articles in the Encyclopedia but what was that after the *Felicia* and the *New Heloise*." It is also known that his executor, Romain Coulomb, in his excessive discretion, burnt 282 passionate letters addressed to him by the Countess Clementine Curial, and very likely of other ladies as well. In the library at Grenoble there is a manuscript designated by number 5896 which contains an unfinished and untitled erotic tale dated 1801. He was famous and notorious as well as a teller of anecdotes. When he was in congenial company he would gladly recount little intimate things. One constantly feared that at any instant he might tumble into the steaming ordure of foulness, but suddenly he would give his anecdote the most innocuous turn and everything would be for the best. One of these little stories has been preserved in a collection by various authors edited by Balzac as *Gloomy Stories*.

Victor Hugo has occasionally been regarded as the author of an obscene work, *The Romance of Violet*. Herein is related the story of a fifteen year old servant girl who flees to an artist to escape the snares of her master. She first serves the artist as model and later as mistress. A young countess casts her eye upon the pretty miss and initiates her into a lesbic cult; after which the artist and the two lesbians form an erotic trio. Violet goes on the stage where she develops her capacities and achievements. Towards the end, other tribadic scenes are enacted. This is obviously an eroticon like hundreds of others, one written without special talent. There certainly is not a trace of Victor Hugo's style. The intense delight depicted in the book of sapphic pleasures, makes one suspect that a woman was the author. Several women have been suspected; e.g., Countess Maurice de Boissiron or a Madame Querouen de Boussiron, but at this late day it is impossible to tell with certainty who the unknown author was. But that Victor Hugo had no hand in this tale is fairly certain. The attribution to him was certainly a shrewd trick by some publisher.

FLAUBERT, MAUPASSANT, ZOLA

FLAUBERT the stylist, acrobat, and the esthetic realist certainly did not put blinkers on to escape erotic problems. His *Madame Bovary* and *The Holy Anthony of Padua* are sufficient proof of his deep interest in this field. The former is the story of an eccentric woman who is chained to a good but dull husband. She neglects her household, gallivants about with lovers, sinks ever more deeply and finally poisons herself. Flaubert was indicted for this novel, but was released because the court recognized that he had remained utterly moral in all his descriptions..

He was always truthful concerning others, and concerning himself as well. His notebook demonstrates this and shows a number of fairly strong erotic passages. This diary of Flaubert's was published in Germany during 1911 and despite the fact that the editor, Wilhelm Herzog, weakened several passages and omitted a number of others, both he and his publisher were indicted for disseminating immoral literature and fined fifty marks each. At the Sunday meetings of Flaubert, Zola, Daudet and Turgenieff there was little attempt at formality. The tone that reigned was that of Rabelais if not that of Villon, and spades were called by name.

Flaubert's friends revelled in their literary productions, in the depiction of fairly free situations. Maupassant particularly showed himself to be an idealizing realist in his works. As critical spirit and cool observer of human weaknesses he naturally does not pass by the differentiated phenomena of sexual life. Indeed many of his works are saturated with sex and built up on the most intimate relationships of both sexes. A few examples will establish the fact that the experience of sex is primary for many if not most of his work. Who does not know the following stories? The comic efforts of the old peasant woman to drive away the gallant whom she has been supporting and whom she has given her tiny estate, when she discovers that he has been unfaithful to her. The young abbé who has been sent to chaperon three boys has to play the mid-wife on the way. The life and doings in a brothel. The cold mondaine who makes her husband so wild by her seductive disrobing that he consents to her conditions, namely, that he can only lie with her if he will pay her, his wife, for her favors. The unfortunate plight of a husband who suffers much because he must love too much, and his subsequent improvement after he provides his wife with a sturdy, powerful lover. All these themes are soaked in sex, and they are just a tiny sampling of the vast production of this prolific raconteur. He tells of the petty adventures of the pretty modiste in her hunt for money and pleasure; of the little sailor girl, when the four fathers of her still-born baby, promise to make another for her; of the hermit who unwittingly cohabits with his own natural daughter; of a lesbian, who drives her lover to suicide because of her tribadic impulses. He shows the surprise of a pair of lovers who have forgotten to bolt the door. He describes the romantic desire of an aging good philistine woman to have at least one idyllic moment in her life; and the first heroism of a boy at boarding school who wins as his mistress not the flapper of his desires, but the dormitory mother. In thoroughly serious and factual fashion he discusses the problem of undesired motherhood. He depicts with masterful conciseness the frivolous conception of marital fidelity entertained by a distinguished matron, who winks from her window to a passing man because such is the fashion of the prostitute across the way. When the man comes up in acknowledgment of her signal, she can find no other way out but of giving herself to him.

In their diary under February 17, 1882, the brothers Goncourt have an entry expressive of their irritation with the dishonest hypocrisy of certain critics. One of these gentry had asserted that he had, much against his will, taken a peep at the works of Marquis de Sade. But at the same time Maupassant informed them, that this very critic had requested him to obtain for him a supply of bawdy books from certain Belgian publishers. The question arises why Maupassant was given the task. It seems reasonable to suppose that the critic suspected that Maupassant had some predilection for, and some knowledge of, this type of literary productions, and that he also had certain connections with publishers of porneia. This would lead us to suppose that either Maupassant himself was a lover of erotic literature, or that among his friends he was known to be active in this field. Actually, the second supposition is true. There is a grotesque eroticon from his pen called *The Turkish House* which was never printed. This work was written in collaboration with Robert Pinchon and the manuscript is in the possession of Maupassant's uncle the painter, Le Pottevin. The piece is, according to the admission of the author, "horribly indecent" and a Parisian journal characterized it as "bawdy enough to make a sargeant blush". The Turkish house is a brothel and Maupassant, the brothel master. This piece was enacted in 1875 in the studio of the painter Leloir, and in 1877, in the studio of another painter Becker. Flaubert, Turgenieff, Zola and others were spectators. Zola remained earnest, Turgenieff applauded, Flaubert refreshed himself with the coarse jesting. A female spectator, Suzane Lazier, protested and left the room. According to a letter of Maupassant, the eight women in the cast appeared with masks on. The remembrance of the marvelous frivolity of this piece was so vivid to Edmond de Goncourt that thirteen years later his conversation would occasionally revert to it.

Two more works sail under Maupassant's name. First, *The Girl Cousins of the Colonel*, which contains the story of two sisters, of whom one is married to a weak husband and the other lives with a man out of wedlock and is disillusioned by her experience. The really erotic scenes are thinly sowed over throughout the book and everything is drawn with the greatest moderation. Maupassant himself absolutely denied any connection with this book. It is likely that the book was written by the same hand that wrote *The Romance of Violet*, Countess Maurice de Boissiron, an intimate friend of George Sand. Both volumes manifest the author's constant predilection for tribadic scenes.

BOOK IV: THE NINETEENTH CENTURY

The second novel attributed to Maupassant is called *The Adventures of a Parisian Cocotte*. There is no way at all of determining Maupassant's authorship but many have assumed it. When he was still young and unknown, he composed a number of ultra-realistic erotic novels. He was impelled to produce this type of literature not merely because of his marked tendencies to erotic representations, which appears so strongly in his recognized immortal masterpieces, but also because he needed money; and an unknown author can always find a publisher in Paris for this sort of thing much more readily than for his serious works. Nevertheless, the book is masterfully done, and if Maupassant was the author he did not have to be ashamed of this natural child. The book is an uncommonly interesting, even fascinating, picture of metropolitan morality, rich in remarkable figures, extraordinary events and thrilling action. All gallant Paris at about 1880 passes in review before our eyes. We become acquainted with the boudoir of a distinguished cocotte, and the separées of aristocratic restaurants. We catch glimpses behind the curtains of great varietés, and of those night quarters which serve the needs of fugitive gallantry. We see the grand cocotte, the highly paid prostitute who seeks her clients only in high society. We see the addicts of lesbian love cults; the journalist who understands how to make all gallant ladies favorably disposed to him; the spendthrift banker who sacrifices thousands to his perverse desires; the clever little ballet dancer who knows just when to rip her tights, etc. The relationships of all these people are drawn with great realistic fidelity and psychological understanding.

Emile Zola belonged to the Flaubert-Maupassant group. In his youth he wrote a little eroticon in the style of Lafontaine called *The Devilish Hermit*, in which he very successfully copied the pleasing style of the good abbé. That Zola's general works abound in erotic situations is known to every one. Take for instance the grandiose scene in *Germinal* when the old women unman the dead Maigrat.

> Now they heard the piercing voice of the Brulé woman:
> "We must mutilate him like a tomcat".
> "Yes, yes! Out upon the tomcat. Out with the tomcat. He has done too much, the filthy fellow."
> Already Mouquette was opening his trousers and pulling them off, while Levaque raised the feet of the dead man. Now Brulé spread apart the thighs of the corpse, and seized with the fleshless hands of old women its genitories. She got hold of everything and tore with such force that her dry old spine bent and her long arms cracked. The soft fleshy parts resisted. She had to grab hold again and finally tore, tore everything out, tore the whole mass out, a filthy bleeding bundle of flesh which she swung in the air with a cry of triumph.
> "I have it, I have it".
> Yawping voices greeted the monstrous trophy with insults.
> "Now you dog, you shall no longer fill the bellies of our girls."
> "Now everything is out. We shall no longer be forced to hold your buttocks for a piece of bread."
> "Hey you, I owe you two francs. Do you want to have something on account? I want it right now, if you can still do it."
> These jests filled them with horrible gayety. They showed each other the bleeding bundle as though it were a wild animal from which they had all had to suffer and which now, finally, they had in their power, dead. They spat upon it, thrust out their chins at it and repeated their mockery in wild expressions.
> "He can no longer do it, he can no longer do it. This is no more a man which will now be hurled into the earth. Now rot, you useless dog."
> Brulé stuck the whole bundle on her stick and holding it on high as though it were a flag, began to move followed by the howling horde of women. Drops of blood fell from it and the lump of flesh dangled from the stick like a piece of refuse meat hangs from the butcher's table.

BOOK IV: THE NINETEENTH CENTURY

If one were to compile all the passages of Zola's work that do not correspond to squeamish taste, one would obtain an integral work of gross obscenity which would undoubtedly fall a prey to the censor. Curiously enough, this attempt at compilation was actually made in France. Towards the close of 1896 a second-hand dealer, Antoine Laporte by name, issued a compilation under the title *Zola against Zola*. It contained all the most daring and realistic scenes of Zola's writings in some sort of order. This anthology was adorned with a frontispiece of exquisitely refined taste. A mass of chamberpots have been set up against the edifice of the forty Academicians and are blocking the way to it. Each of these pots bears the name of a writing of Zola.

If Zola is raw to the point of disgust, if he wallows in the monstrosities of human life, if he fears no stench, if he permits his characters to employ words that are omitted from ordinary lexicons, he is never lascivious. He knows no bawdy illusions. He does not raise curtains half way and invite the imagination to complete the process. If he has something to say or show, he says and shows it with the rawness of truth and indignation.

PAUL VERLAINE

PAUL Verlaine (1844-1896) has given us in his famous poetry, verse of overwhelming power and natural charm. There is something unFrench in his naturalness, and that is why foreigners are so fond of the emotional warmth and truth in his work. But these famous poems in the official collections are not the whole unadulterated Verlaine. To be able to form a correct judgment of the man one must also read his secret books. Having done the latter, we are constrained to admit that he would have remained nearer to us had we been spared the other side of his poetical creation. It is not the fact that Verlaine was an erotic writer that puts us out of humor, but that this factitious eroticism explodes like a cold firecracker, and does not break forth mightily like a hot stream of lava from some glowing interior. It is this which casts a shadow upon his character. *Les Amies* is a series of six extremely candid sonnets which treats of the sapphic exercises of two budding girls. It is delightful despite the passionate eroticism because of its magnificent rhythm. These poems, wonderfully delicate in their sentiment, will not obscure the picture of the poet. But what of the collection, *Men* and *Women*, which appeared clandestinely in Verlaine's last years? Stefan Zweig, the best student of Verlaine's work, holds that in these works Verlaine takes his place among the greatest pornologists of all time. He has sharply broken with the tradition of the charming ribaldry of Grécourt and Piron to record with unparalled shamelessness, subjective pornography. They are, despite their smooth form, the most repulsive in their self-revelation, the most complete lexicon of perverse arts, the most brutal in realistic representation. The sexual gaminerie of Verlaine which, at an earlier stage of his life in the *Fêtes Galantes*, was frequently able to unite with the tender sentiment of his sensitive soul a coquettish, panurgic, lascivious sort, has here become naked and utterly obscene. It is infinitely tragic, this spectacle of an old man on the hospital lists writing with uncertain and trembling hand these pitiful rhymes about his vices and past nakedness, all for a few francs with which to buy some absinthe. And just as the poem, *Le trou de cul*, written together with Rimbaud, and reproduced in the pederastic book *Hombres*, destroyed the legend of a purely psychic and ethereal friendship, so too the existence and distribution of these books banishes the fable of the "pure fool". It is all too pitiful, but the immortal singer still retains the sympathy of all great poets and writers.

BOOK IV: THE NINETEENTH CENTURY

Femmes was published in 1890 in London and Verlaine got twelve pounds sterling for it. As can well be imagined, the edition was almost immediately confiscated so that only a few copies were sneaked away. *Hombres* too was confiscated. In the latter work all those poems were unified that sprang from the love experience of Verlaine with Arthur Rimbaud, and are therefore songs of praise in honor of uranic love. All these shamelessly erotic poems (*Amies, Femmes, Hombres*) were later united and published.

CHARLES BAUDELAIRE

BY THE side of Verlaine we might fittingly place the poet of decadence, of the abnormal, Charles Baudelaire. He regarded divinity and love as merely welcome texts from which to derive stimulus for inhumanly smooth and satanically cool poems. Concepts reversed themselves for him and good became bad, and evil became ideal. In his *Flowers of Evil* there stands revealed his morbid mania, to make the ugly and hateful the subject of poetry. Yet he cannot really be regarded as an erotic writer even though he extols *Venus vulgivaga* in his poetry, though not exactly in the same measure as Verlaine. Six poems in the first edition of this work were branded as immoral by the police and had to be expurgated from all future editions. Nevertheless, Baudelaire printed them privately together with some satirical poems in the volume *Epâves*, which Rops provided with a frontispiece. This volume is practically non-existent today but other editions have been reprinted often. The poem, *A maid complains in midsummer*—"how long will love last?" gave rise to a wide-spread pornographic parody. When he was only twenty-one, Baudelaire chose as the epitaph suitable for him some doggerel to the effect that "here lay a fellow who had hurried to the worms too soon because he had fooled with women too much."

THE EROTIC HISTORY OF FRANCE

Baudelaire had a great love for erotic literature of all sorts as appears from a letter of his to his publisher in 1865. "Thanks for having informed me about the price of Sade's *Justine* and where I could possibly find it. I would also like to know the price of *Aphrodite*, and what in your opinion are the characteristic moral and literary qualities of such slop? You may ask what does Baudelaire want with this package of excrement? The said Baudelaire has enough spirit to study crime and vice in his own heart. Well, the information I want from you is intended for a great man who believes he can study crime in other people." This reference is to Sainte-Beuve who once asked Baudelaire for one of the dirty poems that had appeared in the publishing house of Poulet-Malassis, Baudelaire's own publisher.

CHAPTER XIX
PUBLISHERS OF EROTICA

THE publication of erotic books has meant at all times great risks for both author and publisher, for if discovered both would be liable to hard punishment. It is remarkable that these dangers did not have an intimidating effect, that large monetary and jail sentences just did not impede the propagation of this literature. The author generally does not lose very much when his writings are confiscated. But much more is at stake for the publisher. Under certain circumstances he saw the foundation of his business endangered when the entire edition of a pornographic work into which he had sunk a portion of his fortune fell a prey to the censor. And yet there were innumerable booksellers who though fully aware of these dangers continually sought to outwit the law. What was the attraction? Surely the chief motive was the desire to earn large and quick profits, for obscene books must always obtain a higher price than any other kind of reading matter. There are several reasons for this: the fact that they are prohibited, that they titillate the senses, that they can serve as a help in seduction, that they are good investments for their value increases with the passage of time, and occasionally such books are sold at very high prices indeed. But this economic moment alone will not serve to explain everything satisfactorily. For if the publisher or bookseller reaps profits from the sale of one product, he is exposed to great loss if some other of these books should be confiscated. It appears likely that there was also a very strong bibliophilic interest which impelled the daring publishers to offer a home to new books of value, whatever their eroscenic nature, or to pluck certain old books from oblivion by reprinting them in worthy garb. There was also a degree of spiritual relationship between the publisher and his authors, which impelled the former to gather around him people who were of similar taste for erotics, facetiæ, curiosa, and thus to obtain a more accessible market for his more tolerable publications.

A half dozen of the most important French publishers of erotica in the last century will now be mentioned.

1. Felix Regnier-Becker, born Meru, was a carpenter by trade. In 1829 he issued a collection of his own verses and in 1830 published *The Siege of Paradise*. This brought him a penalty of three months' imprisonment and a fine of 300 francs. However, a certain journal took up a collection for him which was so successful that he could not only pay the fine but had a tidy little sum left, with which he became a bookdealer. He devoted himself to the promulgation of obscene books and put more than a hundred of these into circulation. Indictments and penalties against him multiplied but the more the persecutions increased, the greater became his bookselling activities. Nothing further is known of his later life.

2. Jules Gay was a vagrant bookseller. He lived first at 41 quai des Grands-Augustins, Paris, but fled to Belgium to escape punishment. In 1865 he became a partner of a Belgian publisher, Mertens. Later he left Brussels secretly and we find him successively in Geneva, Turin, Nice and San Remo, and finally in Brussels again where he formed a new firm with a Mlle. Doucé. In 1871 he founded the *Société des bibliophiles cosmopolites* whose only members, however, were himself and his son Jean, who opened a small bookshop in Turin in 1875. The senior Gay was very active, particularly in the domain of erotica. His chief interest was not

BOOK IV: THE NINETEENTH CENTURY

in the publication of original works but in the reprinting of famous masterpieces of erotic literature, which he sent out into the small world of bibliophiles in exceedingly fine editions. Naturally he frequently ran afoul of the law which could not understand his aims, which were ideal from the standpoint of the bibliophile. In order to escape persecution, Gay was careful to hide his identity at least in the most daring books; but as a general rule, he gave the child of his firm, his own name, or that of Gay-Doucé. He circulated his books from one of the metropolitan centers listed above.

As the illustrator for his books, Gay had the virtuoso Félicien Rops who was himself more or less responsible for the publication of a number of books in this genre and was himself, a bookworm. Besides women, his art and flowers, he loved nothing more than to browse about old books. Many of these were found by him and later published, e.g., *The Satirical Cabinet*, *The Devotions of Monsieur Roch*, and others. All the books, about 70, which Rops illustrated were more or less erotic, some in the quarrelsome, humorous old Flemish style, many in the gallant forms of the eighteenth, and the rest in the decadent style of the ninteenth century. All his engravings which were the products of a ripe artist, refer to women. It is difficult to say whose influence was greater: that of contemporary literature upon Rops, or the influence he exerted upon the writing of his contemporaries who began to write about women as he represented her in his lines and planes and colors.

Gay was indicted several times, and in 1863 he had to pay a fine of 100 francs and suffer the confiscation of his books. Two years later he again appeared before the court, this time in the company of other publishers. He was accused of being the publisher of 38 erotic and obscene books, and was sentenced to four months in jail and 500 francs fine. Gay himself reported these trials in a work which he published in a limited edition of but 100 copies. In this he does not polemize against his sentence but merely sets forth the reasons that induced him to become a fervent lover of clandestine literature and an inveterate bibliophile, and hence to undertake the publication of these and other confiscated works.

3. Another publisher sentenced at the same time with Gay was Poulet-Malassis who received one year in jail and 500 francs' fine, in punishment for the 86 erotica he had sent into the world, and the unscrupulousness that characterized this distribution. Undoubtedly monetary motives were paramount with him, but even he was definitely a bibliophile. His de luxe edition of the classics was a terrible failure and well-nigh ruined him. Now he was compelled to move to the suburbs, to Ixelles, where Baudelaire lived, and to take a small house among the philistines. Bibliographic interests and the very natural desire to recoup his fortunes impelled him to take up the publishing and reprinting of piquant works. Here the little slender man sat bent over his manuscripts and proofs, indefatigable and indomitably ambitious, and supervised the editions that were to bring the choicest products to the small community of booklovers. Baudelaire gave him encouragement and stimulus; and Poulet succeeded in obtaining the active cooperation of the distinguished artist, Rops. These delightful little books wandered into the world on strong China or Holland paper, in very limited editions. The most fruitful year was 1864, which saw the publication of about a dozen classics.

4. In the eighties, the work of Gay was carried on by Isidore Liseux. In him too the bibliophile was superior to the tradesman, for what merchant would expose himself to as many hazards as did Liseux? His editions are as much sought after today as Gay's.

5. Kistemaecker in Brussels is at the opposite pole from Liseux. He cultivated pure pornography. Everything that was at all coarse and offensive, be the contents solid or froth, was meat for Kiste-

mæcker. His obscene productions were smuggled over the border to provide France with saucy stuff.

6. At the turn of the century a successor who followed in the footsteps of Gay and Liseux, established himself in Paris, Charles Carrington by name, an Englishman. In excellent editions, provided with prefaces, he issued, both in English and French, the most famous erotica of the world at a cheap price. True bibliophile that he was, no erotic product was outside his domain: anthropology, chronicles of scandal, flagellation, original gallant literature, scientific works on sex, etc. Charles Carrington was harassed by official chicaneries even more than Gay or Liseux. He died after the World War.

A word will be in order about Félicien Rops (1833-1898), whom we have mentioned several times as the illustrator of numerous erotic books. This Flemish artist, of colossal strength, found in Paris the world's center of the striving after pleasure. From the wealth of experience he had here and the multitude of sights that came under his eyes, the notion crystallized in his mind that all life and thought centered around woman. He loved the Parisian mixture of silk, nerves and powder with eyes greatly enlarged through the application of cosmetics. There is nothing more ravishing, colorful, or gallant than the plastic *Decameron* of elegant Paris which Rops undertook. He looked everywhere and saw everything. And every woman that he represented he undressed, but always left her some bit of clothing: a pair of hose, a panty, a corset; anything to make her nakedness more titillating. Rops often pilloried modern woman, representing her as a prostitute, with bony body, with eyes staring and made wild by alcohol, with protruding jaws; a prostitute whose tremendous power is a mixture of base and lusting elements. It is the sexual life destroyed and poisoned by a depraved morality that speaks to us through the medium of

Rops' intellectual art. He represents the lurid tragedies of love of revengeful women, whose passion dotes on the strong spice of sadistic feeling; and by her side, in his inexhaustible gallery of modern women, those grinning children of lust whose prototype is that street Venus bursting with power and strength, appearing in the picture *Pornocraty*. Rops descended into the hell of the brothel and cheap tavern to show us the women in whom immorality has begun its work of disintegration. Weary and nauseated by the endless monotony of their métier, these women for whom the beaker of lust has become flat and stale, have taken refuge in absinthe, which still leaves them a few pitiful illusions, and confers upon them an artificial happiness, and the meagre intoxication of forgetfulness. Hollow-eyed they lie there before us in expectation of the routine embrace, with just a rag of a shirt to cover the nakedness of their withering body, washed out, enervated Messalinas. He shows us these unfortunate creatures on the inexorable decline. The progress of their ruin makes them confused and wasted drunkards in whose eyes only the fire of alcohol glimmers; or they become that mercilessly emaciated woman whose type he draws for us in *Mors syphilitica*. Of all the thrilling beauty of the earthly goddesses, which once could lash male flesh into fury, nothing now remains but a heap of human ruins. What was once a woman, now is entirely debased, debauched, and disintegrated by the foul profusion of modern perversities, now is the broken, shapeless, useless plaything of the devil hurled on the rubbish heap to complete her decay.

Before we get to the end of our forage into the nineteenth century, let us say a little about erotic theatres, particularly the erotic theatre on the Rue de la Santé, previously referred to. This erotic theatre, which actually existed from 1862 to 1864 owes its rise to a drunken jest. In the circle of young bohemians some

BOOK IV: THE NINETEENTH CENTURY

one got the idea of creating a little puppet theatre for the amusement of a few chosen ones. Droll pieces were to be presented and no limits were to be set to the fancies of the poets. The theatre was opened in the presence of twenty-five young authors, publishers and artists. Among the invited guests were Chamfleury, Monselet, Daudet, and Poulet-Malassis. These presentations even found a favorable review in the press. Some of the comments were: Still a new theatre. An intimate theatre. Theatron eroticon that is, a theatre with love arousing marionettes. But without excitation, and everything is held within moral bounds. The harlequin thrusts have at all times been the guardians of morality and when the mother cannot bring her little daughter here, this hospitable place will become the pleasurable gathering place of talented artists and literati.

In order to afford the reader some notion of these plays a few of the more common ones will be summarized.

The Eyes of Love by Lemercier de Neuville is, despite its erotic license, very interesting psychologically. Sylvia, a brothel mistress still young, complains in a monologue that she must always further the intimate relations between her girls and the visitors, while no hour of love comes to her. For this reason she decides to go on the "line" once again. Luck is with her. Dorante, a famous pimp and girl-dealer wants to pay for his female flesh once, for a change. Since Sylvia pleases him he follows her. Deceived by his fine clothing she acquiesces to his terms of paying later. But his end having been gained, the pander in him comes out and he states very brutally that in his own house of prostitution he would not tolerate such a one as stupid as she who did not know enough to insist on payment before the deed. Now Sylvia removes her mask, avows her amorous desires, and proposes that he become her bully, to which he assents.

A Caprice by the same author deals with a married skirt-chaser by the name of Florestan. He comes to a strumpet whose suggestive name is Urinette, but she is still at her toilette. In the introductory monologue he avers that he was on the point of fulfilling his connubial function with his sleeping little wife. But variety is attractive, and so he decides to go out and hunt up a new vessel. Hence he interrupts his siege to his wife and saves his ammunition for later. But when the jade enters and tempts him to the act, he suffers a shameful impotence. Urinette leaves him alone, raging mad. Soon Don Priapus shows his caprice and rises to new life. But Urinette is implacable and Florestan experiences a recrudescence of moral scruples. Why debauch away from home? True happiness is to be found only at home.

Scapin by Glatigny is a peculiar sort of drama. Lucinde, the daughter of Corbin and the betrothed of Pignouflard, does not want to wash her private parts. The father complains to Scapin, a brothel master, about his troubles whereupon the latter offers to bring about the girl's ablution if she will come to his institution. Corbin agrees. By chance the fiancé of Lucinde visits the brothel and naturally meets his bride. The engagement is in danger of being broken. Thereupon the master of the brothel brings in a tub with the bathwater, and the pestilential fumes stream out, a sign that the girl is washing herself. All ends in harmony.

The Sign of Gold by Amadée Rolland and Jean Duboys has been aptly designated as excrement by Deditius. This erotic scatological musical comedy in three acts is the best thing in the collection, after Monnier's contribution. The Marquis who is growing old wants an heir to carry on his name and makes every possible effort to gain his end. But he must have recourse to many artifices, which we shall leave undescribed here. The drama occupies itself as much with infidelities as with excrement but the dialogue is carried out with considerable wit.

BOOK IV: THE NINETEENTH CENTURY

The Anniversary of the Marriage, by Neuville and Duboys, describes two young and now honorably married women, despite their earlier wanton life, who are expecting their former lovers in a separée. Memories are exchanged. Both are dissatisfied with their husbands who do not understand how to love. The only lovely thing is love between women. They become more and more intimate and at the very moment when the waiter outside is ushering the lovers in, both women disappear in order to flee to Lesbos.

The Grisette and the Student of Monnier has already been analyzed. *The Last Day of a Condemned Man* of Tisserand and *The Grand Symphony of the Bug* of Neder and Bataille, possess neither the wit nor the effectiveness of the others.

All in all, one must admit that much effort has been expended on such none too worthy dramas. There seems to be little justification for the expenditure of money and intellectual effort except as a manifestation of French drama and thought during the nineteenth century.

CHAPTER XX
VENUS VICTORIOUS

This final chapter will attempt to bring the erotic history of France up-to-date. It will show the wide-spread eroticism and marital infidelities among the bourgeoisie and how they altered the customs of the houses of prostitution which had been practically unchanged since the birth of France, a thousand years ago. It will also point out the significant consequences of the erotic movies, which have also become an indispensable part of brothels. This history makes no pretence to go beyond the nineteenth century, but in this closing chapter we shall treat somewhat of twentieth-century France.

Venal love has been found at all times and among all peoples, and indeed it will continue to exist as long as social and economic contrasts remain in national life. Poverty compels youth to make capital of its body; indolence and the desire to lead a comfortable life without strenuous labor will always recruit the ranks of prostitutes. This fact is not altered by the circumstance that with the progressive emancipation of women the stigmatization of extra-marital intercourse has begun to disappear. It is true that our social evolution with the difficulties it sets in the way of marriage, especially for those belonging to the middle class, has gradually achieved some measure of recognition for the varied forms of pre- and extra-marital sex relationships. Indeed, this development has already progressed very far. Prostitution still exists in that primitive form which it has had for centuries, with one important difference; the rigid boundaries erected between bourgeoisie and prostitution have become more flexible. But this can scarcely be interpreted as a higher stage of morality.

Although the practices in all the brothels of the world are essentially the same, there are some differences between the French and those of foreign brothels. The satisfaction of the sheerly physical need without any trace of emotional excitation, the practice most common in harbor brothels is, in Paris, found only in the very lowest dives. But the average prostitute in Paris wants to create the impression at least that it was an impulse of the heart, be it ever so ephemeral, that impelled her to give herself. This circumstance probably has its ground in the fact that among the French, almost the whole private and public life is steeped in sex. Hence, physical satisfaction is not simply a whim that appears suddenly and will be submerged by other interests immediately after the act.

The famous sexologist Rohleder who went through the metropolis of France with wide-open impartial eyes characterizes the dominant atmosphere in most telling words. He concluded that one need only to have lived in Paris a very short while and to have observed attentively, to realize how everywhere in public life, in the larger and particularly the smaller theatres, variétés, cafés chantants, the main boulevards, the restaurants down to the vilest absinthe dive, everything turns on the sexual. What makes everything so easy is the system of hotel quarters. There are thousands of smaller and medium sized hostelries which are available to couples for a brief hour or so. One must have seen how immensely large this clandestine prostitution is, how here almost any kind of woman, from the *honorable* matron to the maid and factory operative, give themselves to a greater or less degree to this clandestine prostitution; how here at every moment of the day and in every section of the city sexual debauches are indulged, how almost all pleasure and art itself, serve the sexual. Let the stranger enter Paris from the *Gare du Nord* or the *Gare de l'Est*. Unless it is very early in the morning and even then the stranger will find immediate incitement to sex, his attention will soon be riveted to sex. He has scarcely alighted from the train when he will, not uncommonly, be accosted by individuals who will volunteer to act as his guides *pour les amusements*. When he arrives at the hotel he may have the experience of being smiled at most warmly and lovingly by the *filles de chambre;* and if he is too naïve to understand their smiles or too indifferent, these females will inform him quite directly that they are ready for an hour of love. When he goes to a restaurant, unless it is a grand-café of the most elaborate kind, he will very soon be informed that white meat is on the menu, and which is ready for consumption after his meal. When he goes to an amusement place he will be surprised at the elegance and luxury of the appointments; and also at the naturalness with which prostitution manifests itself.

But in this respect Paris is like other great metropolitan centers, which cater to an enormous contingent of travellers who have to be amused. Since Paris has long borne the odium of being the most wicked capital in the world, it must strive to do justice to all tastes in order to bring gold into the land. But this fact alone will not explain the overplus of prostitution. Indeed, many other motives are at work, particularly the poor economic circumstances which continually recruit the ranks of the daughters of joy. The underpaid salesgirls and shop clerks can practice prostitution as their main vocation for quite a while without passing as official prostitutes. However, only a slight impetus will be necessary to push them in that direction. Sickness, unemployment, domestic quarrels, trouble with the police,—all are just a few causes which may make professional prostitutes out of clandestine ones. If these factors do not come into operation, then the traffic with one's corporeal charms can still contribute a very appreciable addition to the otherwise meagre income. The sinking to the level of purchasable goods is rendered easy by the frivolity of the Parisienne which is inbred and nurtured by the germs of seduction which enter every pore of her body with the very air of Paris.

This frivolity of attitude to mate or lover, this gay evaluation of marital fidelity, had necessarily to seek a vent through which the accumulated sexual tension could be relieved, and whereby the woman with an eye to financial remuneration could realize her desires. The most convenient opportunity for these amusements were offered by the *maisons de rendezvous*. This system of temporary quarters, in which the woman who was willing to sell her body could enter and leave secretly, offered to both sexes all the opportunities and delights of intimate intercourse without subjecting either of the parties to the degrading feeling of venality. The man, who had to pay a higher price for these goods than for the usual prostitute, could enjoy the piquant feeling of having an adventure with a *good* woman, while continuing to enjoy the lure of the forbidden. The woman, on the other hand, earned from these occasional adventures some valuable pin money whereby she could satisfy the extravagant wishes of her capricious little head without molesting the purse of her legitimate consort. Talmeyr, who visited very many of these houses of rendezvous at the behest of the police, has described his experiences in a book entitled: *The End of a Society: New Forms of Corruption in Paris*. He confirms the fact that it was primarily the wish to earn a little something from her escapade that impelled the woman to visit such convenient houses of opportunity. Some came regularly, others infrequently. Whatever class of society they were recruited from, they found here at all times and under the most discreet circumstances whatever sum they were in need of, the fifty or one hundred francs of the little business to the 3,000 or 4,00 francs of the big transaction, in return for the usufruct of their person. But we must not forget the fact that it was men who were the patrons of these houses; it was they who visited these *maisons de rendezvous* to give free rein to their passions and who ultimately guaranteed the profitability of such establishments.

It is self evident that such houses needed many customers to carry on. The mania of the male visitors consisted, as is quite comprehensible, in working for their partners married women and ladies of society; and it was the duty of the mistress of such houses to arouse the belief in these gulls that their wishes were being gratified. There certainly was no lack of married women and even the demand for ladies of society could in most cases be supplied. When the latter was not possible the clever panderesses could always create the illusion that Countess de X or Marquise de Y was ready to give her private favors for a suitable price. Such a pleasure naturally was worth much and there were enough simpletons who bought for a dear price nothing more than the commonest whore. But although ever so often ladies of the peripatetic vocation would be frequenters of such houses, the effort was constantly made to avoid anything that might be offensive and give away baldly the preciously guarded secrets of the house. After all, it was the unsuspected nature of these love-nests that constituted their value to those who made occasional use of them.

Of course these houses did considerable damage to the brothel business but they continued to exist in all shades, from the most luxurious palatial villa to the most miserable hovel. They served all types of perversities including the most fiendishly cruel; and even the most repulsive sadists got what they wanted if they but paid enough for it. No matter how much a girl was tortured, the police could not interfere if she had consented to suffer these perversities.

Doctors agree that the modern cultured person needs variety and that constant physical copulation with the same person requires change. It was but one step further to suggest that the change be a complete alteration of the sexual act, and this change, the Parisian brothels met in the cleverest ways and called into service the most complicated achievements of modern technique. In the illustrated comic weeklies, particularly *Le Sourire*, there are weekly advertisements of these temples of vice where all sorts of "artistic tableaux" and representations of gallant engravings are enacted in the flesh. There is a great appeal about this sort of sextravagance. As soon as the spectators have taken their places and find themselves in good hands, the presentation begins—behind a glass plate. Behind the scenes of suburban theatres, bayaderes from the rue Lepic give themselves to lesbian love just as the collegean student might imagine it. Or the eighteenth century is employed as the milieu of the scene to be enacted. The famous pieces of Schall, Fragonard, Borell, and the lesser masters, follow in order between a bed from the milieu of the Faubourg St. Antoine and two empty easy chairs. They enacted *The Enema, The Lever of the Newly Married Couple*, and many daring illustrations to the tales of Lafontaine. It is understood that all this was amusement for cultured folks only, for one must at least be acquainted with the tales of Lafontaine to appreciate the detailed points of the pantomime.

But no matter how clever and attractive such shows might be for the numerous audiences of well-read people, they could never satisfy the coarser instincts of the average public. Artificial representations no matter how piquant, are not what the visitor to a brothel expects. He desires more powerful fare and this is purveyed in the very numerous pornographic movies. These are, to be sure, no monopoly of the French for they are found in the brothels of all other countries. Curt Moreck, writing about the pornographic film, says that it offers us an insight into the varied erotic tastes and views of the different nations. Thus the French films specialize in depictions of the orgasm, of the acts of discharge, and go into the broadest descriptions of the preparatory acts, though occasionally attention is centered on the latter to such an extent that the sexual act occurs behind the scenes. England produces such stuff principally for consumption by India; and South Africa prefers flagellational scenes and sadistic abuses of negroes. Italy, whose southern extremity is already in the zone of Oriental sexuality, cultivates as its specialty the sotadic film, the representation of sodomitic acts; and only slightly less popular than photographs of sexual acts between men and beasts, are scenes of copulation among beasts. In Germany sin is without grace and indeed in the erotic movies of this land the charge seems quite true. For they generally show well executed, terribly realistic coitus scenes but lack the erotic pictures of animals. One can say, in brief, that the pornographic movie comprehends the whole scale of immorality and includes all variations, from the refined *piquanterie* which shudders at the representation of the sex act and depicts only the immoral flirt in all its dangers, to the most bestial wallowing in the foulest and most extravagant postures. How these scenes were staged and enacted can be imagined from the fact that the actors were in most cases whores and alphonses, or other shady and depraved individuals. They lack every trace of artistic refinement and are merely the witless hackwork of depraved imaginations.

Something should be said about this alphonse or bully concerning whom the reader of newspapers, whose curiosity has been fed by an accommodating press, has got quite false notions. These declassed of society have nothing queer or striking about their exterior. The balloon cap and the red neckerchief, the chief outward signs of the Apaches, have passed from the picture. They are only recreated or called back into life to impress tourists and create local color and the illusion of cruelty, mystery and mad love. There is nothing at all distinctive about the clothing of these *Louis* which would set them apart from the average citizen; and indeed, like American racketeers, they don't like to have too much attention drawn to them in any way. The support of these fellows is worried about by the girls who "run" for them; and in turn, the girls find in these pimps, protectors and lovers. The latter factor is more imaginary than real for when they choose their bully, they virtually contract to support him continuously, to transfer all their earnings to him and if these are sometimes insufficient to suffer abuse and manhandling as punishment. And yet one of these lost creatures will hang on to her pimp and swear every manner of perjury in order to save him from jail, because in a moment of fierce jealousy at his choice of another, she had gotten him into a scrape.

Again, like American racketeers, these bullies had to have a vocation through which they ostensibly support themselves. They usually pretend to be commercial representatives, travelling salesmen of wine, cigars or perfumes, or else they choose some other free profession whose economic possibilities cannot be checked up. Every bourgeois occupation is thoroughly eschewed; and it is understood that everyone who "belongs" will not hesitate to augment his business with a little extra job like theft, fake, swindle, etc., a procedure not only not frowned upon by his fellow workers but rather abetted. Since they are regarded as declassed by the laws of the bourgeoisie, it must not be a matter of surprise if they do not accept such laws. In this respect the Parisian bully differs in no wise from his colleagues in the metropolis of any other land.

THE EROTIC HISTORY OF FRANCE

And so, we come to an end of the erotic history of France, and the history of its erotic literature. There are endless books on the history of France, endless books on its literature, but hitherto one could find no work dealing with the erotic aspects of this, the most erotic of European countries. What is the relation between France's eroticism and its eminence in the arts? What is the relation between France's erotic literature and its eminence in world literature? We do not pretend to know but perhaps this volume may have suggested a few ideas in the mind of the reader. France typifies the highest and noblest peak of Latin civilization in the modern world. Its contributions to the spirit of man are immeasurable. And in the use of leisure, in the art of living and loving, no nation in Europe is its peer. May not this volume contain some kernel of truth to account for this?

Finally, it behooves us to repeat that we have tried to avoid giving any offense to the reader despite the nature of this work. It has been much more difficult to pull in the reins than the reader imagines, for it has only been since the World War that Americans have been able to read many of the books mentioned herein; and even today, despite the general condemnation of censorship by men in all walks of life—except for works of definite and deliberate obscenity—there still remain blue laws and censors to hound the honest and intimidate the free.